Assessment Sourcebook

THE UNIVERSITY OF CHICAGO SCHOOL MATHEMATICS PROJECT

FUNCTIONS, STATISTICS, AND TRIGONOMETRY

INTEGRATED MATHEMATICS

About Assessment
Assessment Forms
Chapter Quizzes
Chapter Tests, Forms A, B, C, and D
Chapter Tests, Cumulative Form
Comprehensive Tests
Answers
Evaluation Guides

D1572868

Scott Foresman
Addison Wesley

Editorial Offices: Glenview, Illinois • Menlo Park, California
Sales Offices: Reading, Massachusetts • Atlanta, Georgia
Glenview, Illinois • Carrollton, Texas • Menlo Park, California

Contents

Pages	Contents
iv	Assessing Student Performance in Mathematics
vi	Portfolios and Notebooks
vii	Using Free-Response and Multiple-Choice Tests
viii	Using Performance Assessment
x	Using Assessment Forms

Student-Completed Forms

Pages	Contents
xi	Student Survey
xii	Student Self-Assessment
xiii	Cooperative Groups Self-Assessment
xiv	About My Portfolio

Teacher-Completed Forms

Pages	Contents
xv	Portfolio Assessment
xvi	Notebooks *Individual Assessment*
xvii	Notebooks *Class Checklist*
xviii	Problem Solving *Individual Assessment*
xix	Problem Solving *Class Checklist*
xx	Observation *Individual Assessment*
xxi	Observation *Class Checklist*
xxii	Cooperative Groups *Class Checklist*
xxiii	Projects *Individual Assessment*
xxiv	Overall Student Assessment *Class Checklist*

Pages	Contents
Tests	
1–2	Quiz Lessons 1-1 Through 1-3
3–4	Quiz Lessons 1-4 Through 1-6
5–8	Chapter 1 Test, Form A
9–12	Chapter 1 Test, Form B
13	Chapter 1 Test, Form C
14	Chapter 1 Test, Form D
15–16	Quiz Lessons 2-1 Through 2-3
17–18	Quiz Lessons 2-4 Through 2-6
19–22	Chapter 2 Test, Form A
23–26	Chapter 2 Test, Form B
27	Chapter 2 Test, Form C
28	Chapter 2 Test, Form D
29–32	Chapter 2 Test, Cumulative Form
33	Quiz Lessons 3-1 Through 3-3
34–35	Quiz Lessons 3-4 Through 3-6
36–39	Chapter 3 Test, Form A
40–43	Chapter 3 Test, Form B
44	Chapter 3 Test, Form C
45	Chapter 3 Test, Form D
46–49	Chapter 3 Test, Cumulative Form
50–53	Comprehensive Test, Chapters 1–3
54	Quiz Lessons 4-1 Through 4-3
55	Quiz Lessons 4-4 Through 4-6
56–59	Chapter 4 Test, Form A
60–63	Chapter 4 Test, Form B
64	Chapter 4 Test, Form C
65	Chapter 4 Test, Form D
66–69	Chapter 4 Test, Cumulative Form
70	Quiz Lessons 5-1 Through 5-3
71	Quiz Lessons 5-4 Through 5-6
72–74	Chapter 5 Test, Form A
75–77	Chapter 5 Test, Form B
78	Chapter 5 Test, Form C
79	Chapter 5 Test, Form D
80–82	Chapter 5 Test, Cumulative Form
83	Quiz Lessons 6-1 Through 6-3
84	Quiz Lessons 6-4 Through 6-6
85–87	Chapter 6 Test, Form A
88–90	Chapter 6 Test, Form B
91	Chapter 6 Test, Form C
92	Chapter 6 Test, Form D
93–95	Chapter 6 Test, Cumulative Form
96–99	Comprehensive Test, Chapters 1–6
100	Quiz Lessons 7–1 Through 7–3
101	Quiz Lessons 7–4 Through 7–6
102–103	Chapter 7 Test, Form A
104–105	Chapter 7 Test, Form B
106	Chapter 7 Test, Form C
107	Chapter 7 Test, Form D
108–109	Chapter 7 Test, Cumulative Form

ISBN: 0-673-45933-0

Copyright
Addison Wesley Longman, Inc.
All Rights Reserved.
Printed in the United States of America.

1 2 3 4 5 6—MH—01 00 99 98

Pages	Contents

Tests

Pages	Contents
110	Quiz Lessons 8-1 Through 8-3
111	Quiz Lessons 8-4 Through 8-6
112–113	Chapter 8 Test, Form A
114–115	Chapter 8 Test, Form B
116	Chapter 8 Test, Form C
117	Chapter 8 Test, Form D
118–120	Chapter 8 Test, Cumulative Form
121	Quiz Lessons 9-1 Through 9-3
122	Quiz Lessons 9-4 Through 9-7
123–124	Chapter 9 Test, Form A
125–126	Chapter 9 Test, Form B
127	Chapter 9 Test, Form C
128	Chapter 9 Test, Form D
129–131	Chapter 9 Test, Cumulative Form
132–136	Comprehensive Test, Chapters 1–9
137	Quiz Lessons 10-1 Through 10-3
138	Quiz Lessons 10-4 Through 10-6
139–140	Chapter 10 Test, Form A
141–142	Chapter 10 Test, Form B
143	Chapter 10 Test, Form C
144	Chapter 10 Test, Form D
145–146	Chapter 10 Test, Cumulative Form
147	Quiz Lessons 11-1 Through 11-3
148	Quiz Lessons 11-4 Through 11-6
149–150	Chapter 11 Test, Form A
151–152	Chapter 11 Test, Form B
153	Chapter 11 Test, Form C
154	Chapter 11 Test, Form D
155–157	Chapter 11 Test, Cumulative Form
158	Quiz Lessons 12-1 Through 12-3
159–160	Chapter 12 Test, Form A
161–162	Chapter 12 Test, Form B
163	Chapter 12 Test, Form C
164	Chapter 12 Test, Form D
165–167	Chapter 12 Test, Cumulative Form
168	Quiz Lessons 13-1 Through 13-3
169	Quiz Lessons 13-4 Through 13-6
170–172	Chapter 13 Test, Form A
173–175	Chapter 13 Test, Form B
176	Chapter 13 Test, Form C
177	Chapter 13 Test, Form D
178–180	Chapter 13 Test, Cumulative Form
181–188	Comprehensive Test, Chapters 1–13

Answers

Quizzes; Tests, Forms A and B, Cumulative Forms; Comprehensive Tests

Pages	Contents
189	Chapter 1
190	Chapter 2
193	Chapter 3
196	Chapter 4
198	Chapter 5
200	Chapter 6
201	Chapter 7
203	Chapter 8
204	Chapter 9
205	Chapter 10
207	Chapter 11
209	Chapter 12
211	Chapter 13

Evaluation Guides

Tests, Forms C and D

Pages	Contents
215	Chapter 1
217	Chapter 2
219	Chapter 3
221	Chapter 4
223	Chapter 5
225	Chapter 6
227	Chapter 7
229	Chapter 8
231	Chapter 9
233	Chapter 10
235	Chapter 11
237	Chapter 12
239	Chapter 13

Assessing Student Performance in Mathematics

The Changing Face of Mathematics Instruction and Assessment

In the past decade, the National Council of Teachers of Mathematics and other mathematics education organizations and professionals have examined the methods teachers use to instruct students in mathematics and have recommended ways to improve this instruction. Their recommendations stress the importance of providing more diverse methods of instruction including activities, open-ended investigations, and long-term projects, many of which utilize cooperative learning. They challenge us to make the goal of mathematics the acquisition of the dynamic processes of critical thinking and problem solving, rather than merely the mastery of a static body of facts and procedures.

Instruction and assessment are closely linked. As instructional methods change, the methods of evaluation need to change. New forms of assessment being proposed provide a more authentic way of evaluating the depth of our students' knowledge of mathematics rather than their ability to memorize facts and procedures. These alternative methods of assessment offer students the opportunity to display how they approach problem situations, collect and organize information, formulate and test conjectures, and communicate their mathematical insights.

An authentic assessment program contains tasks that are appropriate to the topics the students are learning and that provide outcomes that are valuable to the students. Such an assessment program allows for such highly individual factors as a school's curriculum objectives, a teacher's style of instruction, and a student's maturity level and preferred learning style. Each individual teacher determines the assessment program best suited to the needs of his or her students.

In an instructional environment that demands a deeper understanding of mathematics, testing instruments that call for only identification of single correct responses no longer suffice. Instead, our instruments must reflect the scope and intent of our instructional program to have students solve problems, reason, and communicate.

NCTM Standards

To help a teacher select the most appropriate evaluation tools for his or her classroom, this *Assessment Sourcebook* provides the following materials. (See pre-chapter pages in UCSMP *Functions Statistics, and Trigonometry* Teacher's Edition for correlation of test items to chapter objectives.)

Assessment Forms

- student-completed forms
- teacher-completed forms for individual, group, and class activities

Assessment Instruments

- **Chapter Quizzes,** two per chapter, which cover three or four lessons and which contain mostly free-response items
- **Chapter Tests, Forms A and B,** which are alternate versions of each other and which test every chapter objective in primarily free-response format
- **Chapter Tests, Form C,** which consist of 4 to 6 performance-based, open-ended items, many of which assess several chapter objectives
- **Chapter Tests, Form D,** which are performance based and which often assess 5 or more chapter objectives as applied to a single larger task
- **Chapter Tests, Cumulative Form,** which contain mostly free-response items
- **Comprehensive Tests,** every three or four chapters, which are cumulative in nature and consist primarily of multiple-choice items

To assess development of a student's mathematical power, a teacher needs to use a mixture of means: essays, homework, projects, short answers, quizzes, blackboard work, journals, oral interviews, and group projects.

Everybody Counts:
A Report to the Nation on the Future
of Mathematics Education

Guidelines for Developing an Authentic Assessment Program

Developing an authentic program of assessment is an ongoing process. Some assessment instruments will seem perfectly suited to the teacher and his or her students from the start. Others may be effective only after the teacher has had a chance to experiment, and refine them. Still others may be inappropriate for a given class or instructional situation. The following are some guidelines that may be helpful when choosing the types of assessment for a particular program.

Assessment serves many purposes.

- For the teacher, assessment yields feedback on the appropriateness of instructional methods and offers some clues as to how the content or pace of instruction could be modified.
- For the students, assessment should not only identify areas for improvement, but it should also affirm their successes.
- Traditional forms of assessment yield a tangible score.

Make the assessment process a positive experience for students.

- Use a variety of assessment techniques.
- Provide opportunities for students to demonstrate their mathematical capabilities in an atmosphere that encourages maximum performance.
- Emphasize what students *do* know and *can* do, not what they do not know and cannot do.
- Motivate students to achieve by using tasks that reflect the value of their efforts.

Authentic assessment focuses on higher-order thinking skills.

- Provides a picture of the student as a critical thinker and problem solver
- Identifies *how* the student does mathematics, not just what answer he or she gets

Provide assessment activities that resemble day-to-day tasks.

- Use activities similar to instructional activities to assess.
- Use assessment activities to further instruction.
- Give students the immediate and detailed feedback they need to further the learning process.
- Encourage students to explore how the mathematics they are learning applies to real situations.

Include each student as a partner in the assessment process.

- Encourage students to reflect on what they have done.
- Encourage students to share their goals.

Portfolios and Notebooks

A portfolio is a collection of a student's work—projects, reports, drawings, reflections, representative assignments, assessment instruments—that displays the student's mathematical accomplishments over an extended period. The following suggestions for use should be adapted to the needs and organizational style of each situation.

A student notebook should reflect the student's day-to-day activities related to the mathematics class. It may include a section for journal entries as well as sections for homework, tests, and notes.

Getting Started

○ Provide file folders labeled *Portfolio*.

○ Provide guidelines for notebook format.

The Portfolio

○ The Portfolio can be used as the basis for assessing a student's achievements. The focus of the Portfolio should be on student thinking, growth in understanding over time, making mathematical connections, positive attitudes about mathematics, and the problem-solving process.

The Notebook

○ The notebook is for "work in progress." The student should keep in it all class and reading notes, group work, homework, reports and projects, and various student assessment forms, such as *Student Self-Assessment*.

○ Every two to six weeks students review their notebooks to determine the materials they would like to transfer to their Portfolios.

○ The teacher also selects student materials for the Portfolio and includes any appropriate assessment instruments.

○ The student completes the *About My Portfolio* form.

> **The opportunity to share mathematical ideas through portfolios can mark a real turning point in student attitudes.**
>
> *Mathematics Assessment (NCTM Publication)*

○ Portfolios may include:

  student selected items from the notebook; a letter from the student about the work; a math autobiography; other work selected by the teacher including math surveys; various assessment documents.

Evaluating a Portfolio

○ Keep in mind that portfolio evaluation is a matter of ongoing discussion.

○ Set aside time to discuss the Portfolio with the student.

○ Use the Portfolio when discussing the student's progress with his or her family.

○ Use it as a basis for identifying strengths and weaknesses and for setting goals for the next block of work.

○ Consider developing your own criteria for evaluating portfolios, for example, numeric scales.

Evaluating a Notebook

○ Notebooks should be evaluated based on agreed-upon guidelines.

○ Notebooks should be evaluated for organization and neatness, completeness, and timeliness.

○ Notebooks may be evaluated every week, every chapter, or any time you feel is appropriate.

○ You may choose to evaluate notebooks by checking items or by assigning numeric values to specific items.

Functions, Statistics, and Trigonometry © Scott Foresman Addison Wesley

Using Free-Response and Multiple-Choice Tests

Teachers use written tests for many purposes. Particularly when it is objective-referenced, a test can be a relatively quick and efficient method of diagnosing the scope of a student's mathematical knowledge. Tests can also provide valuable instructional feedback. And, of course, grades are a traditional instrument for reporting student achievement to parents, administrators, and the community. This *Sourcebook* provides a large number of both free-response and multiple-choice items.

Free-Response Tests

A free-response test, sometimes called a completion test, is a collection of items for which a student must supply requested information. While free-response tests are generally designed for written responses, they may also be used orally with individual students, especially those with limited English proficiency.

Multiple-choice Tests

A multiple-choice test consists of many well-defined problems or questions. The student is given a set of four or five possible answers for each item and is asked to select the correct or best answer. The other choices, often called distractors, usually reflect common misconceptions or errors.

This *Sourcebook* contains:

- Quizzes covering three or four lessons in each chapter. The quizzes are primarily free response in nature.

- Chapter Tests, Forms A and B, which are alternate forms of each other and which test every chapter objective. The tests contain primarily free-response items, but they may also include several multiple-choice items. These tests can be used as chapter pretests and posttests to help implement needed individualized instruction

- Chapter Tests, Cumulative Form, for Chapters 2-13, which are basically free-response assessment

- Comprehensive Tests for Chapters 1-3, 1-6, 1-9, and 1-13, which consist of mostly multiple-choice items and are cumulative in nature

Functions, Statistics, and Trigonometry © Scott Foresman Addison Wesley

Using Performance Assessment

In order to provide more authentic forms of assessment, this *Sourcebook* provides two forms of chapter tests that focus on students' ability to demonstrate their understanding of mathematical concepts.

Chapter Tests, Form C

The Form C Chapter Test items help you make a judgment of the students' understanding of mathematical concepts and their ability to interpret information, make generalizations, and communicate their ideas. Each assessment contains four to six open-ended questions, each of which is keyed to several chapter objectives.

Administering Form C Tests

The tests can be administered in a way that is best suited for the students. Provide manipulatives, extra paper, and other tools as needed. The use of calculators is assumed.

○ Use all the assessment items.

○ Use only one or two, along with a free-response or a multiple-choice test.

○ Use the assessment items to interview each student.

○ Have students give the explanations orally, and then write the answers.

Evaluating Form C Tests

Each test item is accompanied by a list of two or more evaluation criteria that can be used as a basis for judging student responses.

To rate how well students meet each criterion, a simple scale such as this may be used.

| + excellent |
| ✓ satisfactory |
| − inadequate |

Evaluation Guides for these tests are found starting on page 215 of this *Sourcebook*.

Comparison of Form C Tests and Free-Response Tests

	Form C Tests	Free Response Tests
Number of items	4–6	15–35
Sample Format	○ Draw 3 different rectangles that each have an area of 12 square centimeters.	○ Find the area of a rectangle that is 4 centimeters long and 3 centimeters wide.
Mode of administration	○ Interview ○ Written response ○ Combination of interview and written responses	○ Written response
Answers	○ May have more than one ○ May require an explanation by student	○ Single, short
Scoring	○ 2–4 evaluation criteria given ○ Use of simple rating scale	○ One correct answer for each item
Benefits	○ More accurate determination of instructional needs and strengths of students	○ Easy to score

Functions, Statistics, and Trigonometry © Scott Foresman Addison Wesley

The Form D Chapter Tests in this *Sourcebook* are composed of large mathematical tasks which allow students to demonstrate a broad spectrum of their abilities:

○ how they reason through difficult problems;

○ how they make and test conjectures;

○ how their number sense helps them give reasonable answers;

○ how they utilize alternative strategies.

These performance tasks also give teachers a means of assessing qualities of imagination, creativity, and perseverance.

Administering Form D Tests

Some Classroom Management Tips

○ Whenever possible, use Form D Tests as cooperative group activities, listening as students interact in their groups.	○ Have any needed mathematical tools or manipulatives readily available. The use of calculators is assumed.
○ Ask students questions that will give you information about their thought processes.	○ Be sure all students understand the purpose of the task. Offer assistance as needed.

Evaluating Performance Assessments

For each assessment, a set of task-specific performance standards provides a means for judging the quality of the students' work. These standards identify five levels of performance related to the particular task. The specific standards were created using the following characteristics of student performance as general guidelines.

Level 5: Accomplishes and extends the task; displays in-depth understanding; communicates effectively and completely.

Level 4: Accomplishes the task competently; displays clear understanding of key concepts; communicates effectively.

Level 3: Substantially completes the task; displays minor flaws in understanding or technique; communicates successfully.

Level 2: Only partially completes the task; displays one or more major errors in understanding or technique; communicates unclear or incomplete information.

Level 1: Attempts the task, but fails to complete it in any substantive way; displays only fragmented understanding; attempts communication, but is not successful.

Each test is accompanied by a set of teacher notes that identifies the chapter objectives being assessed, as well as the mathematical concepts and skills involved in the performance task. The notes also list any materials that are needed and provide answers where appropriate. Questions to guide students as they seek solutions are provided, along with ideas for extending the activity. These notes, along with the performance standards as described at the left, are found in the Evaluation Guides starting on page 216 of this *Sourcebook*.

Since performance tasks are open-ended, student responses are as varied and individual as the students themselves. For this reason, it may be helpful to use these general guidelines as well as the task-specific standards when determining the level of each student's performance.

Functions, Statistics, and Trigonometry © Scott Foresman Addison Wesley

Using Assessment Forms

Using Student-Completed Forms

To do meaningful work in our fast-paced and ever-changing technological world, students must learn to assess their own progress. This *Sourcebook* provides four forms that can be used to help students with self-assessment. Use one or more depending on the needs of your students.

Using Teacher-Completed Forms

This *Sourcebook* also provides ten assessment forms that are designed to help you keep a record of authentic assessments. Some forms are for use with individual students, while others are for use with groups of students. Determine which would be best suited for use in your classroom.

	Form	Purpose	Suggested Uses
Student-Completed	Student Survey	Checklist of student attitudes toward various math activities	○ Periodically monitor the change in student attitudes toward math
	Student Self-Assessment	Checklist of student awareness of how well he or she works independently	○ Monitor student progress in working independently
	Cooperative Groups Self-Assessment	Form for students to describe their attitudes and interaction with other students in a cooperative-learning situation	○ Completed at the conclusion of group learning activities ○ Completed by individual students or groups of students
	About My Portfolio	Form for student to describe the contents of his or her portfolio	○ Completed when student transfers work from the notebook to the *Portfolio*
Teacher-Completed	Portfolio Assessment	Form to assess student's mathematical accomplishments over time	○ Use to discuss student's progress in discussions with family
	Notebooks, Individual Assessment	Form to record student's organizational skills and completeness of assignments	○ Describe student's attention to specified daily tasks
	Notebooks, Class Checklist	Checklist to record students' notebook maintenance	○ Use when setting goals for improving study skills
	Problem Solving, Individual Assessment	Form to assess each student in a problem-solving situation	○ Describe level of student performance ○ Modify the level to meet individual needs
	Problem Solving, Class Checklist	Checklist to assess groups of students in problem-solving situations	○ Assess the entire class ○ Assess small groups over time
	Observation, Individual Assessment	Form to determine the student's thought processes, performances, and attitudes	○ Record observation of student in classroom
	Observation, Class Checklist	Checklist for observing several students at one time	○ Provide a mathematical profile of the entire class ○ Identify common strengths and weaknesses ○ Help in modifying content or pace and in determining appropriate groupings
	Cooperative Groups, Class Checklist	Checklist to assess students' abilities to work constructively in groups	○ Assess one or more cooperative groups
	Project Assessment	Form for evaluating extended projects or oral presentations	○ Evaluate an individual or group project or presentation ○ Prepare students for presentations or projects
	Overall Student Assessment, Class Checklist	Checklist summary of students' overall performance	○ Evaluate student performance over an entire instructional period

Functions, Statistics, and Trigonometry © Scott Foresman Addison Wesley

Student Survey

Answer the following questions using the rating scale provided.

5   Always
4   Usually
3   Sometimes
2   Rarely
1   Never

_____   **1.** I read material more than once if I don't understand it.

_____   **2.** I use the reading heads and bold terms to help me preview the material.

_____   **3.** I review for a test more than one day before it is given.

_____   **4.** I concentrate when I study.

_____   **5.** I try all the examples.

_____   **6.** I do all of my assigned homework.

_____   **7.** I pay attention in class.

_____   **8.** I take notes and keep my notebook up-to-date and neat.

_____   **9.** I bring the required materials to class.

_____   **10.** I really try to get good grades.

_____   **11.** I ask questions and try to get help when I need it.

_____   **12.** I use the Progress Self-Test and Chapter Review to prepare for tests.

_____   **13.** I make up work when I have been absent.

_____   **14.** I look for uses of math in real life.

_____   **15.** I can solve most problems.

_____   **16.** I like to try new strategies.

_____   **17.** I give up too easily.

_____   **18.** I work cooperatively.

My favorite kind of math is _____

because _____

List some activities in which you have used math.

_____

_____

_____

Functions, Statistics, and Trigonometry © Scott Foresman Addison Wesley

Student Self-Assessment

Complete the following sentences to describe your learning experience.

I was supposed to learn _____

_____

I started the work by _____

_____

_____

As a group member, I contributed _____

_____

_____

I learned _____

_____

_____

I am still confused by _____

_____

_____

I enjoyed the assignment because _____

_____

_____

I think the assignment was worthwhile because _____

_____

_____

Check the sentences that describe your work on this assignment.

☐ I was able to do the work.
☐ I did not understand the directions.
☐ I followed the directions but got wrong answers.
☐ I can explain how to do this assignment to someone else.
☐ The assignment was easier than I thought it would be.
☐ The assignment was harder than I thought it would be.

Functions, Statistics, and Trigonometry © Scott Foresman Addison Wesley

Cooperative Groups Self-Assessment

Assignment _____

Reader: _____   *Writer:* _____

Materials handler: _____   *Checker:* _____

Others in group: _____

Materials: _____

Check the sentences that describe your work.

☐ We had a new idea or made a suggestion.
☐ We asked for more information.
☐ We shared the information we found.
☐ We tried different ways to solve the problem.
☐ We helped others explain their ideas better.
☐ We pulled our ideas together.
☐ We were reminded to work together.
☐ We demonstrated a knowledge of the mathematical concept.
☐ We encouraged those who did not understand.

Complete each sentence.

We learned

_____

_____

We found an answer by

_____

_____

After we found an answer, we

_____

_____

By working together, we

_____

_____

About My Portfolio

Complete the following sentences about the work you are putting into your portfolio.

Describe the assignment.

_____

_____

_____

I chose this work as part of my portfolio because

_____

_____

_____

I began my work by

_____

_____

_____

Doing this work helped me

_____

_____

_____

The work was   ☐ too easy   ☐ easy   ☐ just right   ☐ hard   ☐ too hard

because _____

_____

_____

Functions, Statistics, and Trigonometry © Scott Foresman Addison Wesley

Portfolio Assessment

The work in this portfolio:

shows growth in the student's mathematical understanding.

exhibits the student's ability to reason mathematically.

makes connections within mathematics.

makes connections to other disciplines.

shows that the student is able to work on mathematical tasks in cooperative groups.

illustrates the appropriate use of a variety of tools.

Notebooks

Rate items, based upon your requirements, as follows:
+   if excellent
✓   if satisfactory
-    if needs improvement
NA   if not applicable

Written Assignments   **Comments**

_____   **1.** Assignment sheet

_____   **2.** Daily homework

_____   **3.** Lesson Warm-ups

_____   **4.** Lesson Masters

_____   **5.** Activities

_____   **6.** Projects

Reading and Class Notes   **Comments**

_____   **7.** Definitions

_____   **8.** Properties

_____   **9.** Examples

_____   **10.** Class notes, handouts

Assessment   **Comments**

_____   **11.** Chapter Quizzes

_____   **12.** Chapter Progress Self-Test

_____   **13.** Chapter Review

_____   **14.** Chapter Tests

_____   **15.** Cumulative Chapter Test

_____   **16.** Comprehensive Test

Other   **Comments**

_____   **17.**

_____   **18.**

_____   **19.**

_____   **20.**

Overall Rating/Comments

Functions, Statistics, and Trigonometry © Scott Foresman Addison Wesley

Class

Rate each item as follows:
+   if excellent
✓   if satisfactory
-     if needs improvement
NA   if not applicable

Students	Date	Written Assignments		Reading/Class Notes		Assessment			
1.									
2.									
3.									
4.									
5.									
6.									
7.									
8.									
9.									
10.									
11.									
12.									
13.									
14.									
15.									
16.									
17.									
18.									
19.									
20.									
21.									
22.									
23.									
24.									
25.									
26.									
27.									
28.									
29.									
30.									

Problem Solving

Check each statement below that accurately describes
the student's work. This list includes suggested student
behaviors to consider. Feel free to modify it to suit your needs.

Reads carefully   **Comments**

☐ Looks up unfamiliar words
☐ Understands lesson concepts and can apply
   them
☐ Rereads
☐ Finds/uses information appropriately
☐
☐

Creates a plan   **Comments**

☐ Chooses an appropriate strategy
☐ Estimates the answer
☐
☐
☐

Carries out the plan   **Comments**

☐ Works systematically and with care
☐ Shows work in an organized fashion
☐ Computes correctly
☐ Rereads the problem if the first attempt is
   unsuccessful
☐ Rereads the problem and interprets the solution
☐ States the answer in required format
☐
☐
☐

Checks the work   **Comments**

☐ Checks by estimating
☐ Tries alternate approaches
☐
☐
☐

Functions, Statistics, and Trigonometry © Scott Foresman Addison Wesley

Problem Solving

Class Checklist

Class

Rate each item as follows:
+   if excellent
✓   if satisfactory
-    if needs improvement
NA   if not applicable

Students	Date	Looks up unfamiliar words	Understands the question/task	Uses information appropriately	Chooses an appropriate strategy	Estimates the answer	Is systematic and careful	Computes correctly	Rereads the problem if necessary	States answer in required format	Tries alternate approaches
1.											
2.											
3.											
4.											
5.											
6.											
7.											
8.											
9.											
10.											
11.											
12.											
13.											
14.											
15.											
16.											
17.											
18.											
19.											
20.											
21.											
22.											
23.											
24.											
25.											
26.											
27.											
28.											
29.											
30.											

Functions, Statistics, and Trigonometry © Scott Foresman Addison Wesley

Name _____ *Date* _____

Observation

Individual Assessment

	Usually	Sometimes	Rarely
Understanding			
Demonstrates knowledge of skills	☐	☐	☐
Understands concepts	☐	☐	☐
Selects appropriate solution strategies	☐	☐	☐
Solves problems accurately	☐	☐	☐
Work Habits			
Works in an organized manner	☐	☐	☐
Works neatly	☐	☐	☐
Submits work on time	☐	☐	☐
Works well with others	☐	☐	☐
Uses time productively	☐	☐	☐
Asks for help when needed	☐	☐	☐
Confidence			
Initiates questions	☐	☐	☐
Displays positive attitude	☐	☐	☐
Helps others	☐	☐	☐
Flexibility			
Tries alternative approaches	☐	☐	☐
Considers and uses ideas of others	☐	☐	☐
Likes to try alternative methods	☐	☐	☐
Perseverance			
Shows patience and perseverance	☐	☐	☐
Works systematically	☐	☐	☐
Is willing to try	☐	☐	☐
Checks work regularly	☐	☐	☐
Other			
_____	☐	☐	☐
_____	☐	☐	☐
_____	☐	☐	☐

Functions, Statistics, and Trigonometry © Scott Foresman Addison Wesley

Observation

Class Checklist

Class _____

Rate each item as follows:
+   if excellent
✓   if satisfactory
-     if needs improvement
NA   if not applicable

Students	Date	Demonstrates knowledge of skills	Understands concepts	Works neatly and systematically	Works well with others	Asks for help when needed	Uses time productively	Displays positive attitude	Tries alternative approaches	Considers and uses ideas of others	Shows patience and perseverance
1.											
2.											
3.											
4.											
5.											
6.											
7.											
8.											
9.											
10.											
11.											
12.											
13.											
14.											
15.											
16.											
17.											
18.											
19.											
20.											
21.											
22.											
23.											
24.											
25.											
26.											
27.											
28.											
29.											
30.											

Functions, Statistics, and Trigonometry © Scott Foresman Addison Wesley

Class

Rate each item as follows:

+   if excellent

✓   if satisfactory

-     if needs improvement

NA   if not applicable

Students	Date	Works with others in the group	Considers and uses ideas of others	Tutors and helps others	Has a positive attitude	Disagrees but is not disagreeable	Shows patience and perseverance	Works systematically	Initiates questions			
1.												
2.												
3.												
4.												
5.												
6.												
7.												
8.												
9.												
10.												
11.												
12.												
13.												
14.												
15.												
16.												
17.												
18.												
19.												
20.												
21.												
22.												
23.												
24.												
25.												
26.												
27.												
28.												
29.												
30.												

Functions, Statistics, and Trigonometry © Scott Foresman Addison Wesley

Project Assessment

Project _____

Rate each item as follows:

+   if excellent
✓   if satisfactory
-      if needs improvement
NA   if not applicable

The Project

_____ Demonstrates mathematical concepts properly

_____ Communicates ideas clearly

_____ Shows connection to another subject

_____ Shows evidence of time spent in planning and preparation

_____ Is original and creative

_____ Includes charts, tables, and/or graphs where appropriate

_____ Uses available technology effectively

_____ Stimulates further investigation of the topic

_____ Includes a short written report if the project is a model or demonstration

_____ Lists resources used

The Oral Presentation

_____ Is organized (includes an introduction, main section, and conclusion)

_____ Uses audio-visual materials where appropriate

_____ Speaks clearly and paces presentation properly

_____ Answers questions and stimulates further interest among classmates

_____ Holds audience's attention

Overall Project Rating/Comments

_____

_____

_____

_____

Overall Student Assessment

Class

Rate each item as follows:

+   if excellent
✓   if satisfactory
-     if needs improvement
NA   if not applicable

Students	Date	Class Work	Discussion	Cooperative Groups	Problem Solving	Homework	Notebooks	Projects	Tests		
1.											
2.											
3.											
4.											
5.											
6.											
7.											
8.											
9.											
10.											
11.											
12.											
13.											
14.											
15.											
16.											
17.											
18.											
19.											
20.											
21.											
22.											
23.											
24.											
25.											
26.											
27.											
28.											
29.											
30.											

Functions, Statistics, and Trigonometry © Scott Foresman Addison Wesley

Name _____

In 1–5, use the table below.

Ownership of the World's Five Hundred Largest Companies, 1995		
Country	Number of Companies	Revenues (billions of dollars)	Profits[2] (billions of dollars)
Total[1]	500	11,378	323
Japan	141	3,985	30
United States	153	3,221	158
Germany	40	1,017	17
France	42	880	3
United Kingdom	32	516	38
Switzerland	16	345	18
South Korea	12	263	7
Italy	12	255	7
Netherlands	8	171	9
Britain/Netherlands	2	160	9
Spain	6	81	4
Canada	6	66	6
Belgium	5	56	2
Sweden	3	54	2
Brazil	4	54	-3

[1] Includes other countries not shown separately.
[2] A minus sign indicates a loss.

Source: *Statistical Abstract of the United States, 1996*

1. What percent of the world's five hundred largest companies are Japanese-owned?

   1. _____

2. What percent of the total profits of the five hundred companies were made by Japanese-owned companies?

   2. _____

3. The companies of which listed country had the least profits?

   3. _____

4. Suppose you make a circle graph of these data. What would be the measure of the central angle, to the nearest degree, for the sector representing the revenues of United States companies?

   4. _____

5. Explain why the sum of the numbers of companies for the listed countries is not 500.

   _____

   _____

Name _____

► **QUIZ for Lessons 1-1 Through 1-3** *page 2*

In 6–8, use the table below. The numbers $a_1, a_2, \ldots, a_{10}$ represent the ages in years of the pupils and the driver on a school bus.

a_1	a_2	a_3	a_4	a_5	a_6	a_7	a_8	a_9	a_{10}
6	6	6	7	7	8	8	10	12	60

6. **a.** Find the mode of the ages of the people on the bus.   6. a. _____

   b. Find the median of the ages of the people on the bus.   b. _____

7. **a.** Evalute $\frac{1}{10}\sum_{i=1}^{10} a_i$.   7. a. _____

   b. What does the expression in part **a** represent?   b. _____

8. Which will change most if the driver's age is excluded   8. _____
   from the data: the mean, the median, or the mode?

In 9–11, use the stemplot at the right. The data represent the average annual pay for residents of each of the fifty states in 1994 as reported in the *Statistical Abstract of the United States 1996*. Each stem indicates $1000. All values have been rounded to the nearest $100.

```
19 | 3 9
20 | 2 4 9
21 | 5 9
22 | 1 2 3 4 4 5 7 8 9
23 | 0 0 2 5 6 9
24 | 1 3 3 6 8 9
25 | 3 5 6 7
26 | 0 0 1 2 4 4 7
27 | 0
28 | 0 4
29 | 1 5 9
30 |
31 | 0
32 | 7
33 | 4 4 8
```

9. What is the range of the average annual pay in the   9. _____
   fifty states?

10. What is the median of the average annual pay   10. _____
    in the fifty states?

11. In how many states is the average annual pay   11. _____
    greater than $30,000?

Functions, Statistics, and Trigonometry © Scott Foresman Addison Wesley

2

Name _____

In 1 and 2, use the following data and graph.

Estimated World Population	
Year	Population (billions)
1650	0.470
1750	0.790
1850	1.260
1900	1.650
1950	2.520
2000	6.090

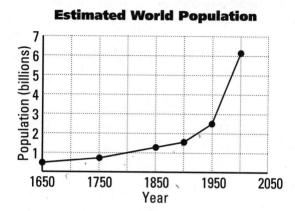

Estimated World Population

1. **a.** Data are given for six years. Between which two of these years is the rate of population growth the greatest?

   1. a. _____

   b. Calculate the average rate of change of the world population over the time interval in part **a**.

   b. _____

2. Find the average rate of change of the world population per year between 1650 and 2000.

   2. _____

In 3 and 4, use the following table, which shows the distribution of 150 hostels affiliated with Hostelling International—American Youth Hostels among the fifty states.

Number of Hostels	0	1	2	3	4	5	6	7	9	11	12	24
Frequency (Number of States)	14	9	10	3	4	1	2	2	2	1	1	1

Source: *1997 Hostelling North America*

3. **a.** Find each measure.

   3. a. _____

   i. Q_1

   i. _____

   ii. Q_3

   ii. _____

   iii. interquartile range

   iii. _____

   b. Use the $1.5 \times$ IQR criterion to find any outliers.

   b. _____

4. What is the percentile ranking of the state with eleven hostels?

   4. _____

In 5 and 6, use the following box plots.

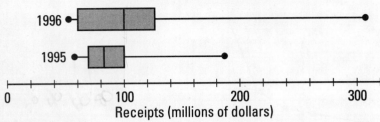

The Year's 25 Top-Grossing Films
(United States and Canada)

Receipts (millions of dollars)

Source: *Daily Variety*

5. Which numbers in the five-number summary for 1995 exceed their counterparts for 1996?

5. _____

6. In 1996, about how many times more films grossed more than $100 million than in 1995?

6. _____

In 7 and 8, use the histograms below, which show the distributions of passenger traffic during 1995 at the busiest United States and foreign airports. There are twenty airports in each group. Each interval includes the left endpoint, but not the right.

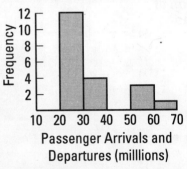

United States Airports

Passenger Arrivals and Departures (milllions)

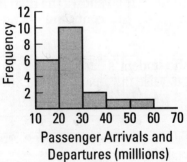

Foreign Airports

Passenger Arrivals and Departures (milllions)

Source: *The World Almanac and Book of Facts 1997.*

7. In which interval does the first quartile for foreign airports lie?

7. _____

8. In 1995, how many more United States airports than foreign airports had at least 30 million passenger arrivals and departures?

8. _____

Functions, Statistics, and Trigonometry © Scott Foresman Addison Wesley

CHAPTER 1 TEST, Form A

You will need a calculator for this test.

1. In a shipment of 100 bags of cookies, each bag contains twenty cookies. Before accepting the shipment, a store owner opened one bag and counted the number of raisins in ten cookies.

   a. What percent of the population does the sample represent?   **1. a.** _____

   b. What is the variable of interest?   **b.** _____

   c. Give a reason for testing only a sample.

   _____

   _____

In 2 and 3, refer to the stemplot at the right, which shows the scores a math student has received on all homework assignments to date.

```
 6 | 1
 7 | 0 2 2 2 4
 8 | 1 1 4
 9 | 3
10 |
```

2. **a.** Find the total number of homework assignments.   **2. a.** _____

   b. Find the mode of the homework scores.   **b.** _____

   c. Find the median of the homework scores.   **c.** _____

3. What must be the total of the student's next two homework scores in order to raise the mean score to 80?   **3.** _____

In 4 and 5, Jack and Jill each tossed a standard six-sided die the same number of times. Each time, they recorded the number tossed. Their results are shown in the dotplots at the right.

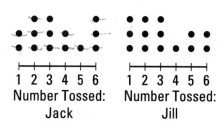

Number Tossed: Jack   Number Tossed: Jill

4. **a.** How many times did each person toss the die?   **4. a.** _____

   b. What is the median number that Jack tossed?   **b.** _____

   c. What is the mean of the numbers that Jill tossed?   **c.** _____

5. Whose data have the greater spread: Jack or Jill? Justify your answer.

   _____

   _____

In 6–8, use the following table.

College Enrollment of High School Graduates by Gender						
	High School Graduates (thousands)			Percent Enrolled in College		
Year	Total	Male	Female	Total	Male	Female
1960	1,679	756	923	45.1	54.0	37.9
1970	2,757	1,343	1,414	51.8	55.2	48.5
1980	3,089	1,500	1,589	49.3	46.7	51.8
1990	2,355	1,169	1,185	59.9	57.8	62.0
1995	2,599	1,238	1,361	61.9	62.6	61.4

Sources: *Statistical Abstract of the United States 1996; The World Almanac and Book of Facts 1997*

6. How many female high school graduates enrolled in college in 1995?

6. _____

7. What information is conveyed by the number 61.9 in the fifth row?

_____

_____

8. Describe one trend in female college enrollment from 1960 to 1995.

_____

_____

In 9 and 10, use the following table, which shows the distribution of a high school's students among four classes.

Class	freshman	sophomore	junior	senior
Students	630	500	475	495

9. **a.** Which would be most suitable for displaying the data: a bar graph, a line graph, or a dotplot?

9. a. _____

   b. Give at least one reason for *not* using each type of graph you rejected in part **a**.

_____

_____

10. Suppose a circle graph were used to display the data. What should be the measure in degrees of the central angle of the sector representing the freshman class?

10. _____

Functions, Statistics, and Trigonometry © Scott Foresman Addison Wesley

In 11–15, *multiple choice.* The numbers $p_1, p_2, \ldots, p_{22}$ represent the annual profits, in decreasing order, of twenty-two companies. Let $P = \sum\limits_{i=1}^{22} p_i$. Choose the expression that represents each measure.

(a) $\frac{1}{22}P$ (b) p_{11} (c) p_{12} (d) $\frac{p_{11} + p_{12}}{2}$

(e) $P - \sum\limits_{i=1}^{11} p_i$ (f) $P - \sum\limits_{i=12}^{22} p_i$ (g) $\frac{1}{22}\sum\limits_{i=1}^{22} p_i^2$ (h) $\frac{1}{21}\sum\limits_{i=1}^{22} p_i^2$

(i) $\frac{1}{22}\sum\limits_{i=1}^{22}\left(p_i - \frac{1}{22}P\right)^2$ (j) $\frac{1}{21}\sum\limits_{i=1}^{22}\left(p_i - \frac{1}{22}P\right)^2$

11. mean profits   11. _____

12. median profits   12. _____

13. sample variance   13. _____

14. population variance   14. _____

15. total profits of the eleven most profitable companies   15. _____

16. The bar graph below shows the distribution of last year's revenues by season for a health club. The circle graph shows the corresponding distribution for a country club.

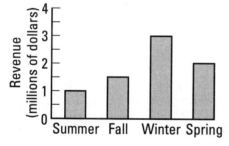

a. By how many dollars did the country club's total annual revenues exceed those of the health club?   16. a. _____

b. In what season(s) did the country club have greater revenues than the health club?   b. _____

17. *True or false.* The median of a data set cannot be less than the mean.   17. _____

18. Refer to the box plot at the right.

Winning Super Bowl Scores, 1967–1997

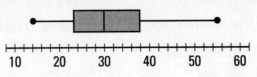

a. What is the range of the scores?   18. a. _____

b. What percent of the scores were between 14 and 23?   b. _____

19. The table shows the twenty United States corporations with the greatest revenues in 1996, as reported in the *Fortune 500* list.

Rank	Company	Revenues ($ billions)	Rank	Company	Revenues ($ billions)
1	General Motors	168	11	Texaco	45
2	Ford Motor	147	12	State Farm	43
3	Exxon	119	13	Prudential	40
4	Wal-Mart Stores	106	14	Du Pont	40
5	General Electric	79	15	Chevron	39
6	IBM	76	16	Hewlett-Packard	38
7	AT&T	75	17	Sears Roebuck	38
8	Mobil	72	18	Procter & Gamble	35
9	Chrysler	61	19	Amoco	33
10	Philip Morris	55	20	Citicorp	33

a. Find each measure.

i.   first quartile   19. a. i. _____

ii. second quartile   ii. _____

iii. third quartile   iii. _____

b. Use the 1.5 × IQR criterion to find any outliers.   b. _____

c. What is IBM's percentile ranking among these 20 companies?   c. _____

d. Construct a box plot of the revenues in the space below.

Now check all your work carefully.

Functions, Statistics, and Trigonometry © Scott Foresman Addison Wesley

Name _____

CHAPTER 1 TEST, Form B

You will need a calculator for this test.

1. A producer's daily output is 1,250 quarts of ice cream. An inspector selects six of these quarts and measures the butterfat content of a 4-oz scoop of ice cream from each.

   a. What percent of the population does the sample represent?   1. a. _____

   b. What is the variable of interest?   b. _____

   c. Give a reason for testing only a sample.

   _____

   _____

In 2 and 3, refer to the stemplot at the right, which shows the scores a math student has received on all homework assignments to date.

```
 6 | 1
 7 | 6 8
 8 | 6 6 6 8 8
 9 | 4 8
10 | 0
```

2. **a.** Find the total number of homework assignments.   2. a. _____

   b. Find the mode of the homework scores.   b. _____

   c. Find the median of the homework scores.   c. _____

3. What must be the total of the student's next two homework scores in order to raise the mean score to 89?   3. _____

In 4 and 5, Jack and Jill each tossed a standard six-sided die the same number of times. Each time, they recorded the number tossed. Their results are shown in dotplots at the right.

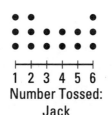
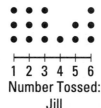

4. **a.** How many times did each person toss the die?   4. a. _____

   b. What is the median number that Jack tossed?   b. _____

   c. What is the mean of the numbers that Jill tossed?   c. _____

5. Whose data have the greater spread: Jack or Jill? Justify your answer.

   _____

   _____

In 6–8, use the following table.

Union Membership in the United States			
Year	Labor Force (thousands)	Union Members (thousands)	Percent of Labor Force
1945	40,394	14,322	35.5
1955	50,675	16,802	33.2
1965	60,815	17,299	28.4
1975	76,945	19,611	25.5
1985	94,521	16,996	18.0
1995	110,038	16,360	14.9

Source: *The World Almanac and Book of Facts 1997*

6. How many people were in the United States labor force in 1995?

6. _____

7. What information is conveyed by the number 18.0 in the fifth row?

_____

8. Describe one trend in union membership from 1945 to 1995.

_____

_____

In 9 and 10, use the following table, which shows the distribution of a city's residents among four groups.

Group	female/ minor	male/ minor	female/ adult	male/ adult
Residents	15,600	15,100	35,000	34,300

9. **a.** Which would be most suitable for displaying the data: a bar graph, a line graph, or a dotplot?

9. a. _____

   b. Give at least one reason for *not* using each type of graph you rejected in part **a.**

_____

_____

10. Suppose a circle graph were used to display the data. What should be the measure in degrees of the central angle of the sector representing the group "male/adult"?

10. _____

Functions, Statistics, and Trigonometry © Scott Foresman Addison Wesley

In 11–15, *multiple choice*. The numbers $p_1, p_2, \ldots, p_{25}$ represent the populations, in increasing order, of the twenty-five smallest towns in a state. Let $P = \sum_{i=1}^{25} p_i$. Choose the expression that represents each measure.

(a) $\frac{1}{25}P$

(b) p_{12}

(c) p_{13}

(d) $\frac{p_{12} + p_{13}}{2}$

(e) $P - \sum_{i=1}^{12} p_i$

(f) $P - \sum_{i=13}^{25} p_i$

(g) $\frac{1}{24} \sum_{i=1}^{25} p_i^2$

(h) $\frac{1}{25} \sum_{i=1}^{25} \left(p_i - \frac{1}{25}P\right)^2$

(i) $\sqrt{\frac{1}{24} \sum_{i=1}^{25} \left(p_i - \frac{1}{25}P\right)^2}$

(j) $\sqrt{\frac{1}{25} \sum_{i=1}^{25} \left(p_i - \frac{1}{25}P\right)^2}$

11. mean population

11. _____

12. median population

12. _____

13. sample standard deviation

13. _____

14. population variance

14. _____

15. total population of the twelve smallest towns

15. _____

16. The bar graph below shows the distribution of last year's revenues by season for a southern resort. The circle graph shows the corresponding distribution for a northern resort.

a. By how many dollars did the southern resort's total annual revenues exceed those of the northern resort?

16. a. _____

b. In what season(s) did the southern resort have greater revenues than the northern resort?

b. _____

17. *True or false.* The mean of a set of data may be less than, equal to, or greater than the median.

17. _____

18. Refer to the box plot at the right.

Losing Super Bowl Scores, 1967–1997

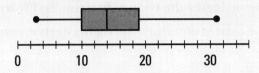

a. What is the range of the scores?

18. a. _____

b. What percent of the scores were between 10 and 19?

b. _____

19. The table shows the twenty United States cities with the greatest populations in 1994.

Rank	City	Population (millions)	Rank	City	Population (millions)
1	New York, NY	7.33	11	San Jose, CA	0.82
2	Los Angeles, CA	3.45	12	Indianapolis, IN	0.75
3	Chicago, IL	2.73	13	San Francisco, CA	0.73
4	Houston, TX	1.70	14	Baltimore, MD	0.70
5	Philadelphia, PA	1.52	15	Jacksonville, FL	0.67
6	San Diego, CA	1.15	16	Columbus, OH	0.64
7	Phoenix, AZ	1.05	17	Milwaukee, WI	0.62
8	Dallas, TX	1.02	18	Memphis, TN	0.61
9	San Antonio, TX	1.00	19	El Paso, TX	0.58
10	Detroit, MI	0.99	20	Washington, D.C.	0.57

Source: *The World Almanac and Book of Facts 1997*

a. Find each measure.

   i.   first quartile

19. a. i. _____

   ii. second quartile

ii. _____

   iii. third quartile

iii. _____

b. Use the $1.5 \times$ IQR criterion to find any outliers.

b. _____

c. What is San Antonio's percentile ranking among the cities?

c. _____

d. Construct a box plot of the populations in the space below.

Now check all your work carefully.

CHAPTER 1 TEST, Form C

1. Create a single set of data for which the following statements are each true. Justify your answer.

$$\sum_{i=6}^{8} g_i = 63 \qquad \frac{1}{8}\sum_{i=1}^{8} g_i = 19$$

2. Explain the difference between a *population* and a *sample*. Then describe a situation in which you might survey a population and a situation in which you might survey a sample.

3. State at least two conclusions that can be drawn from the data in the table below.

United States Population (millions)				
Year	Age in Years			Total
	Under 20	20–64	Over 64	
1930	24.0	34.7	3.3	62.1
1950	25.9	43.1	5.8	74.8
1970	77.0	106.2	20.0	203.2
1990	71.7	145.9	31.1	248.7

4. The box plot and histogram represent the same set of data. What statistical measures can be read from the box plot but not the histogram? from the histogram but not the box plot? from neither?

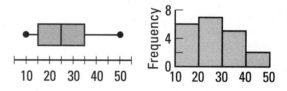

5. At the right are two students' scores on twelve math tests this year. Use statistical measures to compare and contrast the scores.

   What do you think is the most appropriate type of display for these data? Explain your choice. Then draw the display.

Larry		Mary	
85	92	79	79
98	86	77	86
80	88	82	76
85	69	88	84
89	82	74	86
52	78	81	92

CHAPTER 1 TEST, Form D

The mayor of your town is planning a campaign to encourage teens to continue their education beyond high school. You work part-time after school as a teen aide to the mayor. You have been given this table of data.

Educational Attainment and Income of Persons 25 Years of Age and Older: 1991–1995 (Number in Millions with Income/Mean Income in Current Dollars/Median Income in Current Dollars)									
Level of Education Attained	**1991**		**1992**		**1993**		**1994**		**1995**	
	Male	**Female**	**Male**	**Female**	**Male**	**Female**	**Male**	**Female**	**Male**	**Female**
Less than 9th Grade	7.143/ 12,944/ 10,319	7.065/ 7,328/ 6,268	7.000/ 13,208/ 10,374	6.921/ 7,456/ 6,337	6.734/ 13,399/ 10,895	6.423/ 7,650/ 6,480	6.507/ 15,131/ 11,324	6.183/ 8,288/ 6,865	6.277/ 14,748/ 11,723	6.020/ 8,691/ 7,096
9th to 12th Grade (no diploma)	7.759/ 17,703/ 14,736	8.561/ 9,022/ 7,055	7.524/ 17,319/ 14,218	8.248/ 9,235/ 7,293	7.377/ 17,651/ 14,550	8.152/ 9,661/ 7,187	7.286/ 17,924/ 14,584	7.943/ 9,758/ 7,618	7.490/ 19,150/ 15,791	8.122/ 10,263/ 8,057
High School Graduate	25.297/ 24,314/ 21,546	30.149/ 13,104/ 10,818	25.143/ 24,408/ 21,645	29.596/ 13,300/ 10,901	24.682/ 25,501/ 21,782	29.171/ 13,844/ 11,089	24.704/ 26,634/ 22,387	29.110/ 14,236/ 11,390	24.909/ 27,952/ 23,365	28.785/ 15,359/ 12,046
Some College, No Degree	12.366/ 29,897/ 26,591	13.013/ 16,426/ 13,963	12.728/ 29,718/ 26,318	13.615/ 16,941/ 14,401	13.247/ 30,799/ 26,323	14.390/ 17,173/ 14,489	13.573/ 31,339/ 26,768	14.911/ 17,594/ 14,585	13.715/ 33,600/ 28,004	14.619/ 18,574/ 15,552
Associate Degree	4.083/ 32,084/ 29,358	5.236/ 19,223/ 17,364	4.540/ 32,046/ 28,791	5.539/ 19,173/ 17,331	4.901/ 32,713/ 29,736	6.282/ 20,486/ 18,346	5.046/ 34,966/ 30,643	6.573/ 20,496/ 17,954	5.230/ 35,812/ 31,027	6.642/ 22,496/ 19,450
Bachelor's Degree	11.657/ 41,808/ 36,067	10.721/ 23,237/ 20,967	11.938/ 42,801/ 36,745	11.133/ 24,400/ 22,383	12.360/ 46,197/ 37,474	11.447/ 25,579/ 22,452	12.997/ 49,094/ 38,701	11.773/ 26,466/ 23,405	13.065/ 48,856/ 39,040	12.875/ 26,927/ 24,065
Master's Degree	4.356/ 49,589/ 43,125	3.745/ 30,776/ 29,747	4.308/ 50,456/ 44,293	3.873/ 31,545/ 30,169	4.320/ 56,016/ 45,597	4.003/ 34,149/ 31,389	4.558/ 58,041/ 46,635	4.166/ 35,706/ 32,069	4.774/ 60,933/ 49,076	4.205/ 35,512/ 33,509
Professional Degree	1.547/ 73,735/ 63,741	0.556/ 44,818/ 34,064	1.639/ 83,872/ 68,429	0.569/ 48,719/ 36,640	1.650/ 99,323/ 69,678	0.583/ 47,666/ 32,742	1.691/ 92,380/ 61,739	0.709/ 56,406/ 35,806	1.657/ 99,141/ 66,257	0.732/ 47,721/ 38,588
Doctorate Degree	0.929 62,450/ 51,845	0.337/ 40,011/ 37,242	1.053/ 61,134/ 51,681	0.358/ 40,694/ 39,322	1.149/ 76,844/ 55,751	0.447/ 45,389/ 42,737	1.183/ 77,147/ 57,478	0.462/ 49,128/ 40,793	1.149/ 72,831/ 57,356	0.457/ 48,235/ 39,821

Source: United States Department of Commerce, Bureau of the Census, *Historical Income Tables* (P-7 and P-7B)

a. Write a one- or two-sentence description of the data displayed in the table.

b. Can you use these data to find the mean income for all persons in 1991? If you answer *yes,* find the mean. If *no,* explain why it is not possible.

c. Can you use these data to find the median income for all persons in 1991? If you answer *yes,* find the median. If *no,* explain why it is not possible.

d. Suppose you want to analyze incomes of females as compared to incomes of males. Do you think you would use the mean or the median? Explain.

e. Describe a method you might use to analyze any trends in the data from 1991–1995.

f. Create a poster than can be displayed at teen centers throughout the town. Convey the message that it is important to extend your education beyond high school. Incorporate some or all of the data from the table. Display data chosen in the form you think is most appropriate and you believe will have the greatest visual impact.

Functions, Statistics, and Trigonometry © Scott Foresman Addison Wesley

In 1 and 2, f is a real function with $f(m) = 4m^2 + 5.5$.

1. Evaluate.

   a. $f(3)$

   b. $f(-3)$

   c. $f(3 + (-3))$

2. State the range of f.

3. Let $R = \{(2, 0), (4, -1), (5, 0), (10, 7)\}$.

   a. Give the domain of R.

   b. Give the range of R.

   c. *True or false. R is a relation.*

   d. *True or false. R is a function.*

4. Consider the relation graphed at the right.

   a. State the domain of the relation.

   b. State the range of the relation.

   c. Does the graph represent a function from x to y? Justify your answer.

   _____

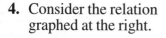

5. For a set of data, the line of best fit is given by $y = -2.32 - 5.96x$, and $r^2 = 0.94$.

   a. What is the correlation coefficient?

   b. *Multiple choice.* Which scatterplot could represent the data?

1. a. _____

   b. _____

   c. _____

2. _____

3. a. _____

   b. _____

   c. _____

   d. _____

4. a. _____

   b. _____

5. a. _____

   b. _____

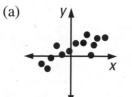 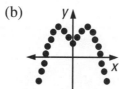 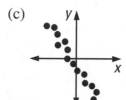

(a) (b) (c) (d)

▶ **QUIZ for Lessons 2-1 Through 2-3** *page 2*

In 6 and 7, refer to the table below, which gives the amount of money Americans spent on hardbound books in selected years from 1982 to 1994.

Year	1982	1985	1990	1992	1994
Amount (millions of dollars)	6,190	7,969	11,789	13,046	14,465

6. The graph at the right is a scatterplot of the data.

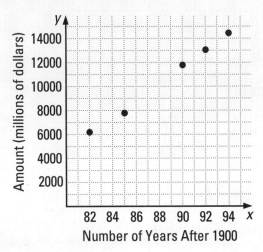

a. Use the points (82, 6190) and (94, 14465) to find a linear model for the relationship between the number of years after 1900 and the amount Americans spent on hardbound books.

6. a. _____

b. Use your model from part **a** to estimate the amount Americans will spend on hardbound books in the year 2005.

b. _____

c. Is your estimate in part **b** an interpolation or an extrapolation?

c. _____

7. **a.** Use a statistics utility to find an equation for the line of best fit for these data.

7. a. _____

b. In 1990, the amount Americans spent on hardbound books was about $11.789 million. Find the error in the value predicted by your model from part **a**.

b. _____

c. What is the correlation coefficient for the line?

c. _____

d. Calculate the center of gravity of the data, and verify that the regression line passes through this point.

_____

_____

QUIZ

In 1–4, state whether the function described by the given equation models exponential growth, exponential decay, or neither.

1. $f(g) = 3^g$

1. _____

2. $m(n) = 12n^4$

2. _____

3. $p(q) = (9.8)\left(\frac{2}{9}\right)^q$

3. _____

4. $A(r) = (0.32)(2.2)^r$

4. _____

5. *Multiple choice.* Which one of the following is *not* a property of the exponential function with equation $y = f(x) = ab^x$, where $a > 0$ and $0 < b < 1$?

5. _____

   (a) For all real numbers $x, f(x) > 0$.

   (b) The function f is strictly decreasing.

   (c) The graph of the function contains the point $(0, a)$.

   (d) As x increases, $f(x)$ increases without bound.

6. The concentrations of many medications in the human blood stream are known to decay exponentially with time. The table below gives such information about a particular medication.

Number of Hours After Medication Was Ingested (h)	Number of Milligrams per Deciliter (mg/dl) in Blood Stream (c)
4	18.0
6	13.9

   a. Give an exponential model for these data.

   6. a. _____

   b. From the model, estimate the initial concentration of the medication in the blood stream.

   b. _____

   c. Estimate the concentration of the medication you would expect to find 12 hours after it was ingested.

   c. _____

7. *Multiple choice.* Which equation could model the data in the scatterplot at the right?

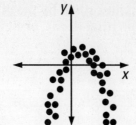

7. _____

(a) $y = -3x^2 - 40x - 20$

(b) $y = 2x^2 - 9x + \pi$

(c) $y = -x^2 + 3x + 1$

(d) $y = 15x^2 - 8$

8. Suppose a ball is thrown upward from the surface of the moon with an initial velocity of $20\frac{m}{sec}$. Then its height h meters above the surface as a function of time t seconds after being thrown is modeled by the following equation:

$$h(t) = -0.8t^2 + 20t.$$

a. What is the height of the ball 3 seconds after being thrown?

8. a. _____

b. How long after being thrown will the ball hit the ground?

b. _____

c. What is the maximum height the ball will reach?

c. _____

d. What is the acceleration due to gravity on the surface of the moon?

d. _____

CHAPTER 2 TEST, Form A

You will need a calculator and a statistics utility for this test.

In 1 and 2, a relation is described.
a. Determine the domain and range of the relation.
b. State whether the relation is a function and justify your answer.

1. $\{(-1, 0), (0, 0), (1, 0), (0, -1)\}$

1. a. _____

   _____

   b. _____

   _____

   _____

2.

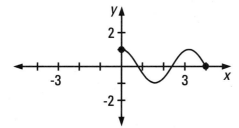

2. a. _____

   _____

   b. _____

   _____

3. Consider $g: x \rightarrow \dfrac{4x^2 + 14}{3}$.

   a. Graph $y = g(x)$ on the domain $-5 \le x \le 5$.

3. a.

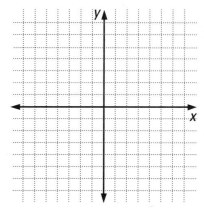

   b. Find the range of the function g if the domain of g is the set of all real numbers.

   b. _____

   c. Give the x-intercepts of the graph of g.

   c. _____

4. In 1790, the official census found the population of the United States to be 3,929,214. In 1800, the census found the population to be 5,308,483.

   a. What was the population growth rate *per decade* in the United States during this period?

   4. a. _____

   b. Suppose the growth rate calculated in part **a** remained unchanged. What would be the population of the United States in the year 2000?

   b. _____

5. Let $f(x) = 3^x$ and $g(x) = \left(\frac{1}{3}\right)^x$.

   a. Which function models exponential decay?

   5. a. _____

   b. What point(s) do the graphs of f and g have in common?

   b. _____

   c. Describe how the graphs of f and g are related.

   _____

   _____

6. Let $k(x) = \dfrac{\lceil x \rceil}{\lfloor x \rfloor}$. Evaluate.

   a. $k(3)$

   6. a. _____

   b. $k\left(-\frac{3}{2}\right)$

   b. _____

   c. $k\left(-\frac{3}{2}\right) \cdot k\left(\frac{3}{2}\right)$

   c. _____

7. Order the scatterplots shown below in increasing order of correlation coefficient.

   7. _____

A. 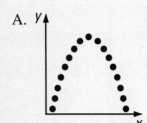 B. 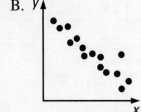 C. 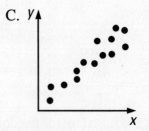 D.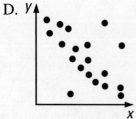

Functions, Statistics, and Trigonometry © Scott Foresman Addison Wesley

In 8 and 9, consider the situation in which a baker charges $2.99 for one dozen muffins and does not sell them in smaller quantities.

8. **a.** How many muffins could you purchase with $20?

8. a. _____

    b. Using the greatest integer function, write an equation that represents the number of muffins m that you can purchase with d dollars.

b. _____

    c. Using the grid at the right, graph your function from part **b** on the domain $0 \leq d \leq 14.95$.

c. _____

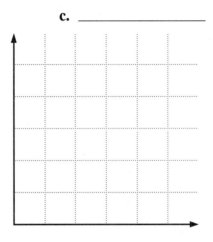

9. Multiple choice. Which equation models the number of muffins m that you can purchase with d dollars?

9. _____

    (a) $m = -12\left\lceil -\frac{d}{2.99} \right\rceil$ (b) $m = 12\left\lceil -\frac{d}{2.99} \right\rceil$

    (c) $m = -12\left\lceil \frac{d}{2.99} \right\rceil$ (d) $m = 12\left\lceil \frac{d}{2.99} \right\rceil$

10. A weather balloon is at an altitude of 10,000 meters when it accidentally bursts. The instruments inside fall to Earth.

    a. Acceleration due to gravity is 9.8 m/s^2. Find an equation that gives the height h meters above Earth of the falling instruments as a function of time t seconds after the balloon bursts.

10. a. _____

    b. How long after the balloon bursts will the instruments hit Earth?

b. _____

11. *Multiple choice.* Suppose all the points of a data set lie on the line of best fit, which has the equation $y = -1.7x + 3$. Which is the correlation coefficient?

11. _____

    (a) -1   (b) -1.7

    (c) 1   (d) cannot be determined from the given information

In 12–14, use the table below. It gives the percent of the U.S. population who had completed at least four years of high school for selected years.

Year	1910	1920	1930	1940	1950	1960	1970	1980	1990	1994
Percent	13.5	16.4	19.1	24.5	34.3	41.4	55.2	68.6	77.6	80.9

Source: *1995 Digest of Education Statistics*

12. **a.** Find an equation for the line of best fit for these data. Let the independent variable be the number of years after 1900.

12. a. _____

b. Use the line of best fit to predict the percent of the U.S. population having completed four years of high school in the years 1985 and 2030.

b. _____

_____

c. For which year in part **b** is your prediction an extrapolation? What problem is there with the prediciton for that year?

_____

13. **a.** Use the points (10, 13.5), (50, 34.3), and (90, 77.6) to find a quadratic model for these data. Let the independent variable be the number of years after 1900.

13. a. _____

b. Use your model from part **a** to estimate the percent of the U.S. population in 1994 who completed at least four years of high school.

b. _____

c. What is the error of your estimate in part **b**?

c. _____

14. Below are graphed the residuals for both the linear and quadratic models. What do these graphs tell you about the appropriateness of each model?

Residuals of Linear Model   **Residuals of Quadratic Model**

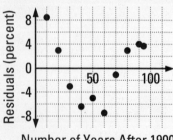 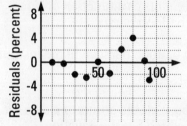

_____

_____

Check all your work carefully.

CHAPTER 2 TEST, Form B

You will need a calculator and a statistics utility for this test.

In 1 and 2, a relation is described.
a. Determine the domain and range of the relation.
b. State whether the relation is a function and justify your answer.

1. $\{(-2, 4), (0, 2), (-1, 0), (4, 5)\}$

1. a. _____

_____

b. _____

_____

_____

2.

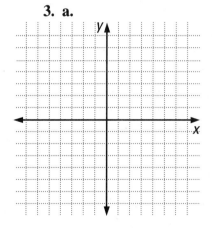

2. a. _____

_____

b. _____

_____

3. Let $g: x \rightarrow \dfrac{5x^2 + 9}{-4}$.

   a. Graph $y = g(x)$ on the domain $-5 \le x \le 5$.

3. a.

   b. Find the range of the function g if the domain of g is the set of all real numbers.

b. _____

   c. Give the x-intercepts of the graph of g.

c. _____

4. In 1800, the official census found the population of the
   United States to be 5,308,483. In 1810, the census found
   the population to be 7,239,881.

   a. What was the population growth rate *per decade*
      in the United States during this period?

   4. a. _____

   b. Suppose the growth rate calculated in part a remained
      unchanged. What would be the population of the
      United States in the year 2000?

   a. _____

5. Let $f(x) = 0.25^x$ and $g(x) = 4^x$.

   a. Which function models exponential decay?

   5. a. _____

   b. What point(s) do the graphs of f and g have
      in common?

   b. _____

   c. Describe how the end behaviors of f and g differ.

   _____

   _____

6. Let 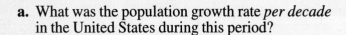 $\dfrac{\lfloor x \rfloor}{\lceil x \rceil}$. Evaluate.

   a. $k(\pi)$

   6. a. _____

   b. $k\left(-\dfrac{3}{2}\right)$

   b. _____

   c. $k\left(-\dfrac{3}{2}\right) \cdot k\left(\dfrac{3}{2}\right)$

   c. _____

7. Order the scatterplots shown below in increasing order
   of correction coefficient.

   7. _____

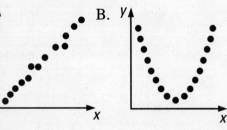
A.  B. C.  D.

In 8 and 9, suppose you are having a party and want to serve each guest one bottle of your favorite root beer. The root beer is sold only in packs of six bottles and costs $3.29 per pack.

8. **a.** What amount must you spend to purchase root beer for 22 guests.

8. a. _____

   b. Using the ceiling function, write an equation that represents the numb er of dollars d that you must spend to purchase root beer for g guests.

b. _____

   c. Using the grid at the right, graph your function from part **b** on the domain $0 \le g \le 30$.

c.

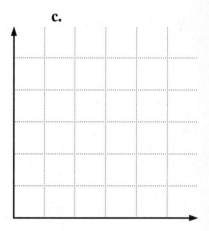

9. *Multiple choice.* Which equation models the number of dollars d needed to purchase root beer for g guests?

9. _____

   (a) $d = 3.29 \left\lfloor -\frac{g}{6} \right\rfloor$ **(b)** $d = 3.29 \left\lfloor \frac{g}{6} \right\rfloor$

   (c) $d = -3.29 \left\lfloor \frac{g}{6} \right\rfloor$ **(d)** $d = -3.29 \left\lfloor -\frac{g}{6} \right\rfloor$

10. A ball is thrown straight upward from ground level with an initial velocity of 25 m/s.

   a. Acceleration due to gravity is 9.8 m/s². Find an equation that gives the ball's height h meters above ground level as a function of time t seconds after it is thrown.

10. a. _____

   b. How long after the ball is thrown will it hit the ground?

b. _____

11. *Multiple choice.* Which is minimized by the line of best fit?

11. _____

   (a) the sum of the residuals **(b)** the sum of the deviations

   (c) the center of gravity   **(d)** the sum of the squares of the errors

In 12-14, use the table below. It gives the percent of the U.S. population
who had completed at least four years of college for selected years.

Year	1910	1920	1930	1940	1950	1960	1970	1980	1990	1994
Percent	2.7	3.3	3.9	4.6	6.2	7.7	11.9	13.9	17.0	17.7

Source: *1995 Digest of Education Statistics*

12. a. Find an equation for the line of best fit for these   **12.** _____
data. Let the independent variable be the number
of years after 1900.

    b. Use your model from part **a** to estimate the percent of   **b.** _____
the U.S. population in 1994 who completed at least
four years of college.

    c. What is the error of your estimate in part **b**?   **c.** _____

13. a. Use the points (10, 2.7), (40, 4.6), and (70, 11.0)   **13. a.** _____
to find a quadratic model for these data. Let the
independent variable be the number of years after 1900.

    b. Use the quadratic model to predict the percent of the   **b.** _____
U.S. population having completed four years
of college in the years 1985 and 2120.

    c. For which year in part **b** is your prediction an extrapolation?
What problem do you find with the prediction for that year?

_____

14. Below are graphed the residuals for both the linear and
quadratic models. What do these graphs tell you about the
appropriateness of each model?

Residuals of Linear Model   **Residuals of Quadratic Model**

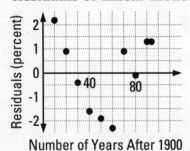   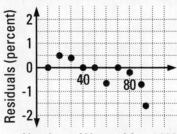

Number of Years After 1900   Number of Years After 1900

_____

_____

Check all your work carefully.

Functions, Statistics, and Trigonometry © Scott Foresman Addison Wesley

CHAPTER 2 TEST, Form C

1. Draw and label a set of coordinate axes. On the axes, sketch the graph of a relation that is *not* a function. State the domain and range of the relation, and explain how you know it is not a function.

2. Compare $f(x) = x^2$ with $g(x) = 2^x$. How are the functions f and g and their graphs alike? How are they different? State at least two significant likenesses and two significant differences.

3. Give an example of a real-life situation that you can model with a floor function and another situation that you can model with a ceiling function. If possible, use Euler's notation to describe each function. If it is not possible, explain why. Then graph each function on a separate set of coordinate axes.

4. The data at the right appear in the *Statistical Abstract of the United States, 1995*. Find a linear model, an exponential model, and a quadratic model for these data. Which model do you think is most appropriate? Explain.

VCRs in U.S. Households	
Year	**Millions**
1980	1
1985	18
1988	51
1989	68
1990	63
1991	67
1992	69
1993	72
1994	74

5. At the right are two scatterplots related to a set of data. Explain what they tell you about the data. What conclusions, if any, might you draw about the data?

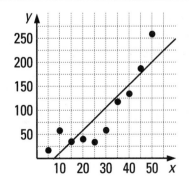
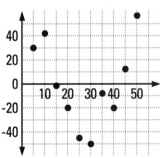

CHAPTER 2 TEST, Form D

Your family is planning to move to the city of Mapleville, which is in a different state. The tables at the right show some historical statistics about Mapleville that were gathered through online resources. Your parents are wondering if it is possible to use these data to make some predictions about the future of Mapleville.

a. Which sets of data are functions? Explain.

b. Which set(s) of data *cannot* be used to make a prediction about a future year? Explain.

c. Use a statistics utility to model the population of Mapleville in each way. Write a regression equation for each model.

   i. linear model

   ii. exponential model

   iii. quadratic model

d. Use each model from part **c** to estimate the population of Mapleville in 1975. Which model, if any, do you think provides the best estimate? Explain.

e. Use each model from part **c** to predict the population in Mapleville in the year 2001. Which model, if any, do you think provides the best prediction? Explain.

f. Prepare a graphic display of each set of data. Whenever appropriate, identify a mathematical model for the data and show both a symbolic and visual representation of it on your display.

g. What do you think Mapleville will be like five years from now? Write a brief report that summarizes any predictions you can make from these data. Justify each prediction.

Year	Population (Thousands)
1970	341.3
1980	413.2
1985	440.0
1987	453.2
1988	464.0
1989	474.6
1990	486.7
1991	501.8
1992	514.6
1993	525.9
1994	534.3
1995	537.0

Year	Median Income
1985	$32,100
1985	35,343
1987	34,624
1988	39,387
1989	37,148
1990	35,406
1991	35,931
1992	34,816
1993	35,555
1994	38,418
1995	35,249
1996	36,803

Year	Median Sale Price of a New House
1970	$25,000
1975	41,600
1980	73,300
1985	91,600
1986	96,700
1987	112,000
1988	127,500
1989	140,000
1990	148,500
1991	142,100
1992	131,400
1993	136,000
1994	141,400
1995	145,300

Individual Income Tax Schedule 1995

Income	Rate
first $5000	0.62%
next $5000	1.24%
next $5000	1.86%
next $5000	2.48%
next $5000	3.1%
next $5000	3.72%
next $5000	4.34%
next $5000	4.96%
next $20,000	5.75%
next $40,000	6.25%
next $100,000	7.0%
next $200,000	8.0%

Month	Normal Daily Mean Temperature (°F)
January	39.1
February	42.5
March	44.6
April	48.2
May	54.1
June	59.9
July	64.2
August	64.5
September	59.6
October	51.8
November	44.3
December	39.5

Functions, Statistics, and Trigonometry © Scott Foresman Addison Wesley

CHAPTER 2 TEST, Cumulative Form

You will need a calculator and a statistics utility for this test.

1. *Multiple choice.* Which is *not* a measure of the spread of a univariate data set?

   1. _____

   (a) variance   (b) interquartile range

   (c) median   (d) standard deviation

2. The scores on the midterm exam in a physics class are shown at the right. The teacher told the class that any student's score at the median or above would get a C or better.

   ```
   3 | 2
   4 |
   5 | 0 8 8
   6 | 1 1 6 9
   7 | 0 2 2 3 8
   8 | 4 7 7 7 8 9
   9 | 1 5 8 9
   ```

   a. How many students took the exam?

   2. a. _____

   b. How many students will get a grade of C or better?

   b. _____

   c. What is the least test score that will receive a grade of C?

   c. _____

3. Let $g(x) = \lfloor 3x - 0.5 \rfloor$. Evaluate.

   a. $g(2.5)$

   3. a. _____

   b. $g(-1.25)$

   b. _____

   c. $g(2.5) \cdot g(-1.25)$

   c. _____

4. Refer to the box plot at the right.

   1996 Birth Rates in Selected African Countries

   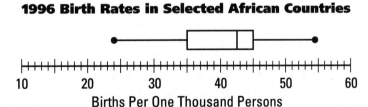

   Births Per One Thousand Persons

   Source: *1995 Statistical Abstract of the United States*

   a. In 1996, the middle 50% of these African countries had birth rates between what two rates?

   4. a. _____

   b. In 1996, the birth rate in the African country Niger was 54.5 per one thousand persons. Is Niger's birth rate and outlier compared to that of the African countries for which data are displayed in the box plot? Justify your answer.

   _____

   _____

In 5 and 6, use the table below.

1994 Average Annual Expenditure per Child (Husband-Wife Families with Income $32,800–$55,000)						
Age of Child (years)	under 2	3–5	6–8	9–11	12–14	15–17
Total (dollars)	7070	7460	7660	7160	7590	8500
Percent Distribution by Expenditure Type						
Housing	37	36	34	31	30	27
Food	13	14	17	21	20	21
Transportation	16	15	18	17	19	20
Clothing	6	6	7	7	11	10
Health Care	6	6	6	7	7	7
Child Care/Education	13	13	7	5	3	5
Miscellaneous	10	10	11	11	11	10

Source: *1995 Statistical Abstracts of the United States*

5. **a.** In 1994, what amount did a family with the given income spend on food for a child 15–17 years of age?

5. a. _____

   b. What expenditure types increase significantly as a percent of total expenditures as a child grows older?

   b. _____

6. **a.** Which expenditure type would include entertainment?

6. a. _____

   b. Consider the expenditure type in part **a**. For which does a family spend the greater amount: a child 12–14 years of age or a child 15–17 years of age?

   b. _____

7. Consider the relation graphed at the right.

   a. State the domain of the relation.

7. a. _____

   b. State the range of the relation.

   b. _____

   c. Is the relation a function? Justify your answer.

8. *True or false.* The center of gravity of a bivariate data set will lie on the line of best fit only if the correlation coefficient is 1 or -1.

8. _____

Functions, Statistics, and Trigonometry © Scott Foresman Addison Wesley

In 9 and 10, the displays below show the number of shares traded on the New York Stock Exchange in the years 1970 through 1996. Both exponential and quadratic models have been fit to the data, and regression equations are given.

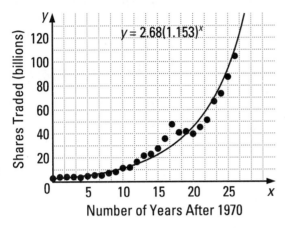

$y = 2.68(1.153)^x$

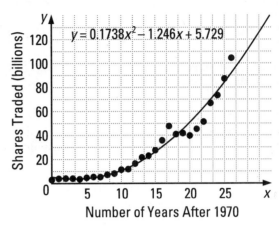

$y = 0.1738x^2 - 1.246x + 5.729$

9. **a.** According to the graphs, how many shares were traded in 1996?

9. a. _____

    b. Calculate the error in each model's prediction of the number of shares traded in 1996.

        i. exponential model

b. i. _____

        ii. quadratic model

ii. _____

    c. Based on your answers in part **b**, which is the better model for the data? Justify your answer.

_____

_____

10. **a.** Use each model to predict the number of shares that will be traded on the NYSE in the year 2100.

        i. exponential model

10. a. i. _____

        ii. quadratic model

ii. _____

    b. Are your answers to part **a** extrapolations or interpolations?

b. _____

    c. Based on your answer to part **b**, which is the better model for the data? Justify your answer.

_____

_____

11. The table below shows ages of cats as related to ages of humans, as observed by French veterinarian Dr. A. Le Beau.

Cat Age (years)	0.5	1	2	4	6	8	10	14	18
Equivalent Human Age (years)	10	15	25	32	40	48	56	72	91

 a. Find an equation for the line of best fit for these data. Let the independent variable be the cat age in years.

11. a. _____

 b. The maximum life span of a cat is said to be 27 years. Use the line of best fit to find the equivalent human age.

b. _____

12. The radioactive isotope actinium-227 decays at a rate of about 3.13% per year. Suppose a 200-milligram sample of actinium-227 is stored in a bottle and left on a laboratory shelf.

 a. How many milligrams of actinium-227 will be in the bottle after one year?

12. a. _____

 b. How many milligrams of actinium-227 will be in the bottle after y years?

b. _____

Check all your work carefully.

Functions, Statistics, and Trigonometry © Scott Foresman Addison Wesley

QUIZ

1. Find equations for all asymptotes of the graph of $f(x) = \dfrac{x^2 - 4}{x^2 - x - 6}$

   1. a. _____

2. **a.** Find an equation for p, the parent function of $f: x \to \dfrac{1}{(x + 1)^2} + 4.$

   2. a. _____

   b. State a rule for the translation T that maps p to f.

   b. _____

3. Consider the function g with $g(x) = (3.2)^x$.

   a. Find an equation for the image of the graph of g under the transformation $T: (x, y) \to (x - 4, y + 3)$.

   3. a. _____

   b. Describe in words the effect T has on the graph of g.

   b. _____

   _____

4. In a clinical study of weight loss, seventy men were each asked to set a goal of losing 12 pounds. Their weights at the outset of the study are described in the *Initial Weights* column of the table below. Complete the *Target Weights* column.

Statistical Measure	Set of Initial Weights (lb)	Set of Target Weights (lb)
mean	188.5	a.
standard deviation	15.6	b.
median	186.5	c.
range	49.0	d.
mode	201.0	e.

   4. a. _____

   b. _____

   c. _____

   d. _____

   e. _____

5. Suppose the point (9, -12) lies on the graph of a function h. Find a point that lies on the image of h under the translation $(x, y) \to (x + 2, y + 2)$.

   5. _____

6. The graph of $y = \sqrt{x}$ is shown at the right together with its image under a translation T. The image of (0, 0) on the graph is the point (2, 3). Find an equation for the translation image.

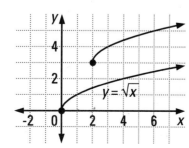

   6. _____

QUIZ

1. Is $f: x \to |x^3|$ an even function or an odd function? Prove your answer using the appropriate definition.

   _____

   _____

2. Show by counterexample that the function g with $g(x) = x^3 - x^2$ is neither an even function nor an odd function.

   _____

   _____

3 **a.** Give an equation for the axis of symmetry of the graph of $y = |x|$.

   b. The translation $T: (x, y) \to (x - 2.5, y + 3.2)$ is applied to the graph of $y = |x|$. Give an equation for the axis of symmetry of the translation image.

   3. a. _____

   b. _____

4. Consider the function with equation $y = (3.2)^x$.

   a. Find an equation for the image of the function under the transformation $S: (x, y) \to \left(\frac{x}{3}, 4y\right)$.

   b. Describe in words the effect of the transformation in part **a** on the graph of g.

   4. a. _____

   _____

   _____

5. The graph of $y = x^3 - 10x^2 + 11x + 70$ has x-intercepts 5, -2, and 7. Find the x-intercepts of the graph of $\frac{y}{9} = 125x^3 - 250x^2 + 55x + 70$.

   5. _____

6. *True or false.* If a data set undergoes a scale change with scale factor -1, the range is unchanged.

   6. _____

Functions, Statistics, and Trigonometry © Scott Foresman Addison Wesley

7. The graph of $y = f(x)$ is shown below. On the coordinate axes at the right, graph $y = -2f(2x)$.

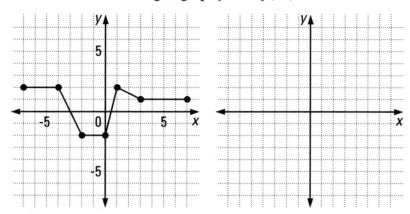

8. An environmental group is measuring the levels of the pesticide thiabendazole found in apples. They bought a sample of apples at each of ten local stores and recorded the thiabendazole levels of the samples in the table at the right. They computed the following statistics for these data.

Store Number	Concentration in Parts per million (ppm)
1	0.510
2	0.775
3	0.812
4	1.000
5	1.500
6	0.333
7	0.147
8	0.311
9	0.001
10	1.131

mean:
0.652 ppm

standard deviation:
0.474 ppm

a. The group wanted to compare the concentration of thiabendazole in each store's apples to the mean concentration. To do this, they divided each concentration in the table by the mean. Give the mean and standard deviation of the transformed data.

8. a. _____

_____

b. How will the median, the first quartile, and the third quartile of the data be affected by the transformation describe in part **a**?

_____

_____

CHAPTER 3 TEST, Form A

You will need a calculator for this test.

1. Consider the function f with $f(x) = 4x^3 - 3x$. Prove that f is an odd function.

   _____

   _____

2. What transformation maps the graph of $y = x^2$ onto the graph of $y = (x - 2)^2 + 4$?

   2. _____

In 3 and 4, a function is described.
a. Describe the inverse using a set of ordered pairs or an equation.
b. State whether the inverse is a function.

3. $y = \dfrac{1}{3 + x} + 2$

   3. a. _____

   b. _____

4. $\{(-5, 3), (-3, 2), (-1, 7), (0, 3)\}$

   4. a. _____

   b. _____

In 5–8, left $f(x) = \dfrac{1}{x}$ and let $g(x) = -x - 2$.

5. Evaluate $(f \circ g)(3)$

   5. _____

6. Evaluate $(g \circ f)(3)$

   6. _____

7. Find a formula for $f \circ g$.

   7. _____

8. Give the domain of $f \circ g$.

   8. _____

In 9 and 10, *true or false*.

9. If the graph of a function passes the vertical-line test, then its inverse is a function.

   9. _____

10. If the mean of a data set is an element of the set, then the z-score of the mean is 0.

    10. _____

11. Explain what is meant by a z-score of 1.2 in terms of the mean and standard deviation.

    11. _____

    _____

    _____

Functions, Statistics, and Trigonometry © Scott Foresman Addison Wesley

12. The graph of a function f has asymptotes with
    equations $x = 5$ and $y = -2$. Find equations for the
    asymptotes of the image of f under the transformation
    $T: (x, y) \rightarrow (x + 5, y + 2)$.

    12. _____

13. The variance of the data set $\{x_1, x_2, x_3, \ldots, x_n\}$ is σ^2.
    What is the variance of the transformed data set
    $\{x_1 + h, x_2 + h, x_3 + h, \ldots, x_n + h\}$?

    13. _____

14. *Multiple choice.* Which scale change has the
    effect on a graph of stretching horizontally by a
    factor of 3 and stretching vertically by a factor of 4?

    14. _____

    (a) $S: (x, y) \rightarrow (3x, 4y)$

    (b) $S: (x, y) \rightarrow \left(3x, \frac{1}{4}y\right)$

    (c) $S: (x, y) \rightarrow \left(\frac{1}{3}x, 4y\right)$

    (d) $S: (x, y) \rightarrow \left(\frac{1}{3}x, \frac{1}{4}y\right)$

15. In a track meet, Corinna competed in two events: the mile
    and the long jump. Corinna's time for the mile was
    6 minutes, 15 seconds. The mean for the mile was
    6 minutes, 20 seconds, and the standard deviation was
    20 seconds. Corinna's distance in the long jump was
    15 feet, 7 inches. The mean for the long jump was 15 feet,
    and the standard deviation was 1 foot.

    a. Find Corinna's z-scores for the mile and for
       the long jump.

    15. a. _____

    _____

    b. In which event did Corinna do better compared to
       other competitors?

    b. _____

16. The graph of
    $y = x^3$ is shown at
    the right together
    with its image under
    a translation T. The
    image of $(0, 0)$ on
    the graph is the point
    $(-2, 4)$. Find an
    equation for the
    translation image.

    16. _____

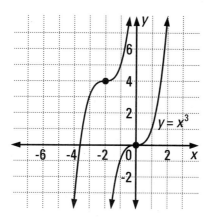

$y = x^3$

Name _____

17. The graph of $y = f(x)$ is shown below. On the coordinate axes at the right, graph $y = f(-\frac{1}{2}x)$.

17.

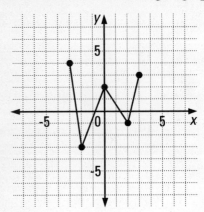

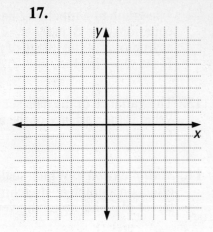

In 18 and 19, consider the following situation. A research team is studying the risks presented to hospital workers by exposure to radiation. The researchers calculated the amount of radiation in millirems (mrem) to which each of 45 randomly selected hospital employees are exposed in one year. They found the following statistical measures from their set of raw data.

mean: 182 mrem   variance: 2116 mrem^2
minimum: 105 mrem   maximum: 260 mrem

18. To account for naturally occurring background radiation, the researchers adjusted the amount of radiation measured for each employee by subtracting 91 mrem from it. Find each statistical measure for the set of adjusted amounts.

   a. mean

   b. standard deviation

   c. maximum

   d. range

18. a. _____

    b. _____

    c. _____

    d. _____

19. Classify the function graphed at the right as odd, even, or neither. Justify your answer in terms of the symmetry of the graph.

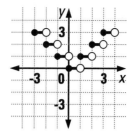

_____

_____

In 20–23, refer to the graph of the function *g* at the right.

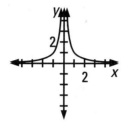

20. Name the parent function studied in this Chapter whose graph most closely resembles the graph of *g*.

21. Describe the symmetry of the graph of *g*.

21. _____

_____

_____

22. *Multiple choice.* Which is the graph of the inverse of *g*?

22. _____

(a) 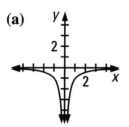 (b) 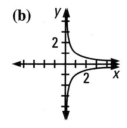 (c) 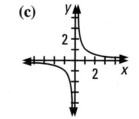 (d)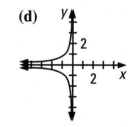

23. Is the inverse of *g* a function? Justify your answer.

_____

_____

Check all your work carefully.

CHAPTER 3 TEST, Form B

You will need a calculator for this test.

1. Consider the function f with $f(x) = 4x^2 - 3$. Prove that f is an even function.

   _____

   _____

2. What transformation maps the graph of $y = 2^x$ onto the graph of $y = 4(2^{3x})$?

   2. _____

In 3 and 4, a function is described.
a. Describe the inverse using a set of ordered pairs or an equation .
b. State whether the inverse is a function.

3. $y = \frac{7}{5x} - 2$

   3. a. _____

   b. _____

4. $\{(0, -1), (1, 1), (2, 2), (3, 3), (4, 5)\}$

   4. a. _____

   b. _____

In 5–8, let $f(x) = \sqrt{x + 2}$ and let $g(x) = 5 - x$.

5. Evaluate $(f \circ g)(3)$

   5. _____

6. Evaluate $(g \circ f)(3)$.

   6. _____

7. Find a formula for $f \circ g$.

   7. _____

8. Give the domain of $f \circ g$.

   8. _____

In 9 and 10, *true or false*.

9. If the graph of a function passes the horizontal-line test, then its inverse is a function.

   9. _____

10. The z-score of the minimum of a data set is 0.

    10. _____

11. Explain what is meant by a z-score of -0.5 in terms of the mean and standard deviation.

    _____

    _____

12. The x-intercepts of the graph of a function f are
-2, .5, and 4. The y-intercept is 7. Find the
x-intercept(s) and y-intercept(s) of the image of f
under the transformation $S: (x, y) \rightarrow \left(6x, \frac{1}{7}y\right)$.

12. _____

13. The variance of the data set $(x_1, x_2, x_3, \ldots, x_n)$ is σ^2.
What is the variance of the transformed data set
$\{ax_1, ax_2, ax_3, \ldots, ax_n\}$?

13. _____

14. *Multiple choice.* Which translation has the effect
on a graph of moving each point 10 units down
and 4 units to the right?

14. _____

   (a) $T: (x, y) \rightarrow (x - 4, y + 10)$

   (b) $T: (x, y) \rightarrow (x + 10, y - 4)$

   (c) $T: (x, y) \rightarrow (x + 4, y + 10)$

   (d) $T: (x, t) \rightarrow (x + 4, y - 10)$

15. Patricia and Maria both ran the 100-meter dash, but they
competed in different heats because of their different ages.
Patricia's time in her heat was 13.15 seconds. The mean
for the heat was 14 seconds, and the standard deviation
was 0.5 seconds. Maria's time in her heat was 14.01
seconds. The mean for her heat was 15 seconds, and the
standard deviation was 0.65 seconds.

   a. Find Patricia's and Maria's z-scores.

15. a. _____

   _____

   b. Who did better compared to other competitors
   in her heat: Patricia or Maria?

   b. _____

16. The graph of
$y = x^3$ is shown at
the right together
with its image under
a translation T. The
image of (0, 0) on
the graph is the point
(2, -4). Find an
equation for the
translation image.

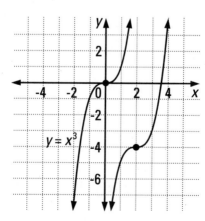

16. _____

17. The graph of $y = f(x)$ is shown below. On the coordinate axes at the right, graph $-\frac{y}{2} = f(x)$

17.

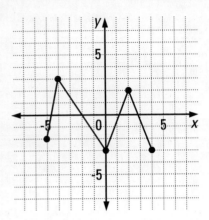

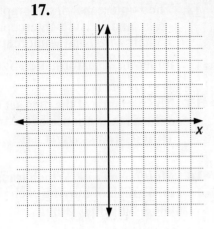

In 18 and 19, consider the following situation. A manufacturer of high-pressure air bags hired an independent laboratory to determine the internal pressure at which their air bags explode. Technicians at the laboratory randomly selected 42 of the air bags, inflated them, and measured the pressure in pounds per square inch (psi) at which each bag burst. They found the following statistical measures for their set of raw data.

mean: 223 psi   variance: 16 psi²
minimum: 208 psi   maximum: 248 psi

18. To account for atmospheric pressure, the technicians adjusted the pressure at which each air bag burst by subtracting 125 psi from it. Find each statistical measure for the set of adjusted pressures.

  a. mean

  b. standard deviation

  c. maximum

  d. range

18. a. _____

b. _____

c. _____

d. _____

Functions, Statistics, and Trigonometry © Scott Foresman Addison Wesley

19. Classify the function graphed at the right as odd, even, or neither. Justify your answer in terms of the symmetry of the graph.

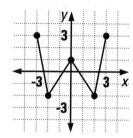

_____

_____

In 20–23, refer to the graph of the function *g* at the right.

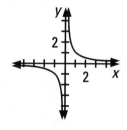

20. Name the parent function studied in this Chapter whose graph most closely resembles the graph of *g*.

20. _____

21. Describe the symmetry of the graph of *g*.

_____

_____

22. *Multiple choice.* Which is the graph of the inverse of *g*?

22. _____

(a) 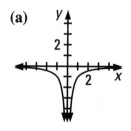 **(b)** 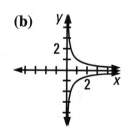 **(c)** 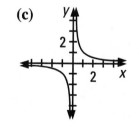 **(d)**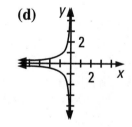

23. Is the inverse of *g* a function? Justify your answer.

_____

_____

Check all your work carefully.

CHAPTER 3 TEST, Form C

1. Identify a transformation S that stretches the graph of $y = \lceil x \rceil$ vertically and shrinks it horizontally. Give an equation for the image of the graph under the transformation.

2. Kioko says that, if a parent function is even, then the function represented by a translation of its graph also is even. Is Kioko's statement always, sometimes, or never true? Explain, using graphs to illustrate your response.

3. Let $f(x) = \frac{3}{x}$. Identify a function g such that $(f \circ g)(1) = 1$. What is $(g \circ f)(1)$? Give a formula for $f \circ g$ and a formula for $g \circ f$. What are the domain and range of $f \circ g$? What are the domain and range of $g \circ f$.

4. A set of data is transformed by a translation. Then the same set of data is transformed by a scale change. Compare the effects of these transformations on the measures of center and spread. How are they alike? different? Give examples to justify your response.

5. The diagram at the right is supposed to appear in a lesson about functions, but someone lost the caption. What do you think the diagram is meant to illustrate? Label the graphs and write an appropriate caption.

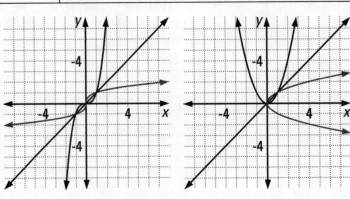

Functions, Statistics, and Trigonometry © Scott Foresman Addison Wesley

CHAPTER 3 TEST, Form D

Sometimes the driver of a car sees a situation that requires a sudden stop. It is estimated that the average person needs about .75 second to react to a situation and apply brakes. The distance the car travels in that time is called the *reaction distance*. Then, once the driver has applied the brakes, the car requires a certain distance to come to a complete stop. This is called the *braking distance*.

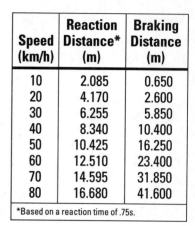

Speed (km/h)	Reaction Distance* (m)	Braking Distance (m)
10	2.085	0.650
20	4.170	2.600
30	6.255	5.850
40	8.340	10.400
50	10.425	16.250
60	12.510	23.400
70	14.595	31.850
80	16.680	41.600

*Based on a reaction time of .75s.

a. Refer to the speed and reaction distance data given in the table.
  i. Give an equation for a function f you can use to find reaction distance in meters for a given speed in kilometers per hour.
  ii. Draw a graph of f.
  iii. Give an equation for p, the parent function of f.

b. If the reaction time of .75 second is multiplied by n, then the reaction distances in the table also are multiplied by n.
  i. Suppose a driver requires a reaction time of 1.5 seconds. Write a rule for the transformation that maps your function f from part **a** to a function g representing this driver's reaction distances.
  ii. What type of transformation is this?
  iii. Draw a graph of g on the same set of axes with the graph of f. What effect did the transformation have on the graph of f?
  iv. Give an equation for q, the parent function of g.

c. Refer again to the speed and reaction distance data as given in the table.
  i. Give an equation for a function h you can use to find speed in kilometers per hour for a given reaction distance.
  ii. How are the functions f and h related?
  iii. Give an equation for r, the parent function of h.

d. The relationship between meters and feet is $1 \text{ m} \approx 3.28 \text{ ft}$.
  i. Write an equation for a function j you can use change a length x in meters to an approximate length $j(x)$ in feet.
  ii. Refer to your function f from part **a**. Give an equation for $(j \circ f)(x)$.
  iii. Explain how you can use $(j \circ f)(x)$ in the context of reaction distances.

e. The sum of the reaction distance and the braking distance is called the *stopping distance*. Give an equation for a function k you can use to find stopping distance in meters for a given speed in kilometers per hour.

f. There are many factors that might increase a driver's reaction time beyond the average, among them being inexperienced, fatigue, and the presence of alcohol or other drugs in the bloodstream. Use the information given here to prepare a poster that advocates responsible driving by teenagers. Your poster should include a chart of speeds, reaction distances, braking distances, and stopping distances and a statement of the function or functions that relate them. Also include at least one graph that illustrates the effects of increased reaction times.

Name _____

CHAPTER 3 TEST, Cumulative Form

You will need a calculator and a statistics utility for this test.

In 1–3, let $f: x \to (.3)(2.5)^x$.

1. Is f an exponential growth function or an exponential decay function?

   1. _____

2. Find an equation for an asymptote to the graph of f.

   2. _____

3. Find an equation for the image of f under the transformation $T: (x, y) \to (x - 1, y + 3)$.

   3. _____

In 4–6, let g be a function defined by $g(x) = \dfrac{-1.5}{x}$.

4. Find an equation for the inverse of g.

   4. _____

5. Is g an even function, an odd function, or neither? Prove your answer using the appropriate definition(s).

   _____

   _____

6. Let h be a function with $h(x) = \dfrac{1}{x}$. State a rule for the transformation that maps h to g.

   6. _____

7. The graphs of any function and its inverse are reflection images of each other. Give an equation for the line of reflection.

   7. _____

8. **a.** On the coordinate axes at the right, graph $y = 2\lfloor .5x \rfloor$ on the domain $-6 \le x \le 6$.

   8. a.

   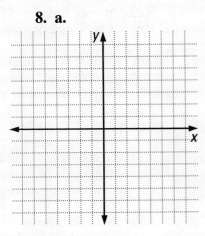

   b. Name three values of x that are points of discontinuity of your graph in part **a**.

   b. _____

Name _____

▶ **CHAPTER 3 TEST,** **Cumulative Form** *page 2*

In 9 and 10, consider the data set $\{x_1, x_2, x_3, \ldots, x_n\}$**, where** $n = 10$ **and** $\bar{x} = 4.5$**.**

9. a. Evaluate $\sum_{i=1}^{n} x_i$.

9. a. _____

   b. Suppose one additional number is included in the data set. What number must it be in order to increase the mean to 5?

   b. _____

10. Evaluate $\frac{1}{n}\sum_{i=1}^{n}(x_i - 6)$.

10. _____

11. In a certain data set, 0 is the z-score for 82 and 0.5 is the z-score for 86. What are the mean and standard deviation of this data set?

11. _____

_____

12. *Multiple choice.* Which statistical measure of a data set is invariant under a translation?

12. _____

   (a) mode   (b) mean

   (c) variance   (d) median

In 13–15, let $g(x) = \lfloor x \rfloor$ **and let** $h(x) = \frac{1}{x}$**.**

13. Evaluate $(g \circ h)\left(\frac{5}{2}\right)$.

13. _____

14. Evaluate $(h \circ g)\left(\frac{5}{2}\right)$.

14. _____

15. Give the domain of $h \circ g$.

15. _____

16. The pages of books are commonly printed in sets called *signatures*. Typically there are 4, 8, 16, 32, or 64 pages in a signature.

   a. What is the minimum number of 32-page signatures needed to print a book that has a total of 284 printed pages?

   16. a. _____

   b. Write a formula for n, the minimum number of 32-page signatures needed to print a book, as a function of p, the total number of printed pages.

   b. _____

17. In general, which is affected more by extreme values in a data set: the mean or the median?

17. _____

Functions, Statistics, and Trigonometry © Scott Foresman Addison Wesley

47 ▶

In 18 and 19, refer to the stemplot at the right, which shows the scores of an 8th-grade class and the scores of a 9th-grade class on the same standardized math test.

8th Grade		9th Grade
	0	
	1	4
6 4	2	7
0	3	
8 8 2	4	3 9
6 6 4 3 3 2	5	5 5 7
5 1 1	6	1 2 3 3 8
	7	4 4 6 7 7
2	8	4
	9	7
	10	

18. a. Give the five-number summary for each class.

_____

_____

b. Use the $1.5 \times$ IQR criterion to find any outliers for each class.

_____

c. Construct box plots of these data in the space below.

19. a. Find the mean and sample standard deviation for the 8th-grade class.

19. a. _____

_____

b. Find the mean and sample standard deviation for the 9th-grade class.

b. _____

_____

c. Who did better compared to others at his or her grade level: the 8th-grade student who scores 65 or the 9th-grade student who scores 74? Justify your answer in terms of *z*-scores.

_____

_____

Functions, Statistics, and Trigonometry © Scott Foresman Addison Wesley

20. A stereo that cost $650 was purchased using a credit card with a monthly interest rate of 1.3%. Suppose no payments are made. What will be the amount owed on the purchase at the end of one year?

20. _____

In 21 and 22, use the table and graph below, which show data about the amount of nuclear-based electricity generated in the United States in five recent years.

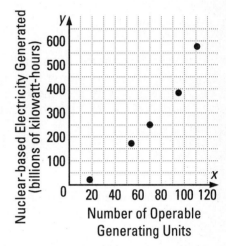

Number of Operable Generating Units	18	54	70	95	111
Nuclear-based Electricity Generated (billions of kilowatt-hours)	21.8	172.5	251.1	383.7	576.9

Source: *1996 Statistical Abstract of the United States*

21. a. Use a statistics utility to find a quadratic model for these data.

21. a. _____

b. Calculate the residual of your model in part **a** for 95 reactors.

b. _____

22. a. Use a statistics utility to find a linear model for these data.

22. a. _____

b. Calculate the center of gravity of the data, and verify that the regression line passes through this point.

_____

_____

Check all your work carefully.

COMPREHENSIVE TEST, CHAPTERS 1-3

Multiple choice. **Give the letter of the correct answer.**

1. Let f be a function with $f(x) = \frac{1}{x} + x$. Which describes the function f?   1. _____
   (a) even
   (b) odd
   (c) both even and odd
   (d) neither even nor odd

2. On each service call, an appliance repair technician charges $30 for one hour of labor or less, then $15 for each additional hour or fraction thereof. Which is a formula for the amount A in dollars the technician charges for t hours of labor on a service call?   2. _____
   (a) $A = 30 + 15t$
   (b) $A = 30 + 15\lfloor t - 1\rfloor$
   (c) $A = 30 + 15\lfloor t\rfloor$
   (d) $A = 30 + 15\lfloor 1 - t\rfloor$

3. Which is an equation of the image of $y = x^3$ under the translation $T: (x, y) \to (x + 1, y - 2)$?   3. _____
   (a) $y = (x - 1)^3 + 2$
   (b) $y = (x - 1)^3 - 2$
   (c) $y = (x + 1)^3 + 2$
   (d) $y = (x + 1)^3 - 2$

4. Let $a_1 = 1, a_2 = 4, a_3 = 5, a_4 = 2, a_5 = 1, a_6 = 2,$ $a_7 = 10,$ and $a_8 = 11.$ Evaluate $\sum_{i=1}^{8} a_i^2 - 5.$ 4. _____
   (a) 1291   (b) 232   (c) 267   (d) 31

5. Let $g: x \to (x + 2)^3 + 4.$ Which is an equation for p, the parent function of g?   5. _____
   (a) $p(x) = x^3$
   (b) $p(x) = x$
   (c) $p(x) = (x + 2)^3$
   (d) $p(x) = \frac{1}{x^2}$

6. Let h be a function with $h(x) = \frac{1}{x + 5}.$ Which is an equation of h^{-1}, the inverse of h?   6. _____
   (a) $h^{-1}(x) = \frac{1}{x} + 5$
   (b) $h^{-1}(x) = \frac{1}{x} - 5$
   (c) $h^{-1}(x) = \frac{x}{5} - 1$
   (d) $h^{-1}(x) = \frac{1}{5} - x$

7. Which best describes the symmetry of the graph of $y = x^5$?   7. _____
   (a) symmetric with respect to the y-axis
   (b) symmetric with respect to the x-axis
   (c) symmetric with respect to the origin
   (d) none of the above

8. The variance of a data set is 7. Suppose each element of the set is multiplied by 15. What is the variance of the new data set?

   (a) 105   (b) 22   (c) 7   (d) 1575

8. _____

9. The range of the scores on a math exam is 40 points. Suppose 9 points are added to each score. What is the range of the new set of scores?

   (a) 58 points   (b) 40 points

   (c) 31 points   (d) 49 points

9. _____

10. The histogram at the right shows data about snowfall in Fargo, North Dakota, for the years 1961-1996. Each interval includes the left endpoint, but not the right. In which interval does the median snowfall occur?

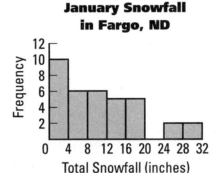

January Snowfall in Fargo, ND

Total Snowfall (inches)

Source: *National Oceanic and Atmospheric Administration, Climate Diagnostics Center*

   (a) $0 \le x < 4$

   (b) $8 \le x < 12$

   (c) $4 \le x < 8$

   (d) $12 \le x < 16$

10. _____

11. Refer to the histogram in Question 10. In approximately what percent of the years did 24 or more inches of snow fall in Fargo in January?

   (a) 4%   (b) 11%   (c) 6%   (d) 24%

11. _____

12. Let $f(x) = \sqrt{x - 4}$ and let $g(x) = x^2$. Find $g(f(8))$.

   (a) $\sqrt{60}$ (b) 16   (c) 4   (d) 0

12. _____

13. Refer to the functions f and g defined in Question 12. What is the domain of $g \circ f$?

   (a) set of all real numbers   (b) $\{x: x \le -2 \text{ or } x \ge 2\}$

   (c) $\{x: -2 \le x \le 2\}$ (d) $\{x: x \ge 4\}$

13. _____

14. Consider the scatterplot at the right. Which best describes the relation between the variables?

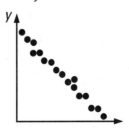

   (a) strong positive correlation

   (b) weak positive correlation

   (c) strong negative correlation

   (d) weak negative correlation

14. _____

15. The *x*-intercepts of the graph of $f(x) = x^2 - 4x - 5$ are   15. _____
    -1 and 5. What are the *x*-intercepts of the image of *f* under
    the transformation $S(x, y) \rightarrow (2x, -4y)$?

    (a) -2 and 10   (b) 4 and -20

    (c) -.5 and 2.5   (d) -.25 and 1.25

16. Let *g* and *h* be inverse functions. Which of the following is true?   16. _____

    (a) For all *x* in the domain of *h*, $g(h(x)) = x$; and for all
        x in the domain of *g*, $h(g(x)) = x$.

    (b) The domain of *g* is the domain of *h*, and the range of *g*
        is the range of *h*.

    (c) The graphs of *g* and *h* are reflection images of each other
        over the line $y = -x$.

    (d) None of the above is true.

17. In 1996, the population of the Republic of Chad was about   17. _____
    6,977,000, with an average annual growth rate of about
    2.7%. Suppose the growth rate remains unchanged. Which
    is an estimate of Chad's population in the year 2000?

    (a) about 7,762,000   (b) about 7,165,000

    (c) about 8,861,000   (d) about 7,971,000

18. The table at the right lists the weights of   18. _____
    several diamonds of the same clarity and
    shows the prices charged for them. Given
    below are two models for these data.

    linear: $p = 10.21w - 7.222$

    quadratic: $p = 3.26w^2 - 4.31w + 4.71$

    The world's largest cut diamond weighs
    530.20 carats. Using the linear model,
    which is a predicted price of this diamond?

    (a) about $2,234,000

    (b) about $5,406,000

    (c) about $914,145,000

    (d) about $5,354,888,000

Weight *w* (carats)	Price *p* ($1000s)
0.70	2.950
0.77	2.125
0.99	5.200
1.00	2.475
1.02	5.250
1.03	2.325
1.07	4.800
1.08	2.775
1.10	4.075
1.70	9.250
1.81	8.700
2.40	11.250
2.66	15.125
4.01	40.500

19. Refer to the information in Question 18.   19. _____
    Using the quadratic model, which is an
    approximation of the residual for the
    price of the 4.01-carat diamond?

    (a) $6520   (b) $33,720

    (c) -$33,720   (c) $0

20. The stemplot at the right give the amount in cents that the federal government returned to each state per dollar of federal taxes paid by its residents in 1995. Which is the mode of these data?

    (a) $1.04
    (b) $0.77
    (b) $1.01
    (c) $1.86

```
 6 | 8 8
 7 | 4 5 6 7 7 7
 8 | 0 4 5
 9 | 2 3 5 5 7 9 9
10 | 0 0 1 1 1 1 3 5 6 9
11 | 3 3 8 8 9 9
12 | 2 3 4 6 7 7 8
13 | 1 4 5 8 9
14 |
15 | 0 3
16 | 1
17 |
18 | 6
```

20. _____

21. Refer to the stemplot in Question 20. Which is the median of the data?

    (a) $1.04
    (b) $1.05
    (b) $1.03
    (c) $1.01

21. _____

22. Refer to the stemplot in Question 20. Using the $1.5 \times$ IQR criterion, which is the complete set of outliers for the data?

    (a) $0.68, $1.86
    (b) $1.86
    (c) $1.61, $1.86
    (d) There are no outliers.

22. _____

23. An object is launched straight up from ground level so that its height h meters above the ground as a function of times t seconds after launch is given by the equation $h = -4.9t^2 + 68.6t$. What is the maximum height the object will reach?

    (a) about 7 meters
    (b) about 240 meters
    (c) about 120 meters
    (d) about 50 meters

23. _____

24. Refer to the situation in Question 23. About how long after launch will the object hit the ground?

    (a) 14 seconds
    (b) 15 seconds
    (c) less than 1 second
    (d) 13 seconds

24. _____

24. Refer to the situation in Question 23. Which describes the type of model used?

    (a) theory-based
    (b) exponential growth
    (c) linear
    (d) impressionistic

25. _____

Check all your work carefully.

QUIZ

1. Fill in the blanks in the table below.

Equivalent Measures of Rotations			
Degrees	**Radians (exact)**	**Radians (nearest tenth)**	**Revolutions**
144°			
	$-\dfrac{4\pi}{3}$		
			3.1
	$\dfrac{61\pi}{15}$		

2. The latitude of St. Louis, Missouri, is 38.63°N, and the latitude of Memphis, Tennessee, is 35.15°N. The longitude of St. Louis is very close to that of Memphis, so assume that St. Louis is directly north of Memphis. Assuming Earth is a sphere of diameter 7920 miles, find the distance between the cities to the nearest mile.

2. _____

3. The area of a sector of a circle of radius 15 centimeters is $\dfrac{45\pi}{2}$ square centimeters. Find the measure of the central angle that forms the sector.

3. _____

4. A hamster ran on a circular wheel of radius 4 inches for 5 minutes. The wheel rotated at a rate of 39.6 radians per minute. How many inches did a point on the rim of the wheel move in this time?

4. _____

5. Fill in the blanks in the table below.

Exact Values of Sines, Cosines, and Tangents			
θ	**sin θ**	**cos θ**	**tan θ**
135°			
$\dfrac{3\pi}{2}$			
7π			
450°			

Functions, Statistics, and Trigonometry © Scott Foresman Addison Wesley

Name _____

QUIZ

1. Suppose $\sin \theta = 0.47$. Evaluate without using a calculator.

   a. $\cos \left(\frac{\pi}{2} - \theta\right)$

   b. $\sin (\pi - \theta)$

   c. $\sin (\text{-}\theta)$

   d. $\sin (\pi + \theta)$

   1. a. _____

   b. _____

   c. _____

   d. _____

2. Justify each lettered step in this proof that, for all θ (in radians) and for all integers n, $\cos \left(\theta - \frac{\pi}{2}\right) = \sin (\theta + 2\pi n)$.

   a. $\cos \left(\theta - \frac{\pi}{2}\right) = \cos \left(\frac{\pi}{2} - \theta\right)$

   b. $\cos \left(\frac{\pi}{2} - \theta\right) = \sin \theta$

   c. $\sin \theta = \sin (\theta + 2\pi n)$

   2. a. _____

   b. _____

   c. _____

   Therefore, by the Transitive Property of Equality, $\cos \left(\theta - \frac{\pi}{2}\right) = \sin (\theta + 2\pi n)$.

3. Give exact values for each.

   a. $\sin \left(\frac{4\pi}{3}\right)$

   b. $\cos \left(\frac{\pi}{6}\right)$

   c. $\tan \left(\frac{5\pi}{4}\right)$

   d. $\cos 420°$

   3. a. _____

   b. _____

   c. _____

   d. _____

4. Consider the tangent function $f(\theta) = \tan \theta$.

   a. Identify two values of x at which f is discontinuous.

   b. Give the range of f.

   c. Describe the symmetry of the graph of f.

   4. a. _____

   b. _____

   c. _____

5. Prove that the function $g(x) = \cos x$ is an even function.

   _____

   _____

CHAPTER 4 TEST, Form A

You will need a calculator and an automatic grapher for this test.

1. Convert $1\frac{1}{6}$ revolutions clockwise to radians exactly.

1. _____

2. Convert $\frac{7\pi}{12}$ radians to degrees.

2. _____

3. Convert $12°$ to radians exactly.

3. _____

4. In a circle of diameter 12 inches, a sector is formed by a central angle of $225°$. Find the area of the sector to the nearest hundredth of a square inch.

4. _____

5. The city of Anchorage, Alaska, has latitude $61.17°N$ and longitude $149.98°W$. The circumference of the meridian is almost exactly 40,000 km. Find the distance between Anchorage and the North Pole, to the nearest kilometer.

5. _____

In 6 and 7, give exact values.

6. $\cos\left(-\frac{3\pi}{4}\right)$

6. _____

7. $\tan 240°$

7. _____

8. Approximate $\tan\left(\frac{4\pi}{5}\right)$ to four decimal places.

8. _____

9. Identify each of the following for the function with equation $y = -2\sin\left(5x + \frac{\pi}{3}\right) + 2$.

   a. domain

   9. a. _____

   b. range

   b. _____

   c. amplitude

   c. _____

   d. period

   d. _____

   e. phase shift

   e. _____

   f. vertical shift

   f. _____

Functions, Statistics, and Trigonometry © Scott Foresman Addison Wesley

10. In what interval(s) between 0 and 2π are cos θ and sin θ both positive? both negative?

10. _____

_____

In 11 and 12, let *P'* be the reflection image of *P* over the *x*-axis in the unit circle at the right. State each value.

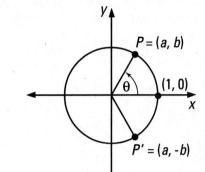

11. sin (-θ)

11. _____

12. cos (π + θ)

12. _____

13. At the right is part of the graph of a function *f*. Which could be an equation for *f*: *f(x)* = sin *x* or *f(x)* = cos *x*? Justify your answer.

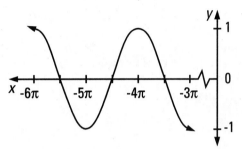

_____

_____

14. At the right is a graph together with a general form of an equation for it. Find each value in the equation.

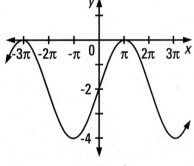

$$y = b\cos\left(\frac{x-h}{a}\right) + k$$

a. *a*

b. *b*

c. *h*

d. *k*

14. a. _____

b. _____

c. _____

d. _____

15. Use theorems about sines and cosines to prove that

    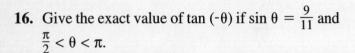

    $\sin(\pi - \theta) = \cos\left(\frac{\pi}{2} - \theta\right)$.

    _____

    _____

16. Give the exact value of $\tan(-\theta)$ if $\sin\theta = \frac{9}{11}$ and $\frac{\pi}{2} < \theta < \pi$.

    16. _____

17. Suppose the transformation $(x, y) \rightarrow \left(\frac{x}{2} + \frac{\pi}{8}, y\right)$ is applied to the graph of $y = \tan x$. State an equation for the image.

    17. _____

18. *Multiple choice.* Which property of a circular function changes under a vertical scale change of its graph?

    18. _____

    (a) frequency   (b) amplitude

    (c) period   (d) phase shift

19. A simple pendulum is shown at the right. The angular displacement from the vertical in radians as a function of time t in seconds is given by

    $f(t) = \frac{1}{4}\sin\left(4t + \frac{\pi}{2}\right)$.

    a. What is the frequency of f?

    19. a. _____

    b. Find the first three times t that the pendulum is at its maximum angular displacement.

    b. _____

Functions, Statistics, and Trigonometry © Scott Foresman Addison Wesley

In 20 and 21, the Ferris wheel shown at the right rotates counterclockwise at a uniform speed of 3 revolutions per minute. It has a radius of 15 m, and its center is 17 m above the ground. After the ride starts, the seat labeled *S* takes 2 seconds to first reach the lowest point on the wheel. The function *h* gives the height in meters of the seat above the ground as a function of the time *t* seconds after the ride starts.

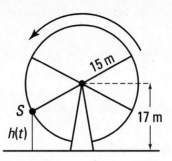

20. *Multiple choice.* Whis is an equation for *h*?

    (a) $h(t) = 17 + 15 \cos\left(\frac{\pi}{10}(t - 2)\right)$

    (b) $h(t) = 17 - 15 \sin\left(\frac{\pi}{10}(t - 2)\right)$

    (c) $h(t) = 17 - 15 \cos\left(\frac{\pi}{10}(t - 2)\right)$

    (d) $h(t) = 17 + 15 \sin\left(\frac{\pi}{10}(t - 2)\right)$

20. _____

21. What will be the height of the seat *S* above the ground 30 seconds after the ride starts? Round to the nearest hundredth of a meter.

21. _____

Functions, Statistics, and Trigonometry © Scott Foresman Addison Wesley

Check all your work carefully.

CHAPTER 4 TEST, Form B

You will need a calculator and an automatic grapher for this test.

1. Convert 2.2 revolutions clockwise to radians exactly.

   1. _____

2. Convert 2 radians to degrees. Give your answer approximated to three decimal places.

   2. _____

3. Convert 144° to radians exactly.

   3. _____

4. In a circle of radius 7 centimeters, a sector is formed by a central angle of $\frac{\pi}{7}$ radians. Find the area of the sector to the nearest hundredth of a square centimeter.

   4. _____

5. The city of Mexico City, Mexico, has a latitude 19.4°N and longitude 99.15°W. The circumference of a meridian is almost exactly 40,000 km. Find the distance between Mexico City and the equator to the nearest kilometer.

   5. _____

In 6 and 7, give exact values.

6. tan 210°

   6. _____

7. $\sin\left(-\frac{13\pi}{6}\right)$

   7. _____

8. Approximate $\cos\left(\frac{21\pi}{10}\right)$ to four decimal places.

   8. _____

9. Identify each of the following for the function with equation $y = -4\cos(2\pi x - 2) - 6$.

   a. domain

   9. a. _____

   b. range

   b. _____

   c. amplitude

   c. _____

   d. period

   d. _____

   e. phase shift

   e. _____

   f. vertical shift

   f. _____

10. In what interval(s) between 0 and 2π are $\sin\theta$ and $\tan\theta$ both positive? both negative?

10. _____

_____

In 11 and 12, let Q' be the reflection image of Q over the x-axis in the unit circle at the right. State each value.

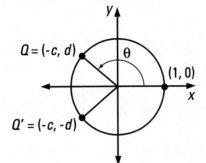

11. $\cos\theta$

11. _____

12. $\sin(\theta + \pi)$

12. _____

13. At the right is part of the graph of a function g. Which could be an equation for g: $g(x) = \sin x$ or $g(x) = \cos x$? Justify your answer.

_____

_____

14. At the right is a graph together with a general form of an equation for it. Find each value in the equation.

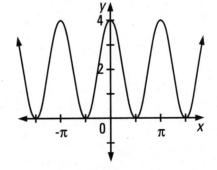

a. a

14. a. _____

b. b

b. _____

c. h

c. _____

$$y = b\sin\left(\frac{x - h}{a}\right) + k$$

d. k

d. _____

15. Use theorems about sines and cosines to prove that
$\sin\left(\frac{\pi}{2} - \theta\right) = \cos(-\theta)$.

_____

_____

16. Give the exact value of $\tan\left(\frac{\pi}{2} - \theta\right)$

if $\cos\theta = \frac{1}{4}$ and $\frac{3\pi}{2} < \theta < 2\pi$.

16. _____

17. Suppose the transformation $(x, y) \to \left(\frac{x}{3} + \frac{\pi}{2}, 3y\right)$
is applied to the graph of $y = \sin x$.
State an equation for the image.

17. _____

18. *Multiple choice.* Which property of a circular function
changes under a horizontal scale change of its graph?

18. _____

(a) maximum   (b) amplitude

(c) period   (d) vertical shift

19. A weight oscillating on a spring is
shown at the right. Its distance from
equilibrium in centimeters as a function
of time t in seconds is given by
$g(t) = 4\sin\left(\frac{\pi}{2}t - \frac{\pi}{2}\right)$.

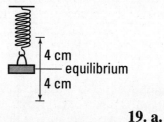
4 cm
equilibrium
4 cm

a. What is the frequency of g?

19. a. _____

b. Find the first three times t that the weight is at its
maximum distance from the equilibrium.

b. _____

Functions, Statistics, and Trigonometry © Scott Foresman Addison Wesley

In 20 and 21, the Ferris wheel shown at the right rotates counterclockwise at a uniform speed of 2.5 revolutions per minute. It has a radius of 20 m, and its center is 22 m above the ground. After the ride starts, the seat labeled *S* takes 4 seconds to first reach the lowest point on the wheel. The function *h* gives the height in meters of the seat above the ground as a function of the time *t* seconds after the ride starts.

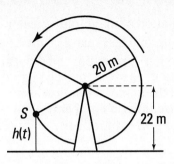

20. *Multiple choice.* Which is an equation for *h*?

20. _____

(a) $h(t) = 22 + 20 \sin\left(\frac{\pi}{12}(t - 4)\right)$

(b) $h(t) = 22 - 20 \cos\left(\frac{\pi}{12}(t - 4)\right)$

(c) $h(t) = 22 - 20 \sin\left(\frac{\pi}{12}(t - 4)\right)$

(d) $h(t) = 22 + 20 \cos\left(\frac{\pi}{12}(t - 4)\right)$

21. What will be the height of the seat *S* above the ground 30 seconds after the ride starts? Round to the nearest hundredth of a meter.

21. _____

Check all your work carefully.

CHAPTER 4 TEST, Form C

1. Choose any rotation of magnitude greater than one full turn and less than $1\frac{1}{4}$ turns. Specify a direction of rotation, and draw a picture to illustrate the rotation. Then give the measure of the angle of rotation as a number of revolutions, a number of degrees, and a number of radians.

2. In circle P, Kelly found the area of the shaded region to be 3240 m² by applying the Circular Sector Area Formula as follows.

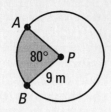

$$A = \tfrac{1}{2}\theta r^2 = \tfrac{1}{2}(80)(9)^2$$

However, Kelly realized that the area of the entire circle is only about 250 m². Identify the error in Kelly's work and correct it.

3. Choose one of these theorems: Opposites Theorem, Supplements Theorem, Complements Theorem, Half-Turn Theorem. State the theorem. Then show how you can use the unit circle to show that it is true.

4. Suppose you are asked *What is cos (-150°)?* and *What is cos (-151°)?* How is answering the first question similar to answering the second? How is it different? Name as many similarities and differences as you can.

5. The functions f and g, graphed at the right, are a parent circular function and its image under a transformation. Identify the parent function and the transformation. Then make a table in which you compare f and g by listing as many properties of each as you can.

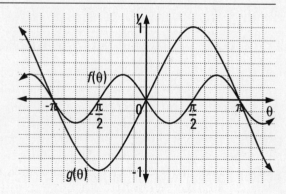

Functions, Statistics, and Trigonometry © Scott Foresman Addison Wesley

CHAPTER 4 TEST, Form D

A friend who creates computer graphics wants to simulate a traditional stopwatch (like the one pictured below) running in real time on a computer screen. Your friend has asked for your help. Your job is to specify the location of the tip of the second hand of the stopwatch as it runs.

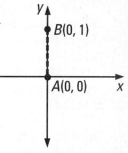

a. On the coordinate axes at the right is a segment $\overline{AB}$ with endpoints $A = (0, 0)$ and $B = (0, 1)$. Suppose $\overline{AB}$ rotates clockwise about point A at the rate of one revolution per minute. Let (p, q) be the *exact* location of point B at a time t seconds after the rotation begins. Complete this table.

t	0	5	10	15	20	25	30	35	40	45	50	55	60
p													
q													

b. Which equation describes the relationship between p and t?

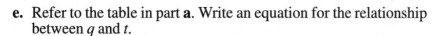

(i) $p = \sin t$ (ii) $p = \sin\left(t + \frac{\pi}{30}\right)$ (iii) $p = \sin\left(\frac{\pi}{30}t\right)$ (iv) $p = \frac{\pi}{30}\sin t$

c. Suppose the endpoints of $\overline{AB}$ were $A = (2, 3)$ and $B = (2, 4)$. Modify the equation from part **b** to model the new relationship between p and t.

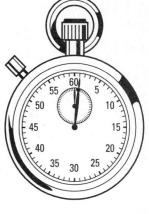

d. Suppose the endpoints of $\overline{AB}$ were $A = (0, 0)$ and $B = (0, 5)$. Modify the equation from part **b** to model the new relationship between p and t.

e. Refer to the table in part **a**. Write an equation for the relationship between q and t.

f. Repeat parts **c** and **d**, this time using your equation from part **e** to analyze the relationship between q and t.

g. Graph your equations from parts **b** and **e**. Identify the amplitude, period, phase shift, and vertical shift of the function each represents.

h. The image on a computer screen is broken into a grid of tiny dots called *pixels*. Each pixel has a numbered *address* that can be determined by a coordinate system with its origin at the lower left of the screen, as shown at the right. The number of pixels on a computer screen is called the *resolution* of the screen. The most common resolution is 640 × 480, which means that the screen is 640 pixels wide and 480 pixels high.

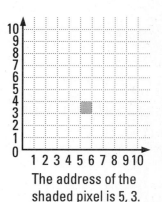

The address of the shaded pixel is 5, 3.

Prepare a set of instructions that your friend can use to locate the tip of the second hand as it runs on a screen with 640 × 480 resolution. Be sure to specify the length of the second hand in pixels and the location of the center of rotation. *Note:* The numbers that identify the address of the pixel must be integers.

CHAPTER 4 TEST, Cumulative Form

1. The histogram at the right shows the age distribution of a town's population. Each interval includes the right endpoint, but not the left.

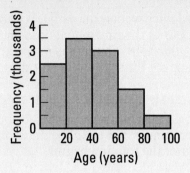

   a. About what percent of the population is age 40 or younger?

                             1. a. _____

   b. In which interval is the third quartile?   b. _____

2. *Multiple choice.* A university sent a questionnaire about income to its most recent graduating class. From the 182 questionnaires returned, they estimated the mean and standard deviation of incomes for all 1250 members of the class. Why might these estimates be very inaccurate?

   (a) Statistical measures of populations cannot be estimated from samples.

   (b) Standard deviations for populations and samples have different formulas.

   (c) The returned questionnaires might not represent a random sample of the population.

   (d) The variable being studied might not be measured in a sample.

                             2. _____

3. Convert 324° to radians exactly.   3. _____

4. Convert 2.25 revolutions counterclockwise to degrees.   4. _____

In 5 and 6, give exact values.

5. $\tan 225°$ 5. _____

6. $\sin\left(-\frac{23\pi}{3}\right)$ 6. _____

Functions, Statistics, and Trigonometry © Scott Foresman Addison Wesley

7. Use circle O at the right, in which $m\angle AOB = 130°$. Compute the area of the sector formed by $\angle AOB$

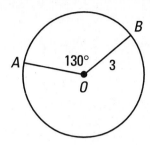

7. _____

8. Justify each lettered step in this proof that, for all θ measured in radians, $\sin\left(\theta - \frac{\pi}{2}\right) = \cos(\theta + \pi)$.

   a. $\sin\left(\theta - \frac{\pi}{2}\right) = -\sin\left(\frac{\pi}{2} - \theta\right)$

   8. a. _____

   b. $-\sin\left(\frac{\pi}{2} - \theta\right) = -\cos\theta$

   b. _____

   c. $-\cos\theta = \cos(\pi + \theta)$

   c. _____

   Therefore, by the Transitive Property of Equality,
   $\sin\left(\theta - \frac{\pi}{2}\right) = \cos(\theta + \pi)$.

9. Demi is starting an exercise program. She plans to do 5 sit-ups per day in the first month. In the next month, she will increase the number by 2, to 7 sit-ups per day. In the month after that, she will increase the number by 4, to 11 sit-ups per day. She plans to continue this pattern for one year, each month increasing the number of sit-ups per day by 2 more than the increase of the preceding month.

   a. Find a quadratic equation that gives the number of sit-ups n per day as a function of the number of the month m of Demi's exercise program.

   9. a. _____

   b. If she adheres to her plan, how many sit-ups per day will Demi do in the twelfth month of her program?

   b. _____

10. If $\sin\theta = \frac{1}{3}$, find all possible values of each. Give the values exactly.

    a. $\cos\theta$

    10. a. _____

    b. $\tan\theta$

    b. _____

11. Write an equation for a function whose parent is $y = \sin x$ and that has phase shift $-\frac{\pi}{2}$ from the parent, period π, and amplitude 3.

11. _____

12. Let f be the function $f(x) = (x - 3)^2 + 5$.

    a. Find an equation for p, the parent function of f.

12. **a.** _____

    b. State a rule for the translation T that maps p to f.

    b. _____

    c. Give an equation for the axis of symmetry of the graph of f.

    c. _____

Consider the following situation. For its first year of operation, a company made \$100,000 in profits p on \$1,000,000 in gross revenues r. In each subsequent year, the company's gross revenues increased by a constant 7% over the preceding year's revenues, but its profit-to-revenue ratio $c = \frac{p}{r}$ decreased by 3%.

13. **a.** Write an equation that gives the company's gross revenues r for its nth year of operation.

13. **a.** _____

    b. What were the company's gross revenues, to the nearest hundred dollars, for its fifth year of operation?

    b. _____

Suppose that, for the set of daily wages of the 12 employees of a small company, the mean is \$80 and the standard deviation is \$21.

14. Suppose that, on the day before Thanksgiving, each employee receives a \$75 bonus.

    a. What is the mean of the wages of the 12 employees on that day?

14. **a.** _____

    b. What is the standard deviation of the wages of the 12 employees on that day?

    b. _____

Functions, Statistics, and Trigonometry © Scott Foresman Addison Wesley

15. Let $h(x) = -2 + 3\cos\left(\frac{x + \pi}{2}\right)$.

    a. Sketch one cycle of the graph of h.

15. a.

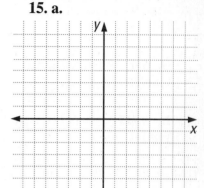

    b. Identify each for the function h.

      i. amplitude

      ii. period

15. b. i. _____

    ii. _____

In 16 and 17, let $j(x) = x - \frac{\pi}{4}$ **and let** $k(x) = \tan x.$

16. Evaluate $(j \circ k)\left(\frac{\pi}{4}\right)$.

16. _____

17. **a.** Find a formula for $k \circ j$.

17. a. _____

    b. Give the range of $k \circ j$.

b. _____

18. Use the Inverse Function Theorem to show that f and g, with $f(x) = 2x + 7$ and $g(x) = \frac{1}{2}x - 7$, are *not* inverses.

_____

_____

Check all your work carefully.

QUIZ

In 1 and 2, refer to △ABC at the right.

1. Find the exact value of tan B.

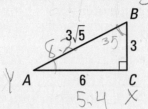

1. _____

2. Find m∠A to the nearest tenth of a degree.

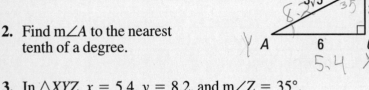

2. _____

3. In △XYZ, $x = 5.4$, $y = 8.2$, and m∠$Z = 35°$. Find z.

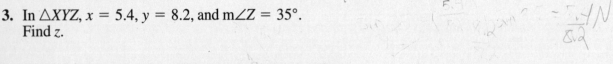

3. _____

In 4–6, find the exact value of the expression in radians.

4. $\cos^{-1}\left(-\frac{1}{2}\right)$

4. _____

5. Arccos 0

5. _____

6. $\cos^{-1}\left(\cos\left(\frac{4\pi}{3}\right)\right)$

6. _____

7. A surveying instrument is positioned 627 feet from the base of a tree. The surveyor determines that the measure of the angle of elevation from the base of the instrument to the top of the tree is 4°36′27″.

   a. Convert 4°36′27″ to decimal degrees.

   7. a. _____

   b. Find the height of the tree to the nearest foot.

   b. _____

8. Is the function f with $f(x) = \cos^{-1}x$ an even function, an odd function, or neither? Justify your answer.

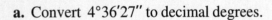

   _____

   _____

9. Use the Law of Cosines to show that a triangle with sides of length 5, 12, and 13 is a right triangle.

   _____

   _____

Functions, Statistics, and Trigonometry © Scott Foresman Addison Wesley

Name _____

QUIZ

In 1–3, find the exact value of the expression in radians.

1. $\sin^{-1}\left(\frac{\sqrt{3}}{2}\right)$

1. _____

2. $\tan^{-1}(-1)$

2. _____

3. $\text{Arcsin}\left(\sin\left(\frac{4\pi}{5}\right)\right)$

3. _____

4. In $\triangle ABC$, m$\angle A = 56°$, m$\angle C = 70°$, and $c = 14$. Find a.

4. _____

5. In $\triangle XYZ$, m$\angle X = 43°$, $x = 7.5$, and $z = 9$. Find all possible values of m$\angle Z$ to the nearest tenth of a degree.

5. _____

6. Find the area of the triangle at the right.

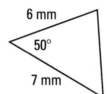

6 mm

50°

7 mm

6. _____

7. Is the function f with $f(x) = \tan^{-1}x$ an even function, an odd function, or neither? Justify your answer.

_____

_____

8. Two stations located on a shoreline and equipped with directional antennas intercept signals transmitted by a ship's radar. By measuring the directions of the signals, it is determined that the ship is 15° east of south from station A and 20° west of south from station B. Given that station B is 15 miles due east of station A, determine each distance to the nearest tenth of a mile.

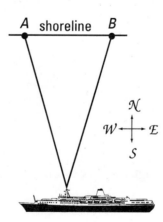

A shoreline B

N

W ←┼→ E

S

a. the distance between the ship and station A

8. a. _____

b. the shortest distance between the ship and the shoreline

b. _____

CHAPTER 5 TEST, Form A

1. Approximate cos 75°48′36″ to the nearest thousandth. 1. _____

In 2–4, refer to △CBS at the right.

2. Find cos S exactly. 2. _____

3. Find tan S exactly. 3. _____

4. **a.** Find sin C exactly. 4. **a.** _____

   b. Find m∠C to the nearest degree. **b.** _____

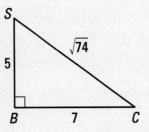

In 5 and 6, find the exact value of the expression in radians.

5. $\sin^{-1}\left(\frac{1}{2}\right)$ 5. _____

6. $\text{Arctan}\left(\tan\left(\frac{3\pi}{4}\right)\right)$ 6. _____

7. For what values of θ is the following statement true? If $k = \cos\theta$, then $\theta = \cos^{-1}k$. 7. _____

8. **a.** The graph of which equation has asymptotes: $y = \sin^{-1}x$, $y = \cos^{-1}x$, or $y = \tan^{-1}x$? 8. **a.** _____

   b. Give equations for the asymptotes. **b.** _____

9. Find x in the triangle at the right. Round your answer to the nearest tenth. 9. _____

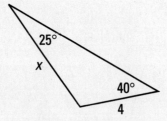

10. A person who is 5 feet 7 inches tall is standing outdoors at a time when the angle of elevation of the sun is 40°. What is the length of the person's shadow, to the nearest inch? 10. _____

Functions, Statistics, and Trigonometry © Scott Foresman Addison Wesley

In 11 and 12, refer to
the diagram at the
right. It shows a
triangular playground
that is bounded by
Main Street, High
Street, and Central
Street.

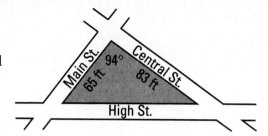

11. The Park District has hired a contractor to pave the
     surface of the playground with asphalt. What is the
     area of the playground to the nearest 100 square feet?

11. _____

12. The contractor also will erect a fence around the
     playground. Assume that the fencing is sold by the
     foot. What is the minimum amount of fencing the
     contractor can buy?

12. _____

In 13 and 14, refer to the playground
swing shown at the right. The seat of
the swing hangs from a rope that is
5 meters long. When the rope's
angular displacement from vertical is
0 radians, the height of the seat above
the ground is 1 meter.

13. **a.** Find a formula for the height *h* of the seat above
             the ground in terms of the angular displacement θ.

13. a. _____

     b. What is the height of the seat above the ground
             when the angular displacement is 0.6 radian?
             Round to the nearest tenth of a meter.

b. _____

14. Suppose the angular displacement of the rope is
     given by θ = .6 sin(1.4*t* − .7), where θ is
     measured in radians and *t* is the time measured
     in seconds. Find the first two values of *t* for which
     the angular displacement of the rope is 0 radians.

14. _____

15. In △*ABC*, *m*∠*B* = 43.8°, *a* = 10, and *b* = 8.
     Find *m*∠*A* to the nearest tenth of a degree.

15. _____

16. Find all values of θ between 0 and 2π such that tan θ = -1.585.

16. _____

17. Give the general solution to $2 \cos \theta - \sqrt{3} = 0$.

_____

_____

18. In $\triangle XYZ$, $ZY = 10$ and $ZX = 7$.

    a. For what measure of $\angle Z$ is the area of $\triangle XYZ$ greatest?

18. a. _____

    b. What is the greatest possible area of $\triangle XYZ$?

b. _____

19. Show that the Pythagorean Theorem is a special case of the Law of Cosines.

_____

_____

Check all your work carefully.

Functions, Statistics, and Trigonometry © Scott Foresman Addison Wesley

CHAPTER 5 TEST, Form B

1. Approximate sin 15°18′24″ to the nearest thousandth.

1. _____

In 2–4, refer to △FOX at the right.

2. Find sin F exactly.

2. _____

3. Find tan F exactly.

3. _____

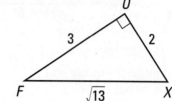

4. **a.** Find cos X exactly.

4. **a.** _____

   b. Find m∠X to the nearest degree.

   b. _____

In 5 and 6, find the exact value of the expression in radians.

5. $\cos^{-1}\left(\frac{\sqrt{2}}{2}\right)$

5. _____

6. $\text{Arcsin}\left(\sin\left(\frac{4\pi}{3}\right)\right)$

6. _____

7. For what values of θ is the following statement true?
If $k = \tan\theta$, then $\theta = \tan^{-1}k$

7. _____

8. Describe the symmetry of the graph of the function g for which $g(x) = \sin^{-1}x$.

_____

_____

9. Find x in the triangle at the right. Round your answer to the nearest tenth.

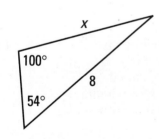

9. _____

10. A person who is 6 feet 1 inch tall is standing outdoors at a time when the angle of elevation of the sun is 75°. What is the length of the person's shadow, to the nearest inch?

10. _____

In 11 and 12, refer to the diagram at the right. It shows a city lot bounded by Chestnut, Walnut, Third, and Fourth Streets. Chestnut and Walnut Streets are parallel, as are Third and Fourth Streets.

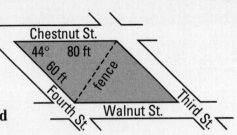

11. The Park District has hired a contractor to lay sod over the entire surface of the lot. What is the area of the lot to the nearest 100 square feet?

11. _____

12. The contractor also will erect a fence diagonally across the lot in the position indicated. Assume that the fencing is sold by the foot. What is the minimum amount of fencing the contractor can buy?

12. _____

In 13 and 14, refer to the playground swing shown at the right. The seat of the swing hangs from a rope that is 4 meters long. When the rope's angular displacement from vertical is 0 radians, the height of the seat above the ground is .75 meter.

13. **a.** Find a formula for the height h of the seat above the ground in terms of the angular displacement θ.

13. a. _____

b. What is the height of the seat above the ground when the angular displacement is 0.4 radian? Round to the nearest tenth of a meter.

b. _____

14. Suppose the angular displacement of the rope is given by $\theta = .4\cos(1.6t - 1.4)$, where θ is measured in radians and t is the time measured in seconds. Find the first two values of t for which the angular displacement of the rope is 0 radians.

14. _____

15. In $\triangle ABC$, m$\angle B = 51.5°$, $a = 15$, and $b = 21$. Find m$\angle A$ to the nearest tenth of a degree.

15. _____

Functions, Statistics, and Trigonometry © Scott Foresman Addison Wesley

16. Find all values of θ between 0 and 2π such that $\sin \theta = -0.358$.

16. _____

17. Give the general solution to $2 \tan \theta - \dfrac{2\sqrt{3}}{3} = 0$.

_____

_____

18. In $\triangle NBC$, $BN = 20$ and m$\angle N = 30°$.

  a. For what measure of $\angle C$ is the length of $\overline{BC}$ shortest?

18. a. _____

  b. What is the shortest possible length of $\overline{BC}$?

  b. _____

19. In $\triangle ABD$ at the right, $DC = CB = y$, $AC = x$, and m$\angle ACB = n°$. Show that $\triangle ABC$ and $\triangle ACD$ are equal in area.

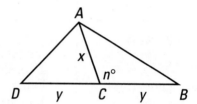

_____

_____

Check all your work carefully.

CHAPTER 5 TEST, Form C

1. On grid paper, draw two different right triangles *ABC* in which ∠*C* is the right angle and tan *B* = .8. Then find the following measures in each triangle: *AC*, *BC*, *AB*, sin *A*, cos *A*, sin *B*, cos *B*, m∠*A*, m∠*B*.

2. In △*RST*, m∠*T* = 52.1° and *s* = 7. Give a length *t* that leads to a unique △*RST*. Then use the given measures and your length *t* to find m∠*R*, m∠*S*, the length *r*, and the area of △*RST*.

3. All the following are true statements.
$$\cos \frac{\pi}{3} = .5 \quad \cos \frac{5\pi}{3} = .5 \quad \cos \frac{7\pi}{6} = .5$$
However, the unique value of $\cos^{-1}(.5)$ is $\frac{\pi}{3}$. Explain how this is possible. Then describe a similar situation involving sines.

4. The following equation can be used to model the average monthly temperature *T* for Cleveland, Ohio, in degrees Fahrenheit, where *n* is the month after January.
$$T = 23.78 \sin(.49n - 1.51) + 48.16$$
Write a problem that you can solve using this equation. Show how to solve your problem.

5. Josh drew the diagram at the right as a summary of the inverse trigonometric functions, but he forgot to label the graphs.

Are Josh's graphs accurate? Do they give a *good* representation of the functions? Explain your reasoning. Modify any graphs that you think are inaccurate or inadequate. Then label the graphs with appropriate equations.

Inverse Trigonometric Functions

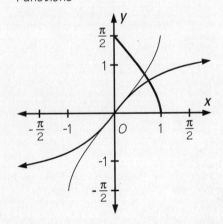

CHAPTER 1 TEST, Form D

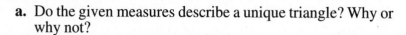

The shaded region of the diagram at the right shows a triangular plot of land and the measures obtained when one person surveyed it.

a. Do the given measures describe a unique triangle? Why or why not?

b. Use the given measures to calculate the measure of the third angle and the lengths of the other sides. Then calculate the area of the plot to the nearest tenth of an acre. (*Note:* 1 acre = 4840 square yards)

c. Suppose a second person surveys the land. This person obtains the same angle measures as given, but finds the length along Morton Street to be 250 yards. Repeat part **b** using this person's measures.

d. Suppose a third person surveys the land. This person obtains the same length as given, but finds the measures of the angles to be 48° and 30°. Repeat part **b** using their person's measures.

e. Suppose you can sell this land for $80,000 per acre. Compare the sale prices of the land using the measures in parts **b**, **c**, and **d**.

f. Your parents own a plot of land that has been in your family for several generations. The only description of the land is the old drawing shown at right below. Now a developer has offered to buy the land at a price of $47,500 per acre. Your job is to help your parents with the sale of the property by performing the following tasks.

- Use the drawing to find measures for the angles at the corners of the property, the length of each side, and the two diagonal lengths across the property. You will need to use a ruler, protractor, and the scale to find some measures, but do this for as few measures as possible. Calculate the rest using trigonometry. Be sure to show all your work.

- Estimate the area of the property and the price this developer will pay for it.

- Prepare an argument to convince your parents of the need to have the plot of land measured *accurately* by a surveyor.

- Recommend a degree of precision for the surveyor's measurements, and explain your reasoning. For example: Angle measures might be measured to the nearest degree, or tenth of a degree, or nearest minute, and so on.

- Describe a plan for measuring that requires making as few measurements as possible, yet specifies the plot of land uniquely.

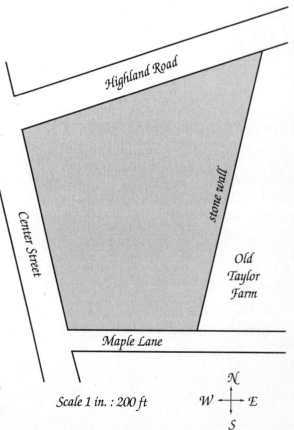

Scale 1 in. : 200 ft

CHAPTER 5 TEST, Cumulative Form

1. Convert 240° to radians exactly.

1. _____

2. In △ACD at the right, find BD. Round your answer to the nearest tenth.

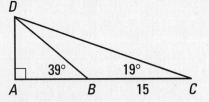

2. _____

3. Find two values of θ on the interval 0° ≤ θ ≤ 360° that satisfy the equation sin θ = -.6293. Round the solutions to the nearest degree.

3. _____

4. Copier paper usually is sold in packs of 500 sheets that are called *reams*. Write a formula for the number of reams *r* needed to make *n* single-sided copies of a 27-page document.

4. _____

5. Find m∠C in the triangle at the right. Round your answer to the nearest degree.

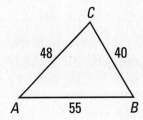

5. _____

6. *True or false.* If sin A > sin B, then A > B. Justify your answer.

_____

_____

Choose from the graphs below.

(i)
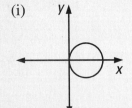

(ii)
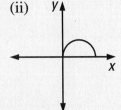

(iii)
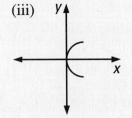

(iv)
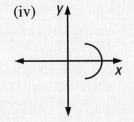

7. Identify all the graphs that represent relations whose inverses are functions.

7. _____

Functions, Statistics, and Trigonometry © Scott Foresman Addison Wesley

8. A ship is 60 nautical miles from port, as a bearing of   8. _____
15° east of north. A second ship is 40 nautical miles from
the same port, at a bearing of 35° west of north. What is
the distance between the ships, to the nearest nautical mile?

9. Consider the function f with $f(x) = x^3$. Find an equation   9. _____
for the image of the graph of f under the translation
$T: (x, y) \rightarrow (x - 5, y + 7)$.

10. Suppose $\cos \theta = .92$. Find $\cos^2 + \sin^2 \theta$.   10. _____

11. The latitude of Pittsburgh, Pennsylvania, is 40°27′N,   11. _____
and its longitude is 79°57′ W. The latitude of Roanoke,
Virginia, is 37°17′N, and its longitude is 79°57′ W.
Assuming Earth is a sphere of radius 3960 miles,
find the distance between the cities to the nearest ten miles.

12. Consider the function described by $y = \tan\left(x + \frac{\pi}{3}\right)$.

    a. State its domain.   12. **a.** _____

    b. State its range.   **b.** _____

13. Give a general solution to $2 \tan \theta - 1 = 0$.   13. _____

14. The area of $\triangle QED$ at   14. _____
the right is 16 square
units, and $\angle Q$ is an
acute angle. Find $m\angle Q$
to the nearest degree.

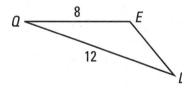

15. A weight on a spring is shown   15. _____
at the right. When the spring
is pulled down 1 inch from
equilibrium, it oscillates
2 inches between its lowest
and highest positions. Its
distance d from the lowest
position in inches as a function
of time t in seconds is given by
$$d = 1 - \cos\left(\frac{\pi}{2}t\right).$$

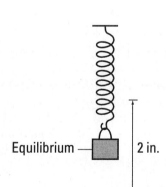

Find all the times t on the interval $0 \le t \le 4$
for which $d = 1.5$.

Functions, Statistics, and Trigonometry © Scott Foresman Addison Wesley

16. Let $f(x) = x^2 - x$ and let $g(x) = \frac{1}{x} + 1$.

    a. Evaluate $g(f(3))$.

    16. a. _____

    b. Find a formula for $g(f(x))$.

    b. _____

17. Suppose the mean score on a test is 82 and the standard deviation is 8. What is the z-score for a raw score of 100 on this test?

    17. _____

18. *Multiple choice.* What function is graphed at the right?

    (a) $y = \sin^{-1}x$

    (b) $y = \cos^{-1}x$

    (c) $y = -\sin^{-1}x$

    (d) $y = -\cos^{-1}x$

    18. _____

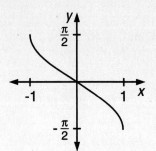

19. A sine wave model for the average temperature T for Newark, New Jersey, during month n can be found using the data and the graph below.

Month	Average Temp. (°F)
January	31
February	33
March	42
April	52
May	63
June	73
July	78
August	76
September	69
October	58
November	47
December	36

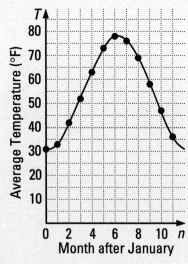

    a. What is the amplitude of the wave?

    19. a. _____

    b. What is the period of the wave?

    b. _____

    c. Write an equations to model these data.

    c. _____

Check all your work carefully.

Functions, Statistics, and Trigonometry © Scott Foresman Addison Wesley

QUIZ

1. List all the real fourth roots of 2401.

   1. _____

2. Simplify $a^3 \cdot a^{-3}$, given $a \neq 0$.

   2. _____

3. Evaluate $125^{-\frac{1}{3}}$.

   3. _____

4. If $x^3 = 32$, what is the value of $x^{\frac{6}{5}}$?

   4. _____

5. Consider two spheres, one with a radius of 2 cm and the other with twice the volume of the first.

   a. The volume V of a sphere is given by the formula $V = \frac{4}{3}\pi r^3$, where r is the radius of the sphere. Find the exact volume of the larger sphere.

   5. a. _____

   b. Find the radius of the larger sphere to the nearest hundredth of a centimeter.

   b. _____

6. a. Rewrite $\left(\sqrt[3]{x}\right)^7$ without a radical sign.

   6. a. _____

   b. For what values of x is the radical expression you wrote in part **a** defined?

   b. _____

7. The concentration [H+] of hydrogen ions in an aqueous solution is given by the formula $[\text{H}+] = 10^{(-\text{pH})}$, where pH is a measure of the acidity of the solution and [H+] is measured in moles per liter.

   a. If the pH of a solution is 1.5, find the concentration of hydrogen ions in the solution to the nearest thousandth of a mole per liter.

   7. a. _____

   b. If the concentration of a solution is .00005, what is the pH of this solution? Round to the nearest tenth.

   b. _____

8. Let $f(x) = x^{\frac{1}{4}}$ and let $g(x) = x^{\frac{1}{3}}$ for all $x \geq 0$.

   a. For what values of x is $f(x) > g(x)$ a true statement?

   8. a. _____

   b. For what values of x is $g(x) > f(x)$ a true statement?

   b. _____

In 9 and 10, find exact values.

9. $\log_3 81$

   9. _____

10. $\log_9 \sqrt{3}$

   10. _____

QUIZ

In 1 and 2, evaluate and round to the nearest hundredth.

1. $e^{-1.64}$

1. _____

2. $\ln 0.32$

2. _____

3. Diane wants to invest \$5000 in a savings account for one year. Which would be a better investment: an account paying 6.3% annual interest compounded twice per year, or an account paying 6.25% annual interest compounded continuously? Justify your answer.

   _____

   _____

4. **a.** Evaluate and round to the nearest whole number.

   i. $\left(1 + \dfrac{7}{100}\right)^{100}$

   4. a. i. _____

   ii. $\left(1 + \dfrac{7}{100}\right)^{1000} = 1070$

   ii. _____

   b. As n increases, what number does $\left(1 + \dfrac{7}{n}\right)^n$ approach?

   b. _____

5. Rewrite as an equation that does not involve logarithms: $\log a = 5 \log b + 2 \log c$

5. _____

6. Evaluate $\log_5 50 + \log_5 2.5$.

6. _____

7. *Multiple choice.* Which is equivalent to $\log_9 5$?

   (a) $\dfrac{\log_5 5}{\log_5 9}$ (b) $\dfrac{\log_5 9}{\log_5 5}$

   (c) $\dfrac{\log_9 9}{\log_5 5}$ (d) $\dfrac{\log_5 9}{\log_9 9}$

7. _____

8. Solve $6^x = 32$. Give the exact solution.

8. _____

9. Solve $7^z = 12$. Round the solution to the nearest thousandth.

9. _____

10. Suppose you deposit \$1000 in an account paying 4.6% annual interest compounded continuously. How long will it take for your money to double?

10. _____

Name _____

CHAPTER 6 TEST, Form A

You will need a calculator and a statistics utility for this test.

1. Evaluate $\left(\frac{8}{27}\right)^{-\frac{1}{3}}$. Give an exact answer.

   1. _____

2. Write $\sqrt[4]{a^5b}$ without a radical sign. Assume $a > 0$ and $b > 0$.

   2. _____

In 3 and 4, let f be a function with $f(x) = x^{\frac{3}{4}}$, where x is a real number.

3. a. State the largest possible domain of f.

    3. a. _____

    b. State the largest possible range of f.

    b. _____

4. Write an expression for $f^{-1}(x)$.

   4. _____

5. The amount of energy an object radiates is given by the equation $R = kT^4$, where R is a rate measured in watts per square meter, T is the temperature of the object measured in degrees Kelvin , and k is a number called the *Stefan-Boltzmann constant*. Write T as a function of R.

   5. _____

6. Rewrite as a single logarithm: $\frac{1}{2}\log_{20} b - 2\log_{20} c$

   6. _____

7. Evaluate $\log_3 21$. Round to the nearest hundredth.

   7. _____

8. Solve $\log_6 x = 5$.

   8. _____

9. Solve $7^n = .14$. Round the solution to the nearest thousandth.

   9. _____

In 10 and 11, use the fact that $\log_b 5 \approx .8271$ and $\log_b 13 \approx 1.3181$ to evaluate the expression.

10. $\log_b 65$

    10. _____

11. $\log_b \left(\frac{13}{5}\right)$

    11. _____

12. Dell bought a $2300 computer using a special type of financing. He will make no payments for the first six months. During this time, however, interest will be charged on the amount he owes at an annual rate of 9.75%, compounded continuously. How much interest will be charged in those first six months?

    12. _____

13. A chemist observes that a particular compound decays continuously, and notes that 45% of the initial amount of the compound remains after 1 hour, 20 minutes. Estimate the half-life of the compound to the nearest minute.

13. _____

14. *Multiple choice.* Let f be a function with $f(x) = 2 \ln x$. Which is an equation for f^{-1}?

14. _____

   (a) $f^{-1} = (x) = \ln\left(\dfrac{2^x}{2}\right)$ (b) $f^{-1} = (x) = \ln\left(\dfrac{x}{2}\right)$

   (c) $f^{-1} = (x) = e^{\frac{x}{2}}$ (d) $f^{-1} = (x) = e^{2x}$

15. Suppose g is a function with $g(x) = \log^3 x$.

   a. Graph $y = g(x)$ and $y = g^{-1}(x)$ on the coordinate axes at the right.

15. a.

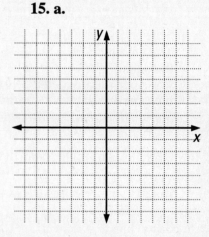

   b. Give the equation(s) of any asymptotes of the graph of g.

   b. _____

   c. Give an equation for g^{-1}.

   c. _____

16. *Multiple choice.* Which could be the equation graphed at the right?

16. _____

   (a) $y = x^{\frac{1}{4}}$

   (b) $y = \log_4 x$

   (c) $y = 4^x$

   (d) $y = \log (x - 3)$

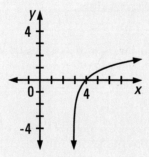

Functions, Statistics, and Trigonometry © Scott Foresman Addison Wesley

In 17–19, find exact values.

17. $\log_9 \sqrt[3]{3}$

17. _____

18. $\log_5 1.25 + 2 \log_5 10$

18. _____

19. $\ln\left(\dfrac{1}{e^5}\right)$

19. _____

20. Let $y = (6.3)(1.5)^x$. Write $\ln y$ as a linear function of x.

20. _____

21. The table below shows the maximum distance D in miles at which a certain size of airplane can be detected by an experimental radar system operating at a power of P kilowatts. In the scatterplot to the right of the table, the logarithms of the data are graphed.

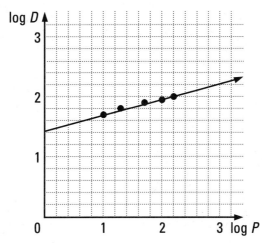

P	D
10	50
20	60
50	75
100	90
160	100

a. Find an equation of the form $\log D = a \log P + b$ to model these data.

21. a. _____

b. The radar's range in miles is related to its power in kilowatts by a function of the form $D = kP^{\frac{1}{n}}$, when n is an integer. What are the values of n and k? Round to the nearest tenth if necessary.

b. _____

Check all your work carefully.

CHAPTER 6 TEST, Form B

You will need a calculator and a statistics utility for this test.

1. Evaluate $\left(\frac{27}{125}\right)^{-\frac{1}{3}}$. Give an exact answer.

   1. _____

2. Write $\sqrt[6]{mn^5}$ without a radical sign. Assume $m > 0$ and $n > 0$.

   2. _____

In 3 and 4, let g be a function with $g(x) = x^{\frac{1}{5}}$, where g is a real number.

3. **a.** State the largest possible domain of g.

   3. **a.** _____

   b. State the largest possible range of g.

   b. _____

4. Write an expression for $g^{-1}(x)$.

   4. _____

5. The maximum distance D at which a radar can detect a target is related to the target's radar cross section A by the equation $D = k\sqrt[4]{A}$, where k is a constant. Write A as a function of D.

   5. _____

6. Rewrite as a single logarithm: $3 \ln b + 2 \ln c$

   6. _____

7. Evaluate $\log_5 17$. Round to the nearest hundredth.

   7. _____

8. Solve $\log_3 x = -2$.

   8. _____

9. Solve $6^r = 1200$. Round the solution to the nearest thousandth.

   9. _____

In 10 and 11, use the fact that $\log_a 4 \approx .7124$ and $\log_a 6 \approx .9208$ to evaluate the expression.

10. $\log_a 96$

    10. _____

11. $\log_a \left(\frac{2}{3}\right)^2$

    11. _____

12. At the time she was born, Melissa's grandparents invested $2000 for her in an account that has an annual interest rate of 7%, compounded continuously. Melissa is not allowed to withdraw the money until her 21st birthday. What will be the total amount in the account at that time?

    12. _____

Functions, Statistics, and Trigonometry © Scott Foresman Addison Wesley

13. A chemist observes that a particular compound decays continuously, and notes that 90% of the initial amount of the compound remains after 1 hour, 10 minutes. Estimate the half-life of the compound to the nearest minute.

13. _____

14. *Multiple choice.* Let f be a function with $f(x) = 2 \log_2 x$. Which is an equation for f^{-1}?

14. _____

    (a) $f^{-1}(x) = \dfrac{2^x}{2}$ (b) $f^{-1}(x) = 2^{\frac{x}{2}}$

    (c) $f^{-1}(x) = \dfrac{1}{2}x^2$ (d) $f^{-1}(x) = 2^{2x}$

15. Suppose h is a function with $h(x) = \log^4 x$.

    a. Graph $y = h(x)$ and $y = h^{-1}(x)$ on the coordinate axes at the right.

15. **a.**

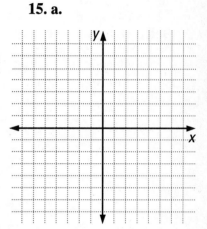

    b. Give the equation(s) of any asymptotes of the graph of h.

b. _____

    c. Give an equation for h^{-1}.

c. _____

16. *Multiple choice.* Which could be the equation graphed at the right?

16. _____

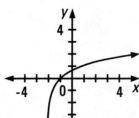

    (a) $y = -\ln x$

    (b) $y = e^x$

    (c) $y = \ln(x + 2)$

    (d) $y = x^{\frac{1}{3}}$

In 17–19, find exact values.

17. $\log_4 \sqrt[4]{8}$

17. _____

18. $\log_{17} 34 - \frac{1}{2} \log_{17} 68$

18. _____

19. $\left(e^{2 \ln 9}\right)^{-\frac{1}{4}}$

19. _____

20. Let $y = (2.5)(.71)^x$. Write $\ln y$ as a linear function of x.

20. _____

21. The table at the right lists six species of mammals, their average body weights Y in kilograms, and their average brain weighs N in grams. In the scatterplot below, the logarithms of the data have been graphed.

Mammal	Y	N
guinea pig	1.04	5.50
monkey	10.00	115.00
sheep	55.50	175.00
donkey	187.10	419.0
cow	465.00	423.00
giraffe	529.00	680.00

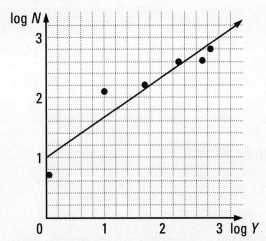

a. Find an equation of the form $\log N = a \log Y + b$ to model these data.

21. a. _____

b. Write an equation equivalent to the equation you wrote in part **a** with N as a function of Y.

b. _____

Check all your work carefully.

Functions, Statistics, and Trigonometry © Scott Foresman Addison Wesley

CHAPTER 6 TEST, Form C

1. a. Consider the expression $a^{\frac{b}{c}}$. Give integral values of the variables *other than 0 or 1* for which it is possible to evaluate the expression without using a calculator. Show how to evaluate the expression

   b. Repeat part **a** for the expression $\log_m n$.

   c. Repeat part **a** for the expression $\ln e^x$.

2. Elena solved $5^n = 24$ as shown at the right. Explain how you can tell without calculating that $n \approx 34.34$ is an unreasonable solution. Then correct Elena's error(s) and give the correct solution.

$$5^n = 24$$
$$n \log 5 = 24$$
$$n = \frac{24}{\log 5}$$
$$n \approx 34.34$$

3. Using the properties of logarithms, write four expressions involving logarithms that are equivalent to $\log_b 36$. In each case, identify the property of logarithms that you applied.

4. Using the coordinate axes below, draw a figure that illustrates this statement: *In general, the logarithm function with base b is the inverse of the exponential function with base b.* Then write a brief description of the figure you drew.

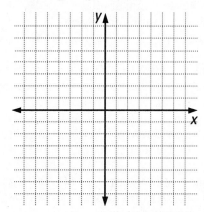

CHAPTER 6 TEST, Form D

The table at the right lists average college costs for selected years from 1959–60 through 1994–95. You will need a statistics utility to work with these data.

a. Let x = the school year after 1959–60 and let y = the average annual total charges at public four-year colleges.

   i. Find an equation of the form $y = ab^x$ that relates these data.

   ii. Transform the data by finding the log of y. Find the line of best fit for the transformed data.

   iii. What conclusion(s) can you draw from our answers to parts i and ii.

b. Show how to use your work from part a to predict:

   i. the average total annual charges at public four-year colleges in the 1996–97 school year.

   ii. the first school year in which the average total annual charges at public four-year colleges will be at least $15,000.

	Average Annual Charges for Full-Time Undergraduate Students 1959–60 to 1994–95 (Current Dollars)					
	Public Four-Year Colleges (In State)			Private Four-Year Colleges		
School Year	Total	Tuition	Room/Board	Total	Tuition	Room/Board
1959–60	$ 810	$ 200	$ 610	$ 1,510	$ 791	$ 719
1964–65	951	255	696	1,914	1,095	819
1969–70	1,237	357	880	2,551	1,557	994
1974–75	1,646	512	1,134	3,397	2,126	1,271
1979–80	2,327	738	1,590	5,013	3,225	1,788
1982–83	3,196	1,031	2,164	7,126	4,639	2,487
1983–84	3,433	1,148	2,285	7,759	5,093	2,666
1984–85	3,682	1,228	2,454	8,451	5,556	2,895
1985–86	3,859	1,318	2,541	9,228	6,121	3,108
1986–87	4,138	1,414	2,724	10,039	6,658	3,381
1987–88	4,403	1,537	2,866	10,659	7,116	3,543
1988–89	4,678	1,646	3,032	11,474	7,722	3,752
1989–90	4,975	1,780	3,195	12,284	8,396	3,888
1990–91	5,243	1,888	3,355	13,237	9,083	4,154
1991–92	5,695	2,119	3,577	14,273	9,775	4,498
1992–93	6,020	2,349	3,670	15,009	10,294	4,716
1993–94	6,365	2,537	3,829	15,904	10,952	4,951
1994–95	6,674	2,689	3,985	16,645	11,522	5,124

Source: United States Department of Education, National Center for Education Statistics

c. A person invests $10,000 in a special fund that pays 6.2% annual interest compounded continuously. There are no additional deposits or withdrawals from this fund.

   i. How much money will be in this account after five years?

   ii. Use logarithms to determine the number of years it would take for the money in this account to grow to $60,000.

d. A student is able to borrow $60,000 at a low annual interest rate of 3%. However, the student can only afford monthly payments of $200 to repay the loan.

   i. Use the *Time-to-Repay Formula* given at the right to determine how long it would take to repay the loan.

   ii. What is the total amount of interest paid on the loan?

Time-to-Repay Formula
$n = \dfrac{\log\left(\frac{a}{a - Pr}\right)}{\log(1 + r)}$
P = amount of loan
r = monthly interest rate
a = amount of each monthly payment
n = number of monthly payments

e. Suppose you must finance a student's college education twenty years from now. Use the information in the table and modeling to predict the cost of that education. Then develop a plan for financing it. Your plan should include a proposal for savings or investment that will cover at least part of the cost. If you also propose to borrow money, be sure the amount of the monthly payments and the time needed to repay are reasonable. Show all your calculations.

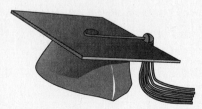

Functions, Statistics, and Trigonometry © Scott Foresman Addison Wesley

CHAPTER 6 TEST, Cumulative Form

You will need an automatic grapher for this test.

1. The stemplot at the right shows the test scores received by students in a math class.

```
 3 | 6
 4 | 1
 5 | 0  3  6  7
 6 | 2  3  5  8  9  9
 7 | 0  1  1  3  4  7  8
 8 | 2  4  5  7  8  8
 9 | 0  3  7  5
10 | 0  0
```

   a. Give the five-number summary of the scores.

   _____

   b. Use the 1.5 × IQR criterion to find any outliers.

   _____

2. *Multiple choice.* For a set of data, the correlation coefficient r is -0.3 and the line of best fit is given by $y = mx + b$. Which is a true statement?

   2. _____

   (a) $m > 0$ (b) $m < 0$

   (c) $m = 0$ (d) m can be any real number.

In 3 and 4, evaluate.

3. $\lfloor \lfloor 8.3 \rfloor + \frac{1}{2} \lceil 14.6 \rceil \rfloor$

   3. _____

4. $\sqrt[3]{-512}$

   4. _____

In 5 and 6, use an automatic grapher to graph the function f with $f(x) = x^5 - 4x^3 + 2x$. Use the graph to answer the questions.

5. Is f an even function, an odd function, or neither?

   5. _____

6. Is the inverse of f a function?

   6. _____

In 7 and 8, refer to $\triangle JKL$ at the right.

7. Find the exact value of $\sin K$.

   7. _____

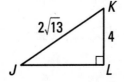

8. Find $m \angle J$ to the nearest tenth of a degree.

   8. _____

In 9 and 10, use the fact that $\log_b 7 \approx 1.20906$ and $\log_b 7 \approx .86135$ to evaluate the expression.

9. $\log_b 14$

9. _____

10. $\log_b \left(\frac{49}{4}\right)$

10. _____

11. A certain substance decays continuously, with 70% of the initial amount of the substance remaining after 20 days. Estimate the half-life of the substance to the nearest tenth of a day.

11. _____

12. Suppose $1000 is invested in an account paying 8.5% annual interest compounded monthly. Assuming no additional money is deposited and none is withdrawn, what is the balance at the end of five years?

12. _____

13. Write the general solution to $4 \cos \theta = 2$.

13. _____

14. Solve for y: $\ln y = 3x + 5$

14. _____

15. Find x in the triangle at the right. Round your answer to the nearest tenth.

15. _____

16. *Multiple choice.* Which equation could *not* model the data displayed in the scatterplot at the right? Assume $a > 0$.

16. _____

(a) $y = a \log x$ (b) $y = a\sqrt{x}$

(c) $y = \frac{a}{x^2}$ (b) $y = a \ln x$

17. A ladder that is 18 feet long rests against a wall so that the top of the ladder is 15 feet above the ground. What is the measure of the angle formed by the ladder and the floor? Round to the nearest degree.

17. _____

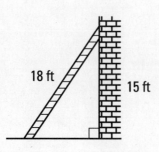

18 ft   15 ft

18. In $\triangle ABC$, $b = 40$, $m\angle A = 20°$, and $m\angle C = 110°$. Find c.

18. _____

19. What transformation maps the graph of $y = x^2$ onto the graph of $y = (x - 5)^2 - 10$?

19. _____

20. If you invest money at 8% annual interest compounded continuously, how long will it take for your money to double?

20. _____

21. Solve $3^x = 10$. Round the solution to the nearest hundredth.

21. _____

22. Solve $\theta = \sin^{-1}\left(\frac{1}{2}\right)$ over the domain $-\frac{\pi}{2} \le 0 \le \frac{\pi}{2}$.

22. _____

23. *True or false.* The function with equation $y = \log_3 x$ is the inverse of the function with equation $y = 3^x$.

23. _____

24. *Multiple choice.* In which interval is $\log_6 50$?

    (a) $\{x: 0 \le x \le 1\}$ (b) $\{x: 1 \le x \le 3\}$

    (c) $\{x: 8 \le x \le 9\}$ (d) $\{x: 9 \le x \le 10\}$

24. _____

25. The radius of circle O at the right is 3 feet. The area of the shaded sector is 4 square feet. Compute each exactly.

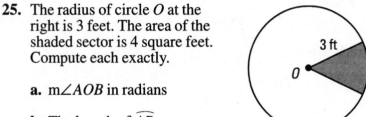

    a. $m\angle AOB$ in radians

25. a. _____

    b. The length of $\overarc{AB}$

    b. _____

26. Find the volume of a cube whose surface area is 294 square centimeters.

26. _____

27. *True or false.* For all θ, $\tan(\pi + \theta) = \tan(\pi - \theta)$. Justify your answer.

_____

_____

Functions, Statistics, and Trigonometry © Scott Foresman Addison Wesley

Check all your work carefully.

Name _____

COMPREHENSIVE TEST, CHAPTERS 1-6

You will need a calculator and a statistics utility for this test.

Multiple choice. **Give the letter of the correct answer.**

1. The table below gives the consumer price index for cable television as related to the year after 1900. What is the correlation coefficient for these data?

1. _____

Year	85	88	89	90	91	92	93	94	95
Index	110.6	132.9	144.0	158.4	175.7	186.2	198.9	197.4	200.7

Source: *Statistical Abstract of the United States, 1996*

(a) -.98   (b) .09   (c) .98   (d) 1

2. Refer to the data in Question 1. Using the index as the dependent variable, which is an equation for the line of best fit?

2. _____

(a) $y = 10.11x - 751.01$ (b) $y = -10.11x - 751.01$

(c) $y = 2.1x - 67.5$ (d) $y = -2.1x + 288.5$

3. The measure of the angle where two roads intersect is 50°. The roads also are joined by a connecting road at junctions that are 10 miles and 15 miles from the intersection, as shown at the right. About what is the length of the connecting road?

3. _____

(a) 11.1 mi   (b) 11.5 mi

(c) 12 mi   (d) 13 mi

4. What is the solution of $\theta = \tan^{-1}\left(\frac{1}{2}\right)$ over the domain $-\frac{\pi}{2} < \theta < \frac{\pi}{2}$?

4. _____

(a) ≈.41 radian   (b) ≈.46 radian

(c) ≈.53 radian   (d) ≈.71 radian

5. What is the exact value of $\cos\left(\frac{\pi}{4} - \pi\right)$?

5. _____

(a) $-\frac{\sqrt{2}}{2}$ (b) $-\frac{1}{2}$ (c) $\frac{1}{2}$ (d) $\frac{\sqrt{2}}{2}$

6. Suppose $10,000 is invested in an account paying 7.5% annual interest compounded annually. Assuming no additional money is deposited and none is withdrawn, what is the balance in this account at the end of five years?

6. _____

(a) $13,472.40   (b) $13,750.32

(c) $14,000.00   (d) $14,356.29

7. Given $\log_b 2 \approx .2354$ and $\log_c b \approx 1.8295$, what is $\log_c b^{\frac{3}{2}}$?

7. _____

    (a) ≈ 1.2197 (b) ≈ 1.4959 (c) ≈ 2.4346 (d) ≈ 2.74425

8. Given $\log_b 2 \approx .2354$ and $\log_c b \approx 1.8295$, what is $\log_c 2$?

8. _____

    (a) $\approx .1278$ (b) $\approx .4307$ (c) ≈ 1.5941 (d) ≈ 7.7719

9. Let $f(x) = 2x + 1$ and let $g(x) = 3x - 5$. If $h(x) = (g \circ f)(x)$, which is an equation for $h^{-1}(x)$?

9. _____

    (a) $h^{-1}(x) = \dfrac{x + 9}{6}$ (b) $h^{-1}(x) = \dfrac{x + 2}{6}$

    (c) $h^{-1}(x) = 6x - 2$ (d) $h^{-1}(x) = 6x - 9$

10. In circle O at the right, the length of $\overset{\frown}{AB}$ is $\dfrac{5\pi}{6}$ meters. What is the area of the shaded region?

10. _____

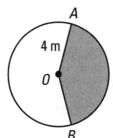

    (a) $\dfrac{8}{3}\pi$ m^2 (b) $\dfrac{20}{3}\pi$ m^2

    (c) $\dfrac{5}{3}\pi$ m^2 (d) $\dfrac{40}{3}\pi$ m^2

11. The figure at the right shows a horizontal beam placed 6 feet above the base of a roof so that it braces the sloping sides of the roof. The length of each side of the roof is 15 feet, and the measure of the angle at the apex is 110°. What is the length of the beam?

11. _____

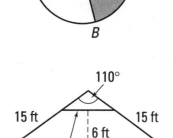

    (a) about 3.64 ft   (b) about 3.72 ft

    (c) about 4.54 ft   (d) about 7.44 ft

12. The charge at an amusement park batting cage is $2.00 to rent a helmet and bat, plus 10¢ for each ball hit. Which is a formula for the total cost C in dollars as a function of the number of balls hit b?

12. _____

    (a) $C = .1b$ (b) $C = 10b + 2$

    (c) $C = 2.1b$ (d) $C = .1b + 2$

13. Which is a formula for the variance s^2 of a sample containing thirty values?

13. _____

    (a) $s^2 = \dfrac{1}{30}\displaystyle\sum_{i=1}^{30} x_i$ (b) $s^2 = \sqrt{\dfrac{1}{29}\displaystyle\sum_{i=1}^{30} (x_1 - \bar{x})^2}$

    (c) $s^2 = \dfrac{1}{30}\displaystyle\sum_{i=1}^{29} (x_1 - \bar{x})^2$ (d) $s^2 = \dfrac{1}{29}\displaystyle\sum_{i=1}^{30} (x_1 - \bar{x})^2$

14. Which increases when 20 is added to each item of a data set?   14. _____

    (a) the standard deviation   (b) the variance

    (c) the mean   (d) none of these

15. A data set has a mean of 50 and a standard deviation of 7.   15. _____
Which member of this data set would have a *z*-score of -8.5?

    (a) -59.5   (b) -51.5   (c) -9.5   (d) -9.5

16. Which translation has the effect on a graph of moving each point   16. _____
7 units to the left and 3 units up?

    (a) $T: (x, y) \rightarrow (x + 7, y - 3)$

    (b) $T: (x, y) \rightarrow (x - 7, y + 3)$

    (c) $T: (x, y) \rightarrow (x + 7, y + 3)$

    (d) $T: (x, y) \rightarrow (x - 7, y - 3)$

17. Which equation could represent the function graphed at the right?   17. _____

    (a) $y = 2 \sin\left(\frac{1}{2}x + \frac{\pi}{4}\right)$

    (b) $y = 2 \sin\left(2x + \frac{\pi}{4}\right)$

    (c) $y = 2 \cos\left(2x + \frac{\pi}{4}\right)$

    (d) $y = \frac{1}{2} \sin\left(2x - \frac{\pi}{4}\right)$

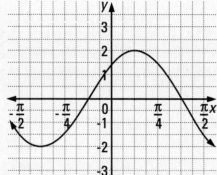

18. $\cos^{-1}\left(\cos \frac{4\pi}{3}\right) =$ ___?___   18. _____

    (a) $-\frac{4\pi}{3}$ (b) $\frac{\pi}{3}$ (c) $\frac{2\pi}{3}$ (d) $\frac{4\pi}{3}$

19. Which equation is *not* an identity?   19. _____

    (a) $\sin^2 \theta - \cos^2 \theta = 1 - 2 \cos^2 \theta$

    (b) $\tan \theta + \tan (\pi - \theta) = 0$

    (c) $\frac{\sin(\pi + \theta)}{\cos (\pi - \theta)} = \tan \theta$

    (d) $\cos (2\theta) = 2 \cos \theta$

20. What is the length *x* in the triangle at the right   20. _____

    (a) ≈ 1.21 (b) ≈ 7.45

    (c) ≈ 9.15 (d) ≈ 9.32

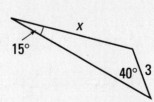

21. Let $f(x) = 4 \sin\left(\frac{x + \pi}{5}\right)$. What is the period of f?

    (a) $\frac{1}{4}$ (b) 4   (c) $\frac{2}{5}\pi$ (d) 10π

21. _____

22. If $2^x = 25$, then $x \approx$ ___?___ .

    (a) 4.64   (b) 5.00   (c) 5.32   (d) 12.50

22. _____

23. Let $f(x) = 3x^2 - 5x$. Which type of function is f?

    (a) an odd function

    (b) an even function

    (c) both an odd function and an even function

    (d) neither an even function nor an odd function

23. _____

24. Which scatterplot represents a set of data that has a strong negative correlation?

24. _____

(a) 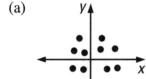   (b)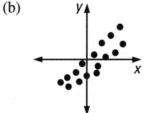

(c) 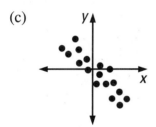   (d)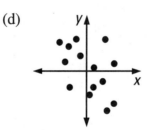

In 25–27, use the stemplot at the right of a set of test scores.

5	8
6	1 3
7	1 3 5 5
8	7 8 8 8 9 9
9	1 6 7 8
10	0 0 0

25. What is the mean?

    (a) 58   (b) 67.5

    (c) 84.35   (d) 100

25. _____

26. What is the median of the scores?

    (a) 74   (b) 84.35   (c) 88   (d) 88.5

26. _____

27. What is the percentile of the score 97?

    (a) 20th   (b) 25th   (c) 75th   (d) 80th

27. _____

Check all your work carefully.

Name _____

1. Suppose that a standard six-sided die is tossed twice. Consider these four events.

   Event A: the first toss is an even number
   Event B: the second toss is an odd number
   Event C: the product of the two numbers tossed is odd
   Event D: the product of the two numbers tossed is even

   Are any of these events mutually exclusive? If so, which ones?

   _____

2. Suppose the sample space for an experiment is the set of all ordered pairs (x, y) where x and y are real numbers. Let A be the event consisting of all ordered pairs (x, y) where $x \neq 0$ and $y \neq 0$. Describe the event which is the complement of A.

   _____

3. In a survey of a group of 60 families, it is found that 38 families own a dog, 45 own a cat, and 26 own both a dog and a cat. What is the probability that a family selected at random from the surveyed group owns neither a dog nor a cat?

   3. _____

4. A small high school has 15 teachers, 40 freshmen, 56 sophomores, 50 juniors and 45 seniors. The school wants to establish a 5-person committee that includes one teacher and one student from each grade. How many different committees are possible?

   4. _____

In 5 and 6, consider an experiment in which the letters "A," "C," and "T" are written on three separate slips of paper and placed in a box. Three slips are then drawn randomly one at a time and the letters appearing on the slips are written down from left to right in the order in which they are drawn.

5. Suppose the experiment is conducted so that the three slips are drawn randomly *without* replacement.

   a. Write out the sample space of possible arrangements.

   5. a. _____

   b. What is the probability that the word "CAT" is formed?

   b. _____

6. Suppose the experiment is conducted so that the three slips are drawn randomly *with* replacement.

   a. How many arrangements are possible?

   6. a. _____

   b. What is the probability that the word "CAT" is formed?

   b. _____

Name _____

QUIZ

1. How many permutations five letters long can be formed from the letters of the word CENTURY?

   1. _____

2. Suppose that in the human population
   gene A occurs in 25% of people,
   gene B occurs in 44% of people, and
   genes A and B occur together in 11% of people.
   Are genes A and B independent? Justify your answer.

   _____

   _____

3. Joan and Jill are on the same softball team.
   Each goes up to bat once during the first inning.
   Suppose that the probability that Joan gets a hit
   whenever she is up to bat is 0.3 and the
   corresponding probability for Jill is 0.2.
   If Joan's hitting is independent of Jill's,
   what is the probability that at least one of them
   gets a hit during the first inning?

   3. _____

4. Solve for n: $_nP_2 = 132$.

   4. _____

In 5–7, use the probability distribution shown below.

x	0	1	2	3	4	5
$P(x)$	$\frac{3}{21}$	0	$\frac{7}{21}$	$\frac{2}{21}$	$\frac{2}{21}$	$\frac{7}{21}$

5. List the values of the random variable.

   5. _____

6. Find $P(x < 3)$.

   6. _____

7. What is the expected value of this probability distribution?

   7. _____

Functions, Statistics, and Trigonometry © Scott Foresman Addison Wesley

CHAPTER 7 TEST, Form A

You will need a calculator for this test.

1. Suppose $P(A) = 0.7$, $P(B) = 0.6$, and $P(A \cup B) = 0.9$.
   Find $P(A \cap B)$.

   1. _____

2. Assume that each of the two spinners shown at the right is equally likely to land in each of the four regions.

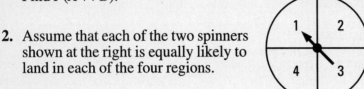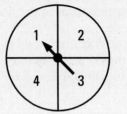

   a. How many outcomes are there in the sample space for the result of spinning both spinners?

   2. **a.** _____

   b. What is the probability that the sum of the two spinners is less than 4?

   b. _____

3. If a fair die is tossed twice, what is the probability that the first toss is an even number and the second is an odd number?

   3. _____

In 4 and 5, evaluate.

4. $\frac{8!}{4!}$

   4. _____

5. $_{15}P_3$

   5. _____

6. **a.** Determine the number of permutations of all the letters in the word MONDAY.

   6. **a.** _____

   b. How many of these permutations begin with A and end with Y?

   b. _____

7. If events A and B are independent and $P(A)$ and $P(B)$ are nonzero, explain why $P(A \cup B) \neq P(A) + P(B)$.

   _____

   _____

8. Solve: $_nP_6 = 6_nP_4$.

   8. _____

In 9 and 10, Jack, Andy, and Kim run for the same office in an election. Determine whether the indicated events are complementary, mutually exclusive but not complementary, or not mutually exclusive. Assume that a tie is not possible.

9. *A*: Jack wins the election.
   B: Kim wins the election.

   9. _____

Functions, Statistics, and Trigonometry © Scott Foresman Addison Wesley

10. *C*: Andy wins the election.
    D: Jack or Kim wins the election.

10. _____

11. A school has 600 male and 400 female students. Three students at random are waiting at a bus stop for a ride to the school. What is the probability that all three are of the same gender? (Assume randomness.)

11. _____

12. A restaurant offers six salads, three soups, five entrees, four desserts, and six beverages. If you want to order one item from each of the five categories, how many different meals can you order?

12. _____

13. A test includes: 8 true-false questions; 5 multiple-choice questions, each with 3 choices; and 5 multiple-choice questions, each with 4 choices. How many different lists of answers are possible for this test?

13. _____

14. Twenty-five percent of the cookies produced by a certain manufacturer are underweight. Design a simulation that does not use a random number generator to estimate the number of packages having no underweight cookies in a box of 100 packages, if each package contains 10 cookies.

_____

_____

_____

15. Explain how to use technology to estimate the area between the graph of $y = \sin x$ and the x-axis from $x = 0$ to $x = \frac{\pi}{2}$.

_____

_____

_____

16. **a.** Verify that the table below shows a probability distribution.

x	1	2	3	4	5	6	7	8
$P(x)$	0.05	0.10	0.15	0.20	0.20	0.15	0.10	0.05

a. _____

b. Find the expected value of the distribution in part **a**.

b. _____

Check all your work carefully.

Functions, Statistics, and Trigonometry © Scott Foresman Addison Wesley

CHAPTER 7 TEST, Form B

You will need a calculator for this test.

1. Suppose $P(A) = 0.5$, $P(B) = 0.3$, and $P(A \cap B) = 0.2$.
   Find $P(A \cup B)$.

   1. _____

2. Assume that each of the two spinners shown at the right is equally likely to land in each of the five regions.

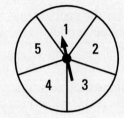 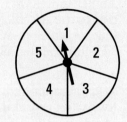

   a. How many outcomes are in the sample space for the result of spinning both spinners?

   2. a. _____

   b. What is the probability that the sum of the two spinners is larger than 7?

   b. _____

3. If a die is tossed twice, what is the probability that the first toss is a smaller number than the second toss?

   3. _____

In 4 and 5, evaluate.

4. $\dfrac{10!}{7!}$

   4. _____

5. $_{12}P_3$

   5. _____

6. a. Determine the number of permutations of the letters in the word TUESDAY?

   6. a. _____

   b. How many of these permutations begin with A and end with Y?

   b. _____

7. A fair coin is tossed twice.
   A is the event that the number of heads is even.
   B is the event that the first toss is a tail.
   C is the event that the number of heads is odd.
   Which, if any, of the events are independent?

   7. _____

8. Solve: $_nP_5 = 30_nP_3$.

   8. _____

In 9 and 10, several high school students are randomly selected for a study. Determine if the indicated events are complementary, mutually exclusive but not complementary, or not mutually exclusive.

9. A: The first student selected is a male senior.
   B: The first student selected is a female senior.

   9. _____

Functions, Statistics, and Trigonometry © Scott Foresman Addison Wesley

10. *A:* The first student selected is a male senior.
    C: The first student selected is a junior, sophomore,
    freshman, or a female.

10. _____

11. Ten percent of the students at a military academy
    are female. If three students at this academy are
    selected at random, what is the probability that
    they are of the same gender?

11. _____

12. Mr. and Mrs. Jones plan to drive into town and stop
    at a restaurant, then a movie theater, and finally a
    gasoline station, before returning home. If there are
    twelve restaurants, two movie theaters, and three
    gasoline stations in town, how many different
    plans are possible?

12. _____

13. A test includes: 10 true-false questions;
    5 multiple-choice questions, each with four choices;
    and 4 multiple-choice questions, each with five choices.
    How many different answer sheets are possible?

13. _____

14. Five trains arrive at a train station every day. Assume that the probability that any given
    train arrives on time is 0.7. Use the following part of a random number table to estimate the
    probability that all five trains will arrive at the station on time. Conduct 25 trials, and circle
    the first digit and the last digit you use in your simulation.

77921	06907	11008	02751	27756	53498	18602	70659	90655	15053	21916	81825	44394	42880
99562	72905	56420	69994	98872	31016	71194	18738	44013	48840	63213	21069	10634	12952
96301	91997	05463	07972	18876	20922	94569	56869	69014	60045	18425	84903	42508	32307

14. _____

15. Explain how to use technology to estimate the area between the graph of $y = \tan x$ and the
    x-axis from $x = 0$ to $x = \frac{\pi}{4}$.

    _____

    _____

    _____

16. **a.** Verify that the table below shows a probability distribution.

x	1	2	3	4	5	6
$P(x)$	0.05	0.075	0.150	0.275	0.400	0.05

    _____

    b. Find the expected value of the distribution in part **a**.   **b.** _____
    Check all your work carefully.

Functions, Statistics, and Trigonometry © Scott Foresman Addison Wesley

CHAPTER 7 TEST, Form C

1. Each regular *octahedral* die at the right is fair and has eight faces numbered 1, 2, 3, 4, 5, 6, 7, 8. Describe an experiment related to the two dice and list the sample space. Then describe four events—E_1, E_2, E_3, and E_4—that satisfy the following conditions.

   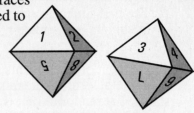

   $P(E_1) = 0$ $P(E_2) = .5$ $P(E_3) = 1$ $.5 < P(E_4) < 1$

2. You and a friend are studying factorials together, and your friend asks why you can't write $(n - 5)! = n! - 5!$. How would you explain?

3. Draw a spinner that has the probability distribution shown below. Then give the expected value of one spin of your spinner.

x	1	2	3	4	5	6
$P(x)$	$\frac{1}{8}$	$\frac{1}{8}$	$\frac{1}{4}$	$\frac{1}{8}$	$\frac{1}{8}$	$\frac{1}{4}$

4. At the right is shown an intersection of two streets. An engineer needs to find probabilities for all possible paths of a car entering this intersection from the south. Which events should the engineer consider? Characterize the events you identify as: complementary, mutually exclusive, dependent, or independent.

5. For their next test, a math class may choose:

   (i) *n* multiple-choice items, with each item having choices A, B, C, and D; or

   (ii) an equal number *n* of "matching" items, with each item in column A matching to exactly one of *n* items in column B.

   The students believe they have a better chance of correctly guessing all the answers with option (ii). Do you agree or do you disagree? Explain your answers.

Functions, Statistics, and Trigonometry © Scott Foresman Addison Wesley

CHAPTER 7 TEST, Form D

Your school is planning a Spring Fair to raise money for a local charity. Students have been asked to submit suggestions for games that might be played to raise some of the money. One student has proposed a game involving the wheel shown at the right, with the following rules.

- A player pays $1 for two spins of the wheel.

- If the amounts on the two spins are equal, the player wins that amount of money.

- If the amounts on the two spins are not equal, the player wins no money.

a. Give the sample space for the result of the two spins.

b. Compute the probability of winning each amount with two spins of the wheel.
  i. $1   **ii.** $5   **iii.** $15   **iv.** $0

c. Show the probability distribution for the result of two spins by making a table of values.

d. What is the expected value of each $1 play of this game?

e. Do you think this game as described will raise a significant amount of money for the charity? Explain your reasoning.

f. Design a simulation for this game and run it several times. Do the results of your simulation support your answer to part **e**?

g. Create an original spinner that might be used at the fair. Then prepare a presentation in which you describe your game to the Spring Fair committee and explain why you think it will be a good fund-raiser. Your presentation should include the following.

- A sketch of the spinner.

- A list of the rules of the game.

- A description of the prize(s). If you plan to have one or more non-monetary prizes (such as a stuffed animal), be sure to indicate their values.

- A statement of the probability of each outcome.

- An estimate of the number of times you think the game will be played.

- An estimate of the amount of money you think the game can raise for the charity.

Functions, Statistics, and Trigonometry © Scott Foresman Addison Wesley

Name _____

CHAPTER 7 TEST, Cumulative Form

1. If two fair dice are tossed, what is the probability that the first yields an odd number or the second yields an even number?

1.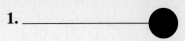

2. *Multiple choice.* Which of the following can be a graph of $y = \log_2 x$?

2.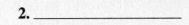

(a)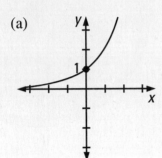

(b)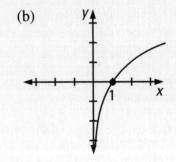

(c)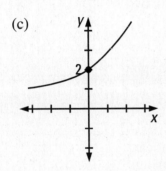

(d)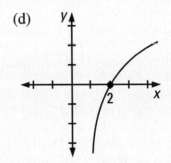

3. If $P(E) = 0.45$, what is $P(\text{not } E)$?

3.

4. In the triangle below, find x.

4. _____

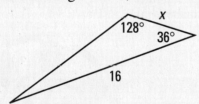

In 5–7, evaluate each expression exactly.

5. $(125c^{12})^{\frac{1}{3}}$

5. _____

6. $e^{\ln a} + \ln e^{-a}$

6. _____

7. $\log\left(\frac{100}{x}\right) + \log x$

7. _____

8. Solve for n: $n! = 90 \cdot (n - 2)!$

8. _____

● Given that $\cos \theta = \frac{1}{3}$ and $-\frac{\pi}{2} < \theta < 0$, find the exact value of $\tan \theta$.

9. _____

10. A cannonball is fired from the top of a rampart. As it leaves the cannon's muzzle, its height above the ground is 80 feet and it rises at a rate of 800 ft/sec. If air resistance is neglected, the height of the cannonball t seconds after it leaves the muzzle is given by the equation $h = 80 + 800t - 16t^2$. To the nearest tenth of a second, how long does it take the cannonball to hit the ground after it leaves the muzzle?

10. _____

11. Find the expected value for the following probability distribution.

11. _____

x	9	10	11	12
$P(x)$	0.30	0.28	0.25	0.17

12. Let $f(x) = 1 + \dfrac{1}{x-1}$.

    a. Sketch a graph of $y = f(x)$ for $-8 \le x \le 8$.

12. a.

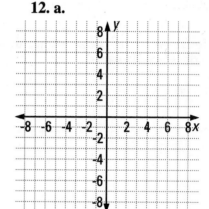

●

    b. Identify the parent function and describe the transformation that maps the graph of the parent function onto the graph of $y = f(x)$.

_____

13. Jack tosses a fair coin twice, and Jill tosses a fair die once. They then add the number of heads obtained to the number of dots appearing on the upper face of the die. What is the probability that the sum is 8?

13. _____

14. Evaluate $\dfrac{63!}{2!61!}$.

14. _____

15. A league has 8 teams. In how many different ways can the eight teams finish?

15. _____

16. Suppose that one percent of brand A fuses and two percent of brand B fuses are defective. If you buy one brand A fuse and one brand B fuse, what is the probability that you will buy a defective fuse?

16. _____

● Check all your work carefully.

Functions, Statistics, and Trigonometry © Scott Foresman Addison Wesley

QUIZ

In 1 and 2, a sequence is described.
a. Give the values of the first five terms.
b. Identify the sequence as arithmetic, geometric, or neither.

1. $\begin{cases} b_1 = 4 \\ b_n = b_{n-1} + 5 \text{ for all integers } n \geq 2 \end{cases}$

1. a. _____

   b. _____

2. $s_n = \left(\frac{1}{3}\right)^{n-2}$, for all integers $n \geq 1$

2. a. _____

   b. _____

3. Suppose that a particular computer depreciates 50% in value each year and has an original cost of $2,000. In what year will the value of the computer first become $100 or less?

3. _____

4. What is the position of 1999 in the arithmetic sequence 7, 13, 19, . . . , 1999, . . . ?

4. _____

In 5–7, decide whether the sequence described has a limit as $n \to \infty$.
If it has one, state its value.

5. $t_n = \frac{1,000,000}{n^2}$

5. _____

6. $q_n = \frac{4n - 3}{2 - 5n}$

6. _____

7. $c_n = \left(\frac{6}{5}\right)^n$

7. _____

8. Suppose that an employee earns $27,000 in the first year on the job. Each year thereafter, the employee receives a raise of $3,000. Find the total amount the employee earns in 10 years.

8. _____

9. Evaluate $\sum_{i=1}^{5} (2i - 5)$.

9. _____

10. Find the sum of the integers from 19 to 50.

10. _____

QUIZ

1. Suppose that the price of cable television increases by 8% each year. If a household currently pays $360 a year, what will their payments total over the next ten years? Round to the nearest dollar.

1. ___5215___

2. After the first circle, the area of each circle in the sequence pictured at the right is one-fourth that of the circle to its left.

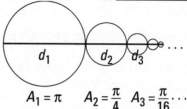

Assume that the first circle has area π cm^2 and that the sequence is infinite. What is the sum of diameters of the circles?

$A_1 = \pi$ $A_2 = \dfrac{\pi}{4}$ $A_3 = \dfrac{\pi}{16} \cdots$

2. _____

3. Evaluate $_{72}C_2$.

3. _____

4. Prove that $\dfrac{r}{n} \cdot {}_nC_r = {}_{n-1}C_{r-1}$ for all integers $n \geq 2$ and $1 \leq r \leq n$.

_____

_____

_____

_____

In 5 and 6, determine whether the series converges. If it does, find its value.

5. $\displaystyle\sum_{n=1}^{\infty} \left(\dfrac{8}{9}\right)^n$

5. _____

6. $\displaystyle\sum_{n=1}^{\infty} \dfrac{1}{2}(3)^n$

6. _____

7. A company owner has 20 employees, and plans to give bonuses to 6 of them. How many different sets of employees could receive bonuses?

7. _____

8. Hugh and Janet are dining out at a cafe that has on its menu 6 entrees, 5 salads, and 10 desserts. They decide they will each order a different entree, salad, and dessert, and share the portions. How many different meals are possible?

8. _____

CHAPTER 8 TEST, Form A

In 1 and 2, consider the sequence defined by the formula
$a_n = n^2 - 1$ **for all integers** $n \geq 1$.

1. Find the first 5 terms of the sequence. 1. _____

2. Is the sequence arithmetic, geometric, or neither? 2. _____

In 3 and 4, evaluate the given series to the nearest whole number.

3. $8 + 17 + 26 + \ldots + 305$ 3. _____

4. $\displaystyle\sum_{n=1}^{30} 13(0.8)^{n-1}$ 4. _____

In 5 and 6, Determine whether the sequence converges.
If so, find the limit of its nth term as $n \to \infty$.

5. $a_n = 356\left(\dfrac{7}{8}\right)^{n-1}$ 5. _____

6. $-\dfrac{1}{2}, \dfrac{1}{4}, \dfrac{19}{26}, 1, \ldots, \dfrac{3n^2 - 8}{2n^2 + 8}, \cdots$ 6. _____

7. The first four terms of an arithmetic sequence are 187, 174, 161, 148.

  a. Give an explicit formula for this sequence. 7. a. _____

  b. Give a recursive formula for this sequence. b. _____

8. The first three terms of a geometric sequence are 3, -51, 867.

  a. Give an explicit formula for this sequence. 8. a. _____

  b. Give a recursive formula for this sequence. b. _____

In 9 and 10, expand the expressions.

9. $(2x - 3)^4$ 9. _____

10. $(4x + 5y)^3$ 10. _____

11. Consider the 50th row of Pascal's triangle.

  a. What are the first three entries in this row? 11. a. _____

  b. What are last three entries? b. _____

▶ **CHAPTER 8 TEST,** Form A *page 2*

12. What is the sum of the entries in the 100th row of Pascal's triangle?

12. _____

In 13 and 14, determine whether the infinite geometric series converges. If so, find its sum.

13. $6 + 4 + \frac{8}{3} + \frac{16}{9} + \ldots$

13. _____

14. $2 - \frac{9}{4} + \frac{81}{32} - \ldots$

14. _____

In 15 and 15, *true or false* for all integers *n* and *r* with $n \geq r + 1$.

15. $_nC_r = {_{n-1}}C_r + {_{n-1}}C_{r-1}$

15. _____

16. $_nC_r = {_n}C_{r-n}$

16. _____

17. A family has lived in an apartment for almost twelve years. Their monthly rent the first year was $300. Each year thereafter their landlord raised the rent by $15 per month.

    a. What is their monthly rent in this, the 12th year?

17. a. _____

    b. In total, how much rent have they paid over the twelve year period?

b. _____

18. A factory has been operating for ten years. The first year of operation its employee payroll was $1.7 million. Each subsequent year, the payroll increased 9% over the previous year. What is the payroll for this, the 10th year?

18. _____

19. A company with 25 employees plans to promote 5 of them. How many different ways can 5 employees be selected for promotion?

19. _____

20. An English teacher requires each student in her class to read 6 books. Four of them are to be selected from a list of 10 novels, and the other two are to be selected from a list of 6 plays. Find the number of different combinations of books that can be selected.

20. _____

21. What is the probability that a student will answer at least three questions correctly by random guessing on an exam with 10 multiple-choice questions each of which has four options?

21. _____

Check all your work carefully.

CHAPTER 8 TEST, Form B

In 1 and 2, consider the following sequence.

$$\begin{cases} a_1 = 5 \\ a_n = a_{n-1} - \frac{1}{2}a_{n-1} \end{cases} \text{ for all integers } n > 1$$

1. Find the first 5 terms of this sequence.

1. _____

2. Is the sequence arithmetic, geometric, or neither?

2. _____

In 3 and 4, evaluate the given series to the nearest hundredth.

3. $6.5 + 8.8 + 11.1 + \ldots 126.1$

3. _____

4. $\sum\limits_{n=1}^{32} 14(0.9)^{n-1}$

4. _____

In 5 and 6, determine whether the sequence converges or diverges. If it converges, find the limit of its nth term as $n \to \infty$.

5. $a_n = 56\left(\frac{8}{7}\right)^{n-1}$

5. _____

6. $\frac{1}{2}, \frac{7}{1}, \frac{2}{3}, \frac{17}{25}, \ldots, \frac{5n-3}{7n-3}, \ldots$

6. _____

7. The first four terms of an arithmetic sequence are 243, 228, 213, 198.

a. Give an explicit formula for this sequence.

7. a. _____

b. Give a recursive formula for this sequence.

b. _____

8. The first three terms of a geometric sequence arc 5, 95, 1805.

a. Give an explicit formula for this sequence.

8. a. _____

b. Give a recursive formula for this sequence.

b. _____

In 9 and 10, expand the expressions.

9. $(5x - 2)^3$

9. _____

10. $(3x + 2y)^4$

10. _____

11. Consider the 20th row of Pascal's triangle.

a. What are the first four entries in this row?

11. a. _____

b. What are the last four entries?

b. _____

12. Given that the middle four entries in a row of
Pascal's triangle are 4,457,400; 5,200,300;
5,200,300; and 4,457,400, what are the middle
three entries in the next lower row?

12. _____

**In 13 and 14, determine whether the infinite
geometric series converges. If so, find its sum.**

13. $8 - 10 + \frac{25}{2} - \frac{125}{8} + \ldots$

13. _____

14. $15474 + 12379.2 + 9903.36 + \ldots$

14. _____

In 15 and 16, *true or false.* **For all integers** n **and** r **with**
$n \geq r + 1.$

15. $_nC_r = {}_{n-1}C_{n-r} + {}_{n-1}C_{r-1}$

15. _____

16. $_nC_r = {}_nC_{n-r}$

16. _____

17. The cost of maintaining a certain type of factory equipment
has increased $120 each year. During the first year after the
equipment was purchased, the maintenance cost was $1,400.

   a. What was the maintenance cost during the
8th year after the equipment was purchased?

17. a. _____

   b. What was the total maintenance cost during the eight-year
period after the equipment was purchased?

b. _____

18. Last year, a jogger decided to gradually increase the distance
she ran. In the first week of her new program, she jogged
7 miles and, each week thereafter, she increased the distance
by 5 percent over the distance she jogged in the preceding week.
She maintained this program faithfully for a full year.
To the nearest mile, what total distance did she
jog during the year?

18. _____

19. A test has 30 questions. Students taking this test may
choose any 25 of the questions. How many
different selections of 25 questions are possible?

19. _____

20. Susan wants to buy three different soft drinks, one type
of chips, and two different dips. The store sells 12 different
soft drinks, 4 types of chips, and 5 different dips. How
many different ways can she choose the refreshments?

20. _____

21. A gardener plants 20 bulbs. The probability that
any given bulb survives is 0.6 and the survival
of each bulb is independent of the survival of the others.
Find the probability that exactly 15 bulbs survive.

21. _____

Check all your work carefully.

Functions, Statistics, and Trigonometry © Scott Foresman Addison Wesley

CHAPTER 8 TEST, Form C

1. Give the first five terms of a geometric sequence. Explain how you know it is geometric. Then write explicit and recursive formulas for the sequence. Show how to find the 10th term using one of the formulas.

2. Calculate the partial sum S_8 for each series below. Then compare the series. How are they alike? different? State as many likenesses and differences as you can.

   (i) $\frac{2}{3} + \frac{4}{3} + \frac{6}{3} + \frac{8}{3} + \frac{10}{4} + \cdots$

   (ii) $\frac{2}{3} + \frac{4}{3} + \frac{8}{3} + \frac{16}{3} + \frac{32}{3} + \cdots$

   (iii) $\frac{2}{3} + \frac{4}{9} + \frac{8}{27} + \frac{16}{81} + \frac{32}{243} + \cdots$

3. a. What is the meaning of $\lim\limits_{n \to \infty} \left(\frac{1-n}{2-n}\right)$?

   b. Maria says the value of this expression is $\frac{1}{2}$. If you agree, justify her statement. If you disagree, find the correct value.

4. Based on your study of Pascal's Triangle in this chapter, make a list of as many facts as you can that lead directly from this statement: *The 5th term in the 30th row of Pascal's Triangle is 27,405.*

5. Write a mathematical statement that describes the relationship between $_nP_r$ and $_nC_r$. For what values of n and r is your statement true?

6. Thinking about a die, write a probability problem whose answer is $_{10}C_2 \left(\frac{1}{6}\right)^2 \left(\frac{5}{6}\right)^8$. Show how to solve your problem.

Functions, Statistics, and Trigonometry © Scott Foresman Addison Wesley

CHAPTER 8 TEST, Form D

In this chapter you have seen that geometric and arithmetic sequences and series often can be represented by a geometric figure or a pattern of geometric figures. Do you think it is possible for a single figure or pattern of figures to represent more than one sequence or series?

For example, the figure at the right is a "nesting" of equilateral triangles called *Triangula*. In forming the figure, the midpoints of the sides of one triangle became the vertices of the triangle nested in its interior. The first few stages of its creation are shown below.

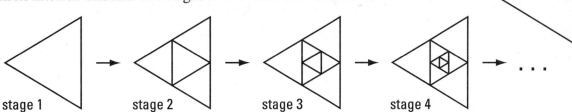

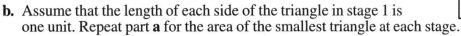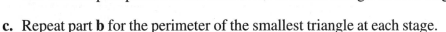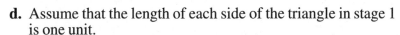

stage 1   stage 2   stage 3   stage 4   . . .

a. Consider the total number of nonoverlapping triangles at each stage.
  i. Write the first four terms of the sequence this represents.
  ii. Tell whether the sequence is arithmetic or geometric.
  iii. Write an explicit formula to represent the nth term of the sequence.
  iv. Write a recursive formula to represent the nth term of the sequence.
  v. Find the tenth term of the sequence.

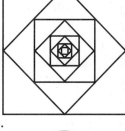

b. Assume that the length of each side of the triangle in stage 1 is one unit. Repeat part **a** for the area of the smallest triangle at each stage.

c. Repeat part **b** for the perimeter of the smallest triangle at each stage.

d. Assume that the length of each side of the triangle in stage 1 is one unit.
  i. Write a series that represents the sum of the lengths of all the nonoverlapping segments in the first ten stages. (*Hint:* This is related to one of the sequences in parts **a** through **c**. Which one?)
  ii. Show how to use a formula to find the sum of all the nonoverlapping segments at stage 10.
  iii. Suppose the pattern could continue forever. Show how to determine the sum of all the nonoverlapping segments.

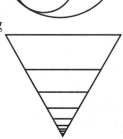

e. Refer back to the figure *Triangula* at the top of the page. Assume that the length of each side of the largest triangle is one unit. Notice that the gray segments form a "spiral" toward the center of the figure. Suppose this spiral could continue forever. What would be its length? Explain.

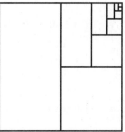

f. Draw a figure that, like *Triangula*, has several sequences and series "embedded" in it. At the right are shown three types of figures you might investigate, or you can create your own original figure. Describe how the figure is formed. Then describe at least three sequences or series embedded in the figure. For each sequence or series, give an explicit formula, recursive formula, or sum as appropriate.

Functions, Statistics, and Trigonometry © Scott Foresman Addison Wesley

CHAPTER 8 TEST, Cumulative Form

1. The mean value of the monthly salaries of the employees of Company X is $2,500 and the standard deviation is $600. Because business has been good, every employee is to be given a $100 per month raise.

   a. What will be the new mean of the employees' annual salaries?

   1. a. _____

   b. What will be the new standard deviation of the employees' annual salaries?

   b. _____

2. The sequence a_n is defined as follows:
$$\begin{cases} a_1 = 3 \\ a_n = \frac{2}{3} a_{n-1} \text{ for } n > 1 \end{cases}$$

   a. Give the first 5 terms of the sequence.

   2. a. _____

   b. Is the sequence arithmetic, geometric, or neither?

   b. _____

3. Sketch the graph of $f(x) = \lceil -x \rceil$.

   3.

   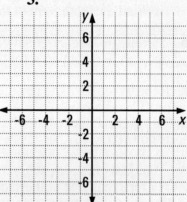

4. What are the period and amplitude of the function f with $f(x) = 3 \cos(5x)$.

   4. period = _____

   amplitude = _____

5. The first 4 terms of an arithmetic sequence are 5, -10, -25, -40. Find an explicit formula for the sequence.

   5. _____

6. A gardener plans to install a triangular flower bed in the corner of his yard. If one side is two feet long, another side is 3 feet long, and the angle between these sides has measure 75°, find the area of the flower bed.

   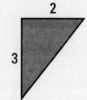

   6. _____

7. Expand $(a - 4b)^4$.

7. _____

8. Solve $2^x = 4096$.

8. _____

9. What is the fourth number in row 10 of Pascal's Triangle?

9. _____

10. To gain access to a secure building, one must enter a code on a keypad on which the digits 0 through 9 appear. If no digit may be included more than once in a code, how many 4-digit codes are possible?

10. _____

11. A company owner, who customarily works 60 hours a week, decides to retire in one year and to reduce his work schedule gradually. He puts in the usual 60 hours in the first week of his final year and, each week thereafter, works one hour less than in the preceding week. How many total hours does he work in his final year?

11. _____

12. Candidates Smith, Johnson, and Harris run for the same office. Let A be the event that Smith wins less than 40% of the vote. Let B be the even that Johnson wins less than 40% of the vote. Are A and B mutually exclusive?

12. _____

13. What is the probability that "doubles" occurs when two fair dice are tossed?

13. _____

14. Does the series $7 + .7 + .07 + \ldots$ converge? If it does, what is its limit?

14. _____

15. A biologist rehabilitates injured birds and returns them to the wild. On average, 70 percent of the birds survive. Design a simulation to estimate the probability that more than 15 birds out of a group of 20 birds survive. Assume that the survivals of the birds are independent of one another.

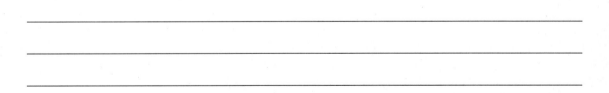

_____

_____

_____

_____

_____

16. Consider the function f defined on the set of
    real numbers by $f(x) = x^3 - 5$.

    a. Find an equation for f^{-1}.

    b. What are the domain and range of f^{-1}?

16. a. _____

b. _____

_____

17. Lena has time to listen to only 4 out of 17 songs on a
    new CD. If she uses the "shuffle" key on her compact disc
    player to play the songs in a random order without
    repeating, what is the probability that Lena will hear
    her 4 favorite songs on the CD?

17. _____

18. John can drive a golf ball over 200 yards 40% of
    the time. If John is at a driving range, estimate the
    probability to the nearest percent that in 30 attempts
    he will drive exactly 15 balls more than 200 yards.
    Assume each drive is independent of the others.

18. _____

Check all your work carefully.

Functions, Statistics, and Trigonometry © Scott Foresman Addison Wesley

QUIZ

1. **a.** Express the volume Y of a box with sides as shown below as a polynomial function in terms of x.

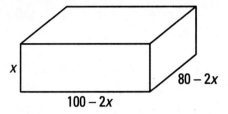

1. a. _____

   b. State the degree of the polynomial.

   b. _____

2. To save money for college, Jim deposits most of his summer job earnings in a savings account at the end of each summer. He deposits $1,000 in the first year and, in each of the next three years, deposits $500 more than he did in the preceding year. Assume that he makes each deposit on the same day of the year, that the annual interest rate is x and remains constant, and that he makes no withdrawals or other deposits.

   a. Find a polynomial in x that expresses Jim's total accumulated savings immediately after he makes his last deposit.

   _____

   b. Evaluate the expression in part **a** when the interest rate is 5.8%.

   b. _____

3. Find a zero of the function f when $f(x) = x^5 + x + 1$ Give your answer accurate to one decimal place.

   3. _____

4. Consider a function g described by the data points below.

n	-2	-1	0	1	2	3
$g(n)$	-47	-8	1	4	25	88

   a. Is g a polynomial function of n of degree less than 5?

   4. a. _____

   b. If the answer to part **a** is yes, find a formula for $g(n)$.

   b. _____

5. Given that $f(x) = 3x^3 - 5x + 2$, use an automatic grapher to graph f on the window $-5 \leq x \leq 5$ and $-5 \leq y \leq 10$.

   a. Identify the y-intercept of f.

   5. a. _____

   b. Estimate the zeros of f to the nearest tenth.

   b. _____

   c. In what interval(s) is f positive?

   c. _____

   d. In what interval(s) is f negative?

   d. _____

   e. In what interval(s) is f increasing?

   e. _____

   f. In what interval(s) is f decreasing?

   f. _____

QUIZ

1. Divide $x^5 + 2x^4 + 5x^2 - x + 3$ by $x^2 + 1$.

1. _____

2. Find the remainder if $v^4 - 3v^3 + 2v + 1$ is divided by $v - 2$.

2. _____

3. When $h(t) = t^3 + 2t^2 - 1$, then $h(-1) = 0$. Use this information to factor $h(t)$ over the set of polynomials with rational coefficients.

3. _____

4. Find an equation for a polynomial function with zeros 1, $-\frac{1}{2}$, and $\frac{2}{3}$.

4. _____

5. Let $x = 1 + 2i$ and $y = 3 - i$. Express each of the following in $a + bi$ form.

   a. $x + y$

   5. a. _____

   b. xy

   b. _____

   c. $\frac{x + y}{xy}$

   c. _____

6. Give the complex conjugate of $3 + \sqrt{-2}$.

6. _____

7. Factor $x^2 - x + 5$ over the set of polynomials with complex coefficients.

7. _____

8. *True or false.* If $2 + 3i$ is a zero of a polynomial $f(x)$ with real coefficients, then $-2 + 3i$ is also a zero of $f(x)$.

8. _____

9. Suppose the graph below is of the polynomial equation $y = f(x)$ with real coefficients. What is the highest possible degree of $f(x)$?

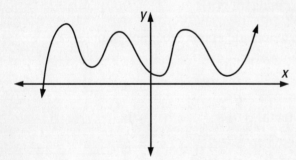

9. _____

Functions, Statistics, and Trigonometry © Scott Foresman Addison Wesley

CHAPTER 9 TEST, Form A

1. In the following table, g is a polynomial function. Determine an equation for $g(x)$.

x	0	1	2	3	4	5	6	7
$g(x)$	-4	-4	-2	8	32	76	146	248

1. _____

2. Find the quotient $q(x)$ and remainder $r(x)$ when $2x^4 - 3x^3 + x^2 - 4x + 7$ is divided by $x - 2$.

   _____

3. *Multiple choice.* If p is a polynomial function and $p(-2) = 0$, which is a factor of p?

   (a) $x - 2$ (b) $2x$

   (c) $x + 2$ (d) $-2x$

   3. _____

4. To the nearest tenth, approximate the largest x-intercept of the graph of $y = x^3 - 3x^2 + x + 1$.

   4. _____

5. Factor $15s^2 + 14s - 8$ over the set of polynomials with integer coefficients.

   5. _____

6. Factor $64m^6 + 27n^3$ over the set of polynomials with integer coefficients.

   _____

7. Let $f(x) = x^4 - x^3 - 5x^2 - x - 6$

   a. *True or false,* $f(i) = 0$.

   7. a. _____

   b. Find all zeros of f.

   b. _____

8. Part of the graph of a polynomial function g is shown below.

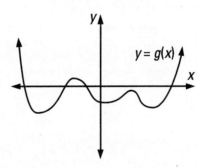

   a. What is the smallest number of real zeros that g can have?

   8. a. _____

b. What is the lowest degree *g* can have?

b. _____

In 9 and 10, let $p = 3 + 2i$ **and** $q = 2 - 3i$.

9. _____

9. Express the conjugate of $p + q$ in $a + bi$ form.

10. _____

10. Express $\dfrac{p}{q}$ in $a + bi$ form.

11. _____

11. *True or false.* Every polynomial of degree $n \geq 1$ must have at least one complex zero.

12. The lengths of the sides of a right triangle are shown below. Find the hypotenuse.

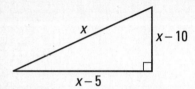

12. _____

In 13–15, $f(x) = (x + 1)^3(2x - 3)^2(3x - 4)$.

13. Which zero of *f* has multiplicity three?

13. _____

14. What is the degree of *f*?

14. _____

15. How many *x*-intercepts does the graph of *f* have?

15. _____

16. A length of pipe 10 m long connects a tank of liquid helium to a superconducting electromagnet. A layer of insulation 8 cm thick surrounds the pipe. Express the volume of the insulation in cubic centimeters as a polynomial function of *r*, the radius of the pipe.

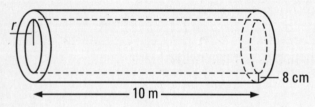

Check all your work carefully.

Functions, Statistics, and Trigonometry © Scott Foresman Addison Wesley

CHAPTER 9 TEST, Form B

1. In the following table, g is a polynomial function. Determine an equation for g.

   1. _____

x	0	1	2	3	4	5	6	7
$g(x)$	5	10	19	26	25	10	-25	-86

2. Find the quotient $q(x)$ and remainder $r(x)$ when $3x^4 - x^3 + 2x^2 - 4x + 10$ is divided by $x + 2$.

   _____

3. *Multiple choice.* If q is a polynomial function and $q(3) = 0$, which is a factor of $q(x)$?

   3. _____

   (a) $3x$ (b) $-3x$

   (c) $3 + x$ (d) $-3 + x$

4. To the nearest tenth, approximate the smallest x-intercept of the graph of $y = x^4 - x^2 - x - 2$.

   4. _____

5. Factor $6n^2 + 5n - 6$ over the set of polynomials with integer coefficients.

   5. _____

6. Factor $125p^3 - 8q^{12}$ over the set of polynomials with integer coefficients.

   _____

7. Let $h(x) = 2x^4 - x^3 - 4x^2 - x - 6$.

   a. *True or false,* $f(-i) = 0$.

   7. a. _____

   b. Find all zeros of h.

   b. _____

8. Part of the graph of a polynomial function p is shown below.

   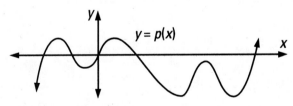

   a. What is the smallest number of real zeros that p can have?

   8. a. _____

   b. What is the lowest degree that p can have?

   b. _____

Name _____

In 9 and 10, let $m = 1 + 2i$ **and** $n = 2 - i$.

9. Express the conjugate of $m - n$ in $a + bi$ form.

9. _____

10. Express $\frac{m}{n}$ in $a + bi$ form.

10. _____

11. *True or false.* Every polynomial with real coefficients of degree $n \geq 1$ must have at least one real zero.

11. _____

12. Find x to the nearest hundredth.

12. _____

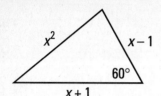

In 13–15, $g(x) = (3x + 1)^4(x - 2)^2(2x - 1)$.

13. Which zero of g has multiplicity four?

13. _____

14. What is the degree of g?

14. _____

15. How many x-intercepts does the graph of g have?

15. _____

16. A cement conduit is constructed so that it has a square exterior and a centered cylindrical interior, as shown below. At its thinnest point, the conduit's wall is 5 cm thick. Express the volume of cement needed to create such a conduit as a polynomial in l and r, where l is the length of a section of conduit and r is the radius of the conduit's interior.

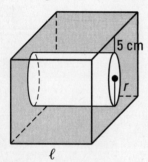

Check all your work carefully.

Functions, Statistics, and Trigonometry © Scott Foresman Addison Wesley

CHAPTER 9 TEST, Form C

1. Your friend is studying geometry and has learned the formula $V = \ell wh$ for finding the volume of a right rectangular prism. So your friend says it is hard to understand how a polynomial *with more than one term* might represent the volume of a right rectangular prism. Explain to your friend why this is possible. Include an illustration.

2. Give two polynomial functions, one of odd degree and one even, each with one zero equal to -3 and another zero of multiplicity 2. Sketch a graph of each function and label all its extrema, giving the value and identifying it as a maximum value, a minimum value, a relative maximum, or a relative minimum.

3. Using the quadratic regression feature of a calculator, a student found the following model for the data below:

$y = 11.5x^2 - 47.5x + 49.5$.
Explain how you know this is not the best model. Show how to find a better model.

x	1	2	3	4	5	6	7	8
y	3	8	21	48	95	168	273	416

4. In this chapter, it is said that the procedure for dividing polynomials is similar to the procedure for dividing integers. List as many similarities as you can. Give examples.

5. a. Is the sum of two complex numbers *always, sometimes,* or *never* complex? Give examples to illustrate your answer.

   b. Repeat part **a**, this time analyzing the product of two complex numbers.

6. Joy says that the solution of $(n - 2)^3 = 0$ is the same as the solution of $n^3 - 8 = 0$. Do you agree or disagree? If you agree, justify your response. If you disagree, show how the solutions of the two equations differ.

CHAPTER 9 TEST, Form D

A group of students wondered about certain characteristics of polynomial functions, such as when the functions are even or odd, when their inverses are functions, and what happens under certain transformations. After some discussion, the students decided to explore the function *f* defined and graphed at the right. Questions **a** through **f** lead you through their investigation.

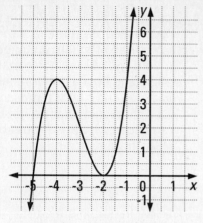

$$f(x) = (x + 2)(x + 2)(x + 5)$$

a. Consider the function *f*.
  i. What are its zeros?   **ii.** Identify any extrema.
  iii. Is it an even function, an odd function, or neither? Explain your choice.
  iv. Is its inverse a function? Explain why or why not.

b. The students believed that the graph of *f* is rotation symmetric.
  i. What are the coordinates of the center of symmetry?
  ii. Give a rule for the translation *T* that maps the center of symmetry to the origin.
  iii. Give a rule for *f'*, the image of the graph of *f* under the translation *T*. Write *f*(*x*) in standard form. That is, write the rule as a sum of terms arranged in order of decreasing degree.

c. Consider the function *f'* from part **b**.
  i. What are its zeros?   **ii.** Identify any extrema.
  iii. Is it an even function, an odd function, or neither? Explain your choice.
  iv. Is its inverse a function? Explain why or why not.

d. Consider the translation *T* from part **b**.
  i. Are the zeros of *f* mapped to the zeros of *f'*?
  ii. Are the extrema of *f* mapped to the extrema of *f'*?

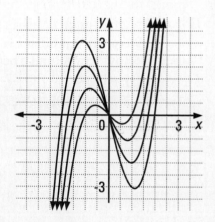

e. The students decided to investigate the whole class of polynomial functions of the form $p(x) = x^3 - kx$ where $k > 0$. They graphed several functions of this form, as shown at the right, then arrived at the conclusions below. Do you think each is true or false? Justify your answers.
  i. Any function of this form is an odd function.
  ii. The zeros of a function of this form are 0, $-\sqrt{k}$, and $\sqrt{k}$.
  iii. The inverse of a function of this form is not a function.

f. Investigate polynomial functions of the form $p(x) = x^3 + kx$ where $k > 0$. State several conclusions about these functions.

g. Prepare a report summarizing your findings.

Name _____

1. *True or false.* If $f(x) = \dfrac{x^4 + 2x^2 - 1}{x^3 + x}$, then f
   is a polynomial function.

   1. _____

2. g is a function with $g(x) = (x^2 + 1)(x - 1)^2(x + 3)^3$.

   a. What is the degree of g?

   2.a. _____

   b. How many x-intercepts does the
   graph of g have?

   b. _____

   c. How many complex zeros (counting
   multiplicities) does g have?

   c. _____

3. Find $\displaystyle\lim_{n \to \infty} \dfrac{1 - n^2}{1 + n^2}$.

   3. _____

4. Solve for n: $4\,_nC_4 = 5\,_nC_5$.

   4. _____

5. Solve the equation $2x^2 - x + 15 = 0$ and
   express the solutions in $a + bi$ form.

   5. _____

6. Find the quotient $q(x)$ and remainder $r(x)$
   when $x^4 - x^3 + 2x^2 - 3$ is divided by $x^2 + 1$.

   6. _____

   _____

7. a. Verify that the table below represents a
   probability distribution.

   7. a. _____

   _____

x	1	2	3	4	5
$P(x)$	0.500	0.385	0.095	0.015	0.005

   b. Calculate the expected value of the distribution.

   b. _____

8. The tent pole pictured at the right has height L, the length of
   rope supporting the pole is $L + 12$, and distance from the
   bottom of the pole to where the rope is anchored to the
   ground is $L + 6$. To the nearest degree, find the angle θ that
   the rope makes with the ground.

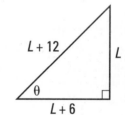

   8. _____

9. The table at the right shows the number of higher education institutions in the ten states with the largest numbers of such institutions in 1994. (Source: *Statistical Abstract of the United States, 1996*)

State	No. of Higher Education Institutions
CA	336
NY	314
PA	218
TX	178
IL	167
OH	157
NC	123
MA	119
GA	118
FL	111

  a. What is the median number of higher education institutions for the ten states?

  b. What is the standard deviation of the number of higher education institutions for the ten states?

9. a. _____

  b. _____

10. Express $\dfrac{2 + 3i}{2 - 3i}$ in $a + bi$ form.

10. _____

11. If $g(m) = 3m^3 - 7m^2 - 7m + 3$, then $g(3) = 0$. Factor $g(m)$.

11. _____

12. A student guessed randomly on an exam with 10 multiple-choice questions, each of which had four options. What is the probability that the student chose exactly 4 correct answers?

12. _____

13. If $f(x) = x^2 + 1$ and $g(x) = \sqrt{1 - x^2}$, evaluate $g(f(-1))$.

13. _____

14. The Louganises are filling up their 1500 ft³ swimming pool by adding 2000 gallons of water per day. Over the course of each day, however, x percent of the water evaporates.

  a. Write a polynomial that expresses the amount of water in the pool at the end of the fourth day as a function of x.

  _____

  b. How much water was in the pool at the end of the fourth day if the daily loss from evaporation was 3 percent?

  b. _____

15. Find the sum of the finite geometric series: $1000 - 200 + 40 - 8 + \cdots + 0.00256$.

15. _____

16. If $f(x) = e^x$, give an equation for f^{-1}.

16. _____

17. *True or false.* If a polynomial function f has a relative maximum at (-1, -5), the graph of $y = f(x)$ never crosses the x-axis.

17. _____

18. Find a polynomial in x and y for the volume V of a right circular cylinder with radius $x + y$ and height $2x$.

18. _____

19. Find the coefficient of a^3b^4 in $(a + 2b)^7$.

19. _____

20. Prove that the product of a complex number and its conjugate is always a real number.

_____

_____

_____

Functions, Statistics, and Trigonometry © Scott Foresman Addison Wesley

Check all your work carefully.

COMPREHENSIVE TEST, CHAPTERS 1-9

1. Which is the median of the data set 4, 8, 10, 12?　　　　1. _____

   (a) 8.5　　　　(b) 8　　　　　　(c) 10　　　　　　(d) 9

2. Evaluate ln 1.　　　　　　　　　　　　　　　　　　　2. _____

   (a) e　　　　　(b) $\frac{1}{e}$　　　　(c) 1　　　　　　(d) 0

3. Which of the following graphs shows the strongest negative correlation?　3. _____

   (a)
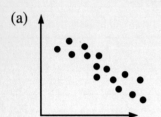
   (b)
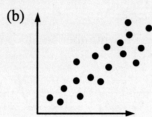

   (c)
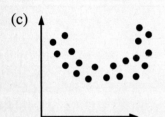
   (d)
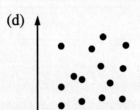

4. Which scale change has the effect on a graph of stretching it horizontally　4. _____
   by a factor of 9 and shrinking it vertically by a factor of $\frac{1}{5}$?

   (a) $S(x, y) = \left(9x, \frac{y}{5}\right)$　　　　　(b) $S(x, y) = \left(\frac{x}{9}, 5y\right)$

   (c) $S(x, y) = \left(5x, \frac{y}{9}\right)$　　　　　(d) $S(x, y) = \left(\frac{x}{5}, 9y\right)$

5. Which is the complex conjugate of 1?　　　　　　　　5. _____

   (a) -1　　　　(b) 1　　　　　(c) i　　　　　　(d) $-i$

6. Which is the coefficient of x^4y^7 in the expansion of $(x - y)^{11}$?　6. _____

   (a) $_{11}C_4$　　(b) $_{11}C_7$　　(c) $-(_{11}C_7)$　　(d) $-(_{11}C_4)$

7. Which of the following statements is false?　　　　　　7. _____

   (a) If events A and B are independent, then $P(A \cap B) = P(A) \cdot P(B)$.

   (b) If events A and B are complementary, then $P(A) + P(B) = 1$.

   (c) If events A and B are mutually exclusive, then
      $P(A \cup B) = P(A) + P(B)$.

   (d) If events A and B are dependent, then
      $P(A \cap B) = P(A) - P(B)$.

8. Which is the graph of $y = \sin(2x) - 1$?

8. _____

(a)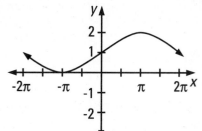

(b)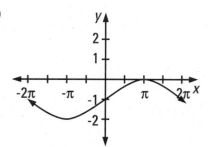

(c)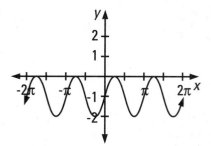

(d)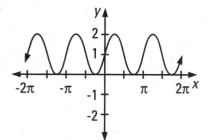

9. A polynomial function f has real coefficients and degree n. Which of the following statements is false?

9. _____

(a) If n is odd, then f has at least one real zero.

(b) If n is even, then f has an even number of complex zeros.

(c) The number of x-intercepts of the graph of $y = f(x)$ is n.

(d) The number of zeros of f, counting multiplicities, is n.

10. Suppose $P(A) = 0.3$, $P(B) = 0.4$, and $P(A \cap B) = 0.2$. Find $P(A \cup B)$.

10. _____

(a) 0.7 (b) 0.9

(c) 0.5 (d) 0.12

11. If both f and g are odd functions, which of the following is not an odd function?

11. _____

(a) $f + g$ (b) $f \cdot g$

(c) $f \circ g$ (d) $g \circ f$

12. Determine $\lim\limits_{n \to \infty} \dfrac{7 - 2n}{5n + 3}$.

12. _____

(a) 0 (b) $\dfrac{7}{5}$

(c) $\dfrac{2}{5}$ (d) $-\dfrac{2}{5}$

13. Which describes all solutions to $\cos x = \frac{\sqrt{3}}{2}$?   13. _____

(a) $2k\pi \pm \frac{\pi}{6}$, for any integer k

(b) $2k\pi \pm \frac{\pi}{3}$, for any integer k

(c) $2k\pi \pm \frac{5\pi}{6}$, for any integer k

(d) $2k\pi + \frac{2\pi}{3}$, for any integer k

14. In a circle of radius 10, how long is an arc with a   14. _____
central angle of 3 radians?

(a) 10   (b) 30

(c) 30π (d) 60π

15. A polynomial $f(x)$ is divided by $x - 2$. The quotient has the   15. _____
factor $x - 1$, and the remainder is 3. Which of the following
points must be on the graph of $y = f(x)$?

(a) $(2, 0)$ (b) $(-2, 0)$

(c) $(1, 3)$ (d) $(-1, -3)$

16. Which of the following could be the graph of $y = \log_a x \ (a > 1)$?   16. _____

(a)

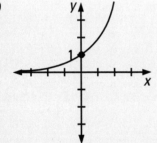

(b)

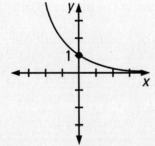

(c)

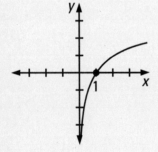

(d)

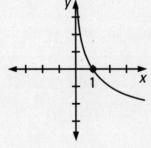

Functions, Statistics, and Trigonometry © Scott Foresman Addison Wesley

17. The following international airmail rates were established in July, 1995, **17.** _____
for letters and letter packages (except to Canada & Mexico): a charge of
$0.60 for the first half ounce or less and a charge of $0.40 for each
additional half ounce or fraction thereof. Which formula gives the cost
of mailing a letter weighing *x* ounces at these rates?

(a) $0.60 + $0.40(x − 0.5)

(b) $0.60 + $0.40\left(\frac{x − 0.5}{0.5}\right)

(c) $0.60 + $0.40\lceil x − 0.5 \rceil

(d) $0.60 + $0.40\left\lceil \frac{x − 0.5}{0.5} \right\rceil

18. The table below shows the number of passenger cars made by General Motors
Corporation in different years.

Models	1995	1990	1985	1980	1975	1970
Chevrolet	665,955	1,025,379	1,691,354	1,737,336	1,687,901	1,504,614
Pontiac	574,455	649,255	702,617	556,429	523,469	422,212
Oldsmobile	391,216	418,742	1,168,982	783,225	654,342	439,632
Buick	393,879	405,123	1,001,461	783,575	535,820	459,931
Cadillac	186,113	252,540	322,765	203,991	278,404	152,859
Saturn	301,540	4,245	—	—	—	
Toyota/Cavalier	1,978	—	—	—	—	

Source: American Automobile Manufacturers Association

For which model did the production decrease the most
from 1970 to 1995?

(a) Buick

(b) Oldsmobile

(c) Chevrolet

(d) Toyota/Cavalier   **18.** _____

19. There are 24 Republicans and 28 Democrats from California in the House of
Representatives of the 105th Congress. If a journalist interviews five Representatives
selected randomly from the California delegation, what is the probability that all
five are Democrats?

(a) $\frac{5}{52}$

(b) $\frac{28}{43}$

(c) $\frac{1}{{}_{52}C_5}$

(d) $\frac{{}_{28}C_5}{{}_{52}C_5}$ **19.** _____

20. If *f(x)* is a polynomial, and *f(-a)* = 0, which is a factor of *f(x)*?   **20.** _____

(a) *a*

(b) *-a*

(c) *x − a*

(d) *x + a*

21. Evaluate $\ln[(e^{-3.1})^2 \cdot \sqrt{e^{2.4}}]$.   **21.** _____

(a) -0.7

(b) 11.16

(c) 0.15

(d) -5

22. How many permutations consisting of four letters each starting with the letter N can be formed from the letters of PERSON?

(a) 60　　　　　　　　　　　(b) 120

(c) 360　　　　　　　　　　 (d) 10

22. _____

23. What is the value of the following sum?

$$2^{50} - 50 \cdot 2^{49} \cdot 7 + \frac{50!}{2!48!} \cdot 2^{48} \cdot 7^2 - \cdots + \frac{50!}{2!48!} \cdot 2^2 \cdot 7^{48} - 50 \cdot 2 \cdot 7^{49} + 7^{50}$$

(a) $(-5)^{50}$　　　　　　　　(b) 9^{50}

(c) 14^{50}　　　　　　　　　(d) 5^{50}

23. _____

24. Find x in the triangle at the right.

(a) $\sqrt{19}$　　　　　　　　(b) $\sqrt{39}$

(c) $\frac{5}{2}$　　　　　　　　　 (d) $\frac{7}{2}$

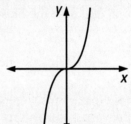

24. _____

25. Which of the functions graphed below has an inverse which is a function?

(a) 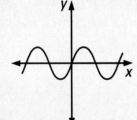　　　　　(b)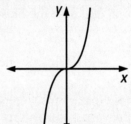

(c) 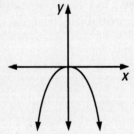　　　　　(d)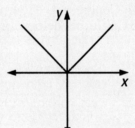

25. _____

Check your work carefully.

Functions, Statistics, and Trigonometry © Scott Foresman Addison Wesley

QUIZ

1. **a.** Write a formula for distribution function B for a binomial experiment that has 35 trials where the probability of success in each trial is .80.

   1. a. _____

   b. Evaluate $B(28)$.

   b. _____

2. Calculate the mean and standard deviation for the binomial distribution described in Question 1.

   2. _____

   _____

3. *True or false.* The area under the graph of a binomial distribution with fixed probability increases as the number of trials increases. Justify your answer.

   _____

4. For what probability is the graph of a binomial distribution symmetric with respect to the mode of the distribution?

   4. _____

5. During the 1997 WNBA regular season, Cynthia Cooper of the Houston Comets had a free-throw percentage of .864. During the post-season semifinal and championship games, Cooper had 27 free-throw attempts.

   a. Assuming the independence of free-throw attempts, what is Cooper's expected number of made free throws in the post-season games?

   5. a. _____

   b. In the post-season games, Cooper actually made 20 of her 27 free throws. How many standard deviations is this number from the expected value?

   b. _____

6. Clare boasted to her friend Debby that she is at least a 90% free-throw shooter. Debby asked Clare to prove it by shooting 20 consecutive free throws.

   a. State a null and alternative hypothesis for testing whether Clare is being honest about her free-throw percentage.

   _____

   _____

   b. If Clare makes 16 out of the 20 free throws, is Debby justified in saying that Clare does not have a 90% free-throw percentage at the 0.05 significance level? Justify your answer.

   _____

   _____

   _____

Name _____

QUIZ

Lessons 10-4 Through 10-6

You will need a standard normal distribution table for this quiz.

1. *Multiple choice.* Which of the following is a
   reason why the parent normal curve, given
   by $f(x) = e^{-x^2}$, cannot represent a probability
   distribution?

   1. _____

   (a) The area under the curve is not 1.

   (b) The curve never intersects the x-axis.

   (c) It is not symmetric to the y-axis.

   (d) It has no inflection points.

2. *True or false.* The standard normal curve and
   the parent normal curve are translation images
   of each other.

   2. _____

3. Estimate the probability represented by the shaded
   area under the standard normal curve graphed below.

   3. _____

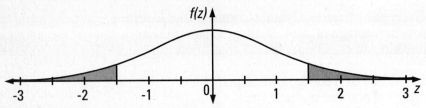

4. Suppose z is a continuous random variable
   with a standard normal distribution and
   $P(z < a) \approx .7140$. Evaluate each.

   a. $P(z > a)$

   4. a. _____

   b. $P(0 < z < a)$

   b. _____

5. Should a binomial distribution with a mean of 17 and a standard deviation
   of 1.6 be approximated by a normal distribution? Justify your answer.

   _____

   _____

6. Suppose you are helping to organize a conference, and it is your responsibility to order
   the buses which will transport the participants from the hotel to the conference site.
   There are 370 participants, but at previous conferences, only about 82% of participants
   needed bus transportation. So you order 7 buses, each of which has a capacity of
   44 people. What is the probability that you did *not* order enough buses to
   accommodate everyone who will need transportation?

   6. _____

Functions, Statistics, and Trigonometry © Scott Foresman Addison Wesley

138

CHAPTER 10 TEST, Form A

You will need a calculator and a standard normal distribution table for this test.

1. Draw a histogram of the binomial probability
distribution for the number of times a two appears
when a fair six-sided die is tossed 5 times.

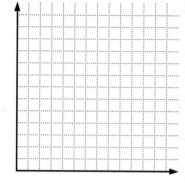

2. Describe how the domain, range, and the shape
of the binomial distribution in Question 1 would
change if the die were tossed 100 times.

_____

_____

_____

3. Consider a test with 50 multiple-choice
questions, each with 5 options. If students
guess randomly on the test, what is the
expected mean and standard deviation?

3. _____

_____

4. *Multiple choice.* Which of the following
is *not* true of the standard normal curve?

4. _____

   (a) The area under the curve is 1.

   (b) The curve has inflection points at $x = 1$ and $x = -1$.

   (c) The curve never intersects the x-axis.

   (d) The curve is always concave down.

**In 5 and 6, z is a continuous random variable with a standard
normal distribution. Estimate the given probability.**

5. $P(z > 1.25)$

5. _____

6. $P(-1.5 < z < -0.5)$

6. _____

**In 7 and 8, consider this statistical data reported by the College
Board. The 1997 SAT I test was administered to 1,127,021 students.
The composite scores (verbal + math) were approximately normally
distributed with a mean of 1,016 and a standard deviation of 206.**

7. Estimate the number of students who scored
1,400 or above.

7. _____

8. Suppose you were to randomly sample
100 of the SAT I test takers. What is the
probability that the mean score of your
sample is less than 1,000?

8. _____

9. The graph below represents a normal probability distribution with mean 25 and standard deviation 2.5. Estimate the area of the shaded region.

9. _____

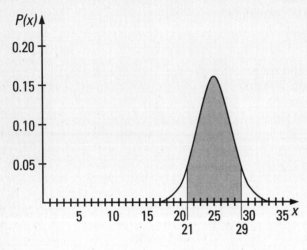

10. A coin is tossed 15 times and comes up heads 13 times.

   a. State a null and alternative hypothesis for testing whether the coin is fair.

   _____

   _____

   b. Can the coin be considered fair at the .01 significance level? Justify your answer.

   _____

11. *True or false.* The graph of every normal distribution is symmetric to the mean.

11. _____

12. Suppose the 90% confidence interval for the lifetime of the rechargeable battery in a cellular phone is 4 hr ± 1 hr. What is the probability that the cellular phone can be used for more than 5 hours without recharging?

12. _____

13. A random sample of 175 salaries was taken from a certain population of teachers' salaries. The mean of the sample was found to be $37,250 and the standard deviation was $4,300. Assuming the standard deviation of the sample is the same as that for the entire population, find the 95% confidence interval for the mean salary of the population of teachers.

13. _____

Check all your work carefully.

CHAPTER 10 TEST, Form B

You will need a calculator and a standard normal distribution table for this test.

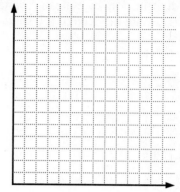

1. A basketball player has a free throw percentage of .82. Draw a histogram of the binomial probability distribution for the number of free throws the basketball player will make in 6 attempts.

2. Describe how the domain, range, and the shape of the binomial distribution in Question 1 would change if the basketball player's free throw percentage were .5.

   _____

   _____

   _____

3. An experiment is conducted in which a fair six-sided die is tossed 60 times and the number of times a five appears is counted. What is the expected mean and variance for this experiment?

   3. _____

      _____

4. *Multiple choice.* Which of the following is *not* true of of the function $f(x) = e^{-x^2}$?

   4. _____

   (a) $f(0) = 1$ 　　　　　　　　(b) $f(x) = f(-x)$ for all x

   (c) The function is always decreasing. 　　(d) The function has no minimum.

In 5 and 6, z is a continuous random variable with a standard normal distribution. Estimate the given probability.

5. $P(0 < z < .69)$ 　　　　　　　　　　　　5. _____

6. $P(|z| \leq 1.2)$ 　　　　　　　　　　　　6. _____

In 7 and 8, consider this statistical data reported by the College Board. The 1997 SAT I-Mathematics test was administered to 1,127,021 students. The scores were approximately normally distributed with a mean of 511 and a standard deviation of 112.

7. Estimate the number of students who scored 600 or above. 　　　　　7. _____

8. Suppose you were to randomly sample 50 of the SAT I test takers. What is the probability that the mean score of your sample is between 500 and 520? 　　8. _____

9. The graph below represents a normal probability distribution with mean 25 and standard deviation 2.5. Estimate the area of the shaded region.

9. _____

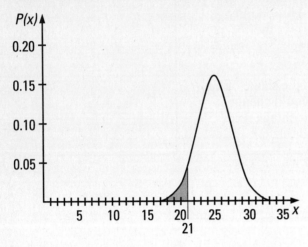

10. A coin is tossed 14 times and comes up tails twice.

   a. State a null and alternative hypothesis for testing whether the coin is fair.

   _____

   _____

   b. Can the coin be considered fair at the .01 significance level? Justify your answer.

   _____

   _____

11. Give the inflection points for the graph of the function $f(z) = \dfrac{1}{\sqrt{2\pi}}e^{-z^2/2}$.

11. _____

12. The pollster determined that, if the election were held tomorrow, 53% of the population would vote for candidate A, with a margin of error of $\pm 3\%$ for the 95% confidence interval. What is the probability that candidate A will win the election?

12. _____

13. A manufacturer of speakers randomly sampled 35 of their new speakers and measured the maximum power output. The mean maximum power output of the sample was found to be 125.2 watts with a standard deviation of 7.4 watts. Assuming the standard deviation of the sample is the same as that for the entire population, find the 90% confidence interval for the mean maximum power output of the speakers.

13. _____

Check all your work carefully.

CHAPTER 10 TEST, Form C

1. In baseball, "success" for a batter is getting a hit when at bat. Choose a number of times at-bat n and a reasonable nonzero probability of success p. (Average major league batters have a success of about 27% in one season.) Draw a binomial probability distribution for your choices. Show how to find the mean and standard deviation of the distribution. What is the meaning of these statistics.

2. A six-sided die that came with a new board game has a visible defect, and you suspect the die is not fair. Describe a binomial experiment you might conduct to test whether it is fair. Explain how you can use a binomial distribution to evaluate your experiment.

3. An equation of the curve graphed at the right is: $y = \dfrac{1}{\sqrt{2\pi}}\, e^{-z^2/2}$. Label the vertical and horizontal scales of the axes. Then state as many facts as you can about the curve and what it represents

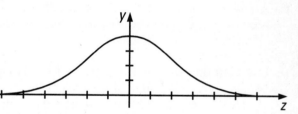

4. The average life of a certain type of light bulb is said to be 3000 h, with a standard deviation of 250 h. Explain how a consumer interest group can use the Central Limit Theorem to verify this claim.

5. Using the Standard Normal Distribution Table, Joe found $P(z < 1.28) \approx .8997$ and $P(z < 1.29) \approx .9015$. He concluded that the z-score 1.28 corresponds to a 90% confidence level. Do you agree? Why or why not?

CHAPTER 10 TEST, Form D

For your summer job, you are working at a company that makes snack mixes. A certain machine in the factory fills about 20,000 packages per day with one particular type of mix. The machine is supposed to fill each package with at least 16 ounces of the mix, but the management is wondering whether the machine is functioning properly.

Yesterday your supervisor selected a random sample of forty packages that this machine filled and measured the weight of the mix in each package. At the right is a list of the weights in ounces. You have been told to analyze the sample.

You will need a statistics utility to answer the following questions.

a. Find each of the following statistics for the weights in the list. When rounding is necessary, round to the nearest hundredth.
  i. mean
  ii. median
  iii. mode(s)
  iv. standard deviation

b. Draw a relative frequency distribution for the weights. Use intervals such as $16.01 \leq x < 16.03$ and $16.03 \leq x < 16.05$.

c. Analyze your distribution from part **b**. What characteristics does it seem to share with a normal distribution? List as many characteristics as you can.

d. Use your distribution from part **b**. Lightly sketch a smooth curve that connects the midpoints of the tops of the bars.
  i. How does the curve you sketched appear similar to a normal curve? How does it appear different from a normal curve?
  ii. What adjustment to the frequency distribution might yield a curve that looks more like a normal curve?

e. Although a sample size of forty is small, assume temporarily that the standard deviation of the weights in this sample is the standard deviation for all the weights in the packages the machine fills. Choose a confidence level and give the confidence interval for the mean weight of the mix in the packages.

f. Prepare a report for your supervisor in which you summarize your results from parts **a** through **e** and make recommendations for future actions. Be sure to give specific instructions. For instance, if you recommend additional sampling, specify the number of samples to be taken and the sample size. Describe any statistical analysis to be done on the samples, and explain the nature of any inferences you expect to draw from the analysis.

16.010
16.031
16.018
16.055
16.019
16.022
15.974
16.048
15.968
16.020
16.022
15.970
16.000
16.011
16.004
16.099
16.020
16.088
15.992
16.033
16.069
16.051
16.027
15.947
16.033
15.921
16.029
16.023
15.988
16.019
16.087
16.006
16.016
15.957
16.068
16.021
16.116
16.008
16.040
15.983

Functions, Statistics, and Trigonometry © Scott Foresman Addison Wesley

CHAPTER 10 TEST, Cumulative Form

1. Suppose you conduct 125 trials of a binomial experiment where each trial has a probability of failure of 0.75. Find the mean and standard deviation for the distribution of the number of failures expected.

1. _____

_____

2. Estimate the area shaded under the standard normal curve below.

2. _____

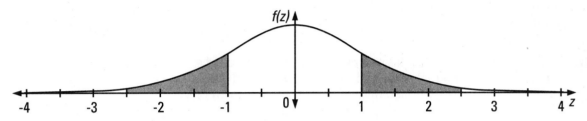

3. In each of the following, identify the events as independent, mutually exclusive but not complementary, complementary, or none of these.

   a. E_1: spending all afternoon July 14th at the beach
      E_2: spending all afternoon July 14th at an art museum

   3. a. _____

   b. E_1: having a male first child
      E_2: having a female second child

   b. _____

   c. E_1: on one toss, hitting the bulls-eye with a dart
      E_2: on one toss, missing the dartboard completely

   c. _____

4. In the U.S. the probability that a baby will be born female is .48. Suppose a large hospital has 2500 live births in a given year. Estimate the probability that more than 1250 will be female. (Hint: Use a normal approximation to this binomial situation.)

4. _____

5. Express $\frac{2 + 4i}{3 + i}$ in $a + bi$ form.

5. _____

6. Find a formula for a polynomial of degree 7 with the following zeros: $x = -2$ of multiplicity 4, $x = 7$ of multiplicity 2, and $x = -\frac{3}{2}$ of multiplicity 1.

6. _____

7. Fran and Paul have lived in their apartment for 7 years. The first year their rent was $845 per month. Each year thereafter the monthly rent increased by 3.5%. How much did Fran and Paul pay in rent over the seven-year period?

7. _____

8. Find the remainder when $10x^4 + 6x^3 - 5x - 3$ is divided by $x + 2$.

8. _____

9. Find an equation for the image of the graph

   of $y = e^{-x^2}$ under the transformation $S(x, y) = \left(x\sqrt{3}, \dfrac{y}{\sqrt{3}}\right)$.

9. _____

   _____

10. A normal probability distribution function
    is given by the equation

    $$f(x) = \frac{1}{.7\sqrt{2\pi}} e^{-\frac{1}{2}\left(\frac{x-98.2}{.7}\right)^2}$$

    What are the mean and standard deviation
    of the distribution?

10. _____

11. To test her friend Sally's claim of clairvoyance, Alice used a
    computer to generate 10 random digits from 0 to 9 and asked
    Sally to guess each generated digit. Sally was able to correctly
    guess 4 of the 10 generated digits. At the .01 significance level,
    is Sally's claim of clairvoyance justified? Justify your answer.

    _____

    _____

12. Suppose you were to randomly sample 64 of
    the 1,127,021 students who took the SAT-I in
    1997. For your sample, you find a mean verbal
    score of 520 and a standard deviation of 110.

    a. Find the 95% confidence interval for
       the mean score of all test takers. (Assume
       the standard deviation for the sample is
       the same as that for the entire population.)

    12. a. _____

    b. How large should your sample size be if
       you wanted to determine the mean verbal
       score with 99% confidence to within 10 points?

    b. _____

13. Let $f(x) = x^4 - 12x^3 + 42x^2 - 36x - 91$. If
    $f(3 - 2i) = 0$, factor $f(x)$ completely over the
    set of polynomials with complex coefficients.

    13. _____

Check all your work carefully.

Functions, Statistics, and Trigonometry © Scott Foresman Addison Wesley

QUIZ

In 1 and 2, multiply.

1. $\begin{bmatrix} 4 & 3 \\ 7 & 1 \end{bmatrix} \begin{bmatrix} 5 & 3 & 1 \\ 6 & 2 & 3 \end{bmatrix}$

1. _____

2. $\begin{bmatrix} \frac{2}{3} \\ \frac{1}{2} \end{bmatrix} [4 \quad 6]$

2. _____

3. The dimensions of P, Q, and R are 3×4, 4×2, and 2×4, respectively, what are the dimensions of the matrix $(PQ)R$?

3. _____

4. An amusement park charges \$30 for adults and \$20 for children. The matrix below represents the attendance for a three-day holiday weekend. Find a matrix representing the total revenue for each day.

	adults	children
Fri	2,000	5,482
Sat	2,100	7,141
Sun	1,975	5,132

4. _____

5. Find a matrix that represents the composite transformation $r_{y=x} \circ r_y$, where

$r_{y=x}(x, y) = (y, x)$ and $r_y(x, y) = (-x, y)$.

5. _____

6. What matrix corresponds to a transformation that multiplies the length of each side of a polygon by 7?

6. _____

7. Find a matrix that represents the composite of rotating a figure 270° around the origin followed by reflecting it over the y-axis.

7. _____

8. Consider $\triangle ABC$ and $\triangle A'B'C'$ graphed below.

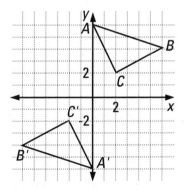

a. Find two matrices which represent the two triangles.

8. a. _____

b. Find the matrix that represents a transformation mapping $\triangle ABC$ onto $\triangle A'B'C'$.

QUIZ

1. If $\sin 17° \approx .2924$ and $17° \approx .9563$, find
the image of the point $P = (2, -1)$ under R_{17}.

    1. _____

2. *Multiple choice.* Which equals
$R_{20} \circ R_{-80}$?

    2. _____

    (a) R_{1600} (b) R_{60}

    (c) R_{-60} (d) $-R_{60}$

In 3–5, give the exact value of each expression.

3. $\cos(-15°)$

    3. _____

4. $\sin \frac{11\pi}{12}$

    4. _____

5. $\sin 71.2° \cos 18.8° + \cos 71.2° \sin 18.8°$

    5. _____

6. Prove that $\cos\left(x - \frac{\pi}{2}\right) \sin x$, for all x.

    6. _____

_____

_____

_____

7. Suppose $\angle A$ is an angle in the second quadrant
and $\sin A = \frac{1}{3}$. Find the exact value of $\sin 2A$.

    7. _____

8. Given $\theta = 22.5°$, use a formula for $\cos 2\theta$ to
find an exact value of $\cos 22.5°$.

    8. _____

Functions, Statistics, and Trigonometry © Scott Foresman Addison Wesley

CHAPTER 11 TEST, Form A

In 1 and 2, multiply the matrices if possible.

1. $\begin{bmatrix} 17 & 3 \\ -6 & -2 \end{bmatrix} \begin{bmatrix} 5 \\ 9 \end{bmatrix}$

1. _____

2. $\begin{bmatrix} 6 & 3 \\ 5 & 1 \end{bmatrix} \begin{bmatrix} 2 & 4 & 1 \\ 14 & 3 & 9 \end{bmatrix}$

2. _____

In 3 and 4, find the inverse, if one exists.

3. $\begin{bmatrix} 5 & 9 \\ 2 & 7 \end{bmatrix}$

3. _____

4. $\begin{bmatrix} 7 & 1 \\ 77 & 11 \end{bmatrix}$

4. _____

5. Find the exact value of sin 195°.

5. _____

6. Given θ is an acute angle and $\sin \theta = .4$, find the exact value of $\sin 2\theta$.

6. _____

7. Find all values of x such that $\begin{bmatrix} x & 2 \\ 6 & x \end{bmatrix}$ has no inverse.

7. _____

8. If M is a 3 × 3 matrix and N is a 3 × 6 matrix, what are the dimensions of MN?

8. _____

9. Consider the following system of equations.
$\begin{cases} 7x + 2y = 53 \\ 2x + 3y = 37 \end{cases}$

   a. Write a matrix equation to represent the system.

9. a. _____

   b. Solve the system.

   b. _____

10. Write the matrix for R_{34} with each element given to the nearest thousandth.

10. _____

11. Give the 2 × 2 matrix for the scale change $S(x, y) = \left(x, \frac{1}{4}y\right)$.

11. _____

12. An automobile manufacturer has three dealers in a certain city and produces three different models. The matrix below displays the numbers of cars sold by each dealer.

$$
\begin{array}{c}
\quad\quad \text{Model} \quad \text{Model} \quad \text{Model} \\
\quad\quad\quad A \quad\quad\quad B \quad\quad\quad C
\end{array}
$$

Dealer 1 $\begin{bmatrix} 672 & 571 & 511 \\ 272 & 258 & 706 \\ 407 & 299 & 646 \end{bmatrix}$
Dealer 2
Dealer 3

a. How many of Model *A* did Dealer 2 sell?

b. If Model *A* sells for $17,000, Model *B* sells for $25,000, and Model *C* sells for $14,000, calculate the sales revenue of each dealer. Express your answer as a matrix.

12. a. _____

b. _____

13. Write the matrix which represents a transformation that rotates a polygon 90° about the origin.

13. _____

14. Given that the matrix *A* represents R_{50} and the matrix *B* represents R_{17}, find the product matrix $A^2 B^{10}$.

14. _____

15. Refer to the square *ABCD* below.

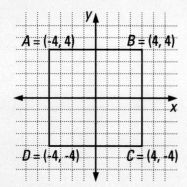

a. Find a matrix representation of *ABCD*.

15. a. _____

b. Find the matrix for the image *A'B'C'D'* of *ABCD* under the transformation represented by $\begin{bmatrix} -\frac{1}{4} & -\frac{3}{2} \\ \frac{3}{2} & -\frac{1}{4} \end{bmatrix}$

b. _____

c. Draw the image *A'B'C'D'* on the grid above.

16. Fill in the blanks with the names of appropriate transformations. The matrix equation

$$
\begin{bmatrix} -1 & 0 \\ 0 & 1 \end{bmatrix}\begin{bmatrix} 1 & 0 \\ 0 & -1 \end{bmatrix} = \begin{bmatrix} -1 & 0 \\ 0 & -1 \end{bmatrix} \text{ implies that}
$$

___**a.**___ followed by ___**b.**___ equals ___**c.**___.

16. a. _____

b. _____

c. _____

Check all your work carefully.

Functions, Statistics, and Trigonometry © Scott Foresman Addison Wesley

CHAPTER 11 TEST, Form B

In 1 and 2, multiply the matrices if possible.

1. $\begin{bmatrix} 15 & -7 \\ -4 & 3 \end{bmatrix} \begin{bmatrix} 2 \\ 3 \end{bmatrix}$

1. _____

2. $\begin{bmatrix} 9 & 4 \\ 7 & 1 \end{bmatrix} \begin{bmatrix} 3 & 6 & 1 & 0 \\ 6 & 4 & 8 & -1 \end{bmatrix}$

2. _____

In 3 and 4, find the inverse, if one exists.

3. $\begin{bmatrix} 1 & 1 \\ 1 & 1 \end{bmatrix}$

3. _____

4. $\begin{bmatrix} 3 & 8 \\ 2 & 5 \end{bmatrix}$

4. _____

5. Evaluate $\cos 165°$ exactly.

5. _____

6. Given $0 < \theta < \frac{\pi}{2}$ and $\theta = \frac{\sqrt{5}}{4}$, find the exact value for $\cos 2\theta$.

6. _____

7. _____

7. For what value(s) of y does the matrix
$\begin{bmatrix} y & 3 \\ y & 5 \end{bmatrix}$ not have an inverse?

8. If M is a 4×2 matrix and N is a 2×7 matrix, what are the dimensions of MN?

8. _____

9. Consider the following system of equations.
$$\begin{cases} 7x + 391y = 426 \\ 5x - 21y = 4 \end{cases}$$

   a. Write a matrix equation to represent the system.

9. a. _____

   b. Solve the system.

   b. _____

10. Write the matrix for R_{-42} with each element given to the nearest thousandth.

10. _____

11. Give the 2×2 matrix for the scale change $S(x, y) = \left(\frac{3}{7}x, y\right)$.

11. _____

Name _____

12. Three tourists taking separate vacation trips to Europe traveled by air, rail, and rental car at various times during their vacations. The following matrix shows the number of hours spent by each tourist on each mode of travel during his or her own vacation. Assume that the average speeds for the various modes of travel were the same for all three tourists and were 800 kph for air, 130 kph for rail, and 60 kph for rental car travel. Find a matrix that represents the total distance in kilometers traveled by each tourist.

	Air	Rail	Retail car
Tourist A	15	20	10
Tourist B	18	30	8
Tourist C	21	15	16

12. _____

13. What matrix represents a transformation that rotates a polygon 270° around the origin?

13. _____

14. Given that the matrix C represents R_{30} and the matrix D represents R_{-100}, find $C^4 D^3$.

14. _____

15. Refer to the square $ABCD$ graphed below.

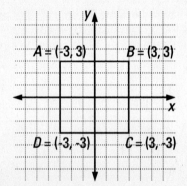

a. Write a matrix that represents $ABCD$.

15. a. _____

b. Find the matrix for the image $A'B'C'D'$ under the transformation represented by $\begin{bmatrix} -\frac{1}{3} & \frac{2}{3} \\ \frac{1}{6} & -\frac{1}{6} \end{bmatrix}$

b. _____

c. Draw the image on the given grid.

16. Fill in the blanks with the names of appropriate transformations. The matrix equation

$\begin{bmatrix} 0 & -1 \\ -1 & 0 \end{bmatrix} \begin{bmatrix} 0 & 1 \\ 1 & 0 \end{bmatrix} = \begin{bmatrix} -1 & 0 \\ 0 & -1 \end{bmatrix}$ implies that

_____a.____ followed by ____b.____ equals ___c.___ .

16. a. _____

b. _____

c. _____

Check all your work carefully.

CHAPTER 11 TEST, Form C

1. a. Identify two matrices, *A* and *B*, for which *AB* and *BA* both exist. Find *AB* and *BA*.

b. Identify two matrices, *A* and *B*, for which *AB* exists, but *BA* does not. Justify your answer.

2. Below is an unfinished exercise. What is the goal of the exercise? For each numbered step of the exercise, write a sentence explaining what was done in that step. Then complete the exercise, continuing to number each step and writing a sentence that explains it.

1. $\begin{cases} 2x - 3y = 7 \\ 3x + y = 5 \end{cases}$

2. $\begin{bmatrix} 2 & -3 \\ 3 & 1 \end{bmatrix}\begin{bmatrix} x \\ y \end{bmatrix} = \begin{bmatrix} 7 \\ 5 \end{bmatrix}$

3. $\begin{bmatrix} 2 & -3 \\ 3 & 1 \end{bmatrix}^{-1}\begin{bmatrix} 2 & -3 \\ 3 & 1 \end{bmatrix}\begin{bmatrix} x \\ y \end{bmatrix} = \begin{bmatrix} 2 & -3 \\ 3 & 1 \end{bmatrix}^{-1}\begin{bmatrix} 7 \\ 5 \end{bmatrix}\cdots$

3. Choose a real-world situation and show how a matrix can be used to organize information related to it. Use real data if it is available, or create a reasonable set of fictional data. Write a question you can answer using the matrix. Give the answer to your question.

4. Use only the exact values of sin 30°, cos 30°, sin 45°, cos 45°, sin 60°, and cos 60°. From these, obtain several other exact values of sin θ and cos θ for 0° < θ < 180°. Show your work.

5. Write a matrix for △*ABC* at the right. Then choose **a.** a reflection, **b.** a rotation, **c.** a scale change, and **d.** a composite of transformations so that each of the four images of △*ABC* under the transformations lies in a different quadrant from the others. Write a matrix for each transformation and show how to use it to find the image.

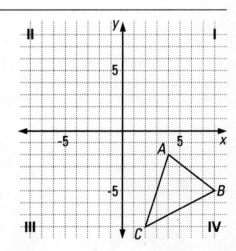

CHAPTER 11 TEST, Form D

A friend of your family owns a company that sells software. The marketing manager of the company would like to have an animation appear as the company's "signature" whenever a customer starts up one of their programs. The figures at the right show eight stages of a proposed animation.

In the first stage of this animation, a simple triangle appears. In each stage thereafter, a new triangle is added by transforming the most recent triangle from the stage before. You have to been asked to help write the matrix multiplications that will achieve this effect.

a. Draw a set of coordinate axes. On the axes, draw a triangle that would be suitable for the figure in stage 1. Write a matrix for your triangle.

b. Explain how the new triangle in stage 2 could be the image of the triangle in stage 1 after:

   i. a single transformation.

   ii. a composite of two transformations.

c. Write a matrix for each transformation you described in part **b**. Then show how to use that matrix to find the image triangle in stage 2.

d. Identify a transformation or composite of transformations that will transform the most recent triangle from stage 2 into the new triangle in stage 3. Write a matrix for the transformation or composite. Show how to use that matrix to find the new triangle in stage 3.

e. Repeat part **d** to proceed from stage 3 to stage 4, from stage 4 to stage 5, and so on to stage 8.

f. What single matrix represents the composite of all the transformations used in proceeding from stage 1 to stage 8?

g. Other people in the company have seen the proposed animation, and they like the basic concept. That is, they approve of the idea of a geometric figure progressively filling all the space around one point. However, they would like to see other possible designs.

   Create a second animation that might be proposed to them. You may work with one of the figures below, or you may design an entirely original figure. Draw all the stages of your animation and show the matrix multiplications that allow you to proceed through all the stages.

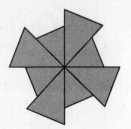

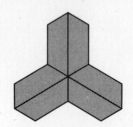

1

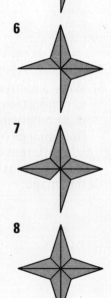

2

3

4

5

6

7

8

Functions, Statistics, and Trigonometry © Scott Foresman Addison Wesley

CHAPTER 11 TEST, Cumulative Form

1. Find the exact value of cos 285°.

1. _____

2. Find $\begin{bmatrix} 4 & 7 \\ 2 & 3 \end{bmatrix}^{-1}$.

2. _____

3. *True or false.* A data set can have a line of best fit with a positive slope but a negative correlation coefficient. Explain your answer.

_____

_____

4. Write the 2 × 2 matrix for a reflection over the *y*-axis.

4. _____

5. The weights of a certain type of apple are normally distributed with a mean of 4 oz and a standard deviation of 1 oz. Find the probability that a randomly chosen apple weighs more than 5.5 oz.

5. _____

6. Determine whether the infinite series $9 + 3 + 1 + \frac{1}{3} + \cdots$ converges. If it does converge, state the value of the limit.

6. _____

7. Show that $\begin{bmatrix} 3 & 4 \\ 9 & 12 \end{bmatrix}$ does not have an inverse.

7. _____

8. Four building contractors with different specialties contributed to three different construction projects. The matrix below represents the percentages of the total construction expenses for each project that were contributed by each firm. If each company receives a share of the proceeds from each project according to the percent of the construction expenses it contributed, and the proceeds from projects 1, 2, and 3 were $21 million, $30 million, and $18 million, respectively, what total proceeds did each firm receive? Express your answer in matrix form.

$$\begin{array}{c} \\ \text{Firm 1} \\ \text{Firm 2} \\ \text{Firm 3} \\ \text{Firm 4} \end{array} \begin{array}{ccc} \text{proj 1} & \text{proj 2} & \text{proj 3} \\ \begin{bmatrix} .33 & .20 & .10 \\ .10 & .40 & .30 \\ .20 & .35 & .40 \\ .37 & .05 & .20 \end{bmatrix} \end{array}$$

8. _____

Functions, Statistics, and Trigonometry © Scott Foresman Addison Wesley

Name _____

► **CHAPTER 11 TEST,** **Cumulative Form** *page 2*

9. A manufacturer molds plastic pieces for use in various products. Each time the machine molds a piece there is a .1 chance that the piece will be defective. If 300 pieces are molded in one day, determine the mean and variance of the distribution of the number of defective pieces in the output for that day.

9. _____

_____

10. Write the matrix representation of R_{21} with each element given to the nearest ten-thousandth.

10. _____

In 11 and 12, the matrix $\begin{bmatrix} 4 & 2 & 0 \\ 1 & -5 & 4 \end{bmatrix}$ represents the triangle *ABC*. Use the same grid for both questions.

11. Graph $\triangle ABC$.

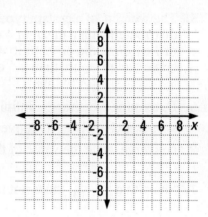

12. If the transformation $\begin{bmatrix} 2 & -.5 \\ .5 & 2 \end{bmatrix}$ is applied to $\triangle ABC$, what is the matrix of the image $\triangle A'B'C'$? Graph $\triangle A'B'C'$.

12. _____

13. What is the remainder when $x^7 + 4x^4 - 5x$ is divided by $x + 1$?

13. _____

14. *True or false.* The graph of every normal distribution is symmetric with respect to the mean of the distribution.

14. _____

156 ►

Functions, Statistics, and Trigonometry © Scott Foresman Addison Wesley

15. *Multiple choice.* Which of the following is true of matrix multiplication?

    (a) It is both commutative and associative.
    (b) It is commutative but not associative.
    (c) It is associative but not commutative.
    (d) It is neither associative nor commutative.

15. _____

16. Solve $2^x = 45$ to the nearest thousandth.

16. _____

17. Let z be a continuous random variable with a standard normal distribution. Estimate each probability.

    a. $P(|z| > 1)$

17. a. _____

    b. $P(|z| = 1)$

      b. _____

18. Find the exact matrix representing the composite transformation $r_x \circ r_{45}$.

18. _____

19. Ben received an 80 on a German test, for which the mean was 75 and the standard deviation was 4. On an English test with a mean of 80 and a standard deviation of 5, he received an 84.

    a. Find the z-scores corresponding to Ben's two test scores.

19. a. _____

    b. In which test was his percentile ranking higher?

      b. _____

20. A quality control inspector takes a sample of 30 two-liter bottles filled by a machine at a bottling plant and measures the volume of liquid in each bottle. The mean volume for the sample is 1995.4 mL and the standard deviation is 10 mL. Assuming the standard deviation for the sample is the same as that for the entire population, find the 95% confidence interval for the mean volume of the population.

20. _____

Check all your work carefully.

Functions, Statistics, and Trigonometry © Scott Foresman Addison Wesley

Name _____

QUIZ

1. **a.** Sketch a graph of the ellipse with equation
   $\frac{(x + 3)^2}{9} + \frac{(y - 6)^2}{16} = 1$.

   b. What are the coordinates of its foci?

   _____

1. a.

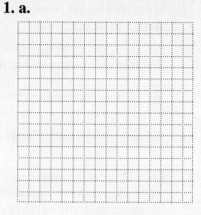

2. **a.** Sketch a graph of the hyperbola with equation
   $x^2 - \frac{y^2}{4} = 4$.

   b. What are the equation(s) of its asymptotes?

   _____

2. a.

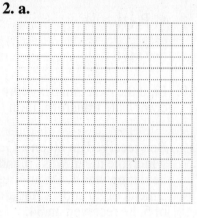

3. An ellipse has its major axis along the line $y = x$ and its
   minor axis along the line $y = \text{-}x$. If the point $(3, \text{-}5)$
   is on this ellipse, name three other points on the ellipse.

   3. _____

4. The comet Kohoutek has an elliptical orbit with the sun as one focus.
   The orbit has a major axis of 6.8 a.u. (astronomical units) and a minor axis
   of 5.7 a.u. Find the orbit's perihelion distance (closet distance to the sun)
   and aphelion distance (farthest distance from the sun).

   _____

   _____

5. A hyperbola has foci at $(7, 6)$ and $(5, \text{-}2)$ and focal constant 8.
   Is the point $(10, 10)$ on the hyperbola? Justify your answer.

   _____

   _____

Functions, Statistics, and Trigonometry © Scott Foresman Addison Wesley

CHAPTER 12 TEST, Form A

1. Draw an ellipse for which the distance between the foci is 6 and the focal constant is 10.

1. a.
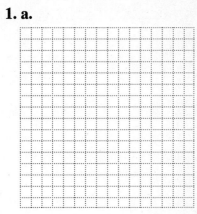

2. Find an equation for the hyperbola with foci $(4, 0)$ and $(-4, 0)$ and focal constant 6.

2. _____

In 3–5, a quadratic relation is given. a. Graph the equation. b. Give the coordinates for the foci of the curve.

3. $\dfrac{x^2}{9} + \dfrac{y^2}{4} = 1$

b. _____

3. a.
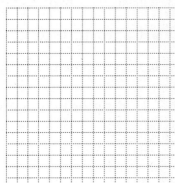

4. $\dfrac{y^2}{16} - \dfrac{x^2}{9} = 1$

b. _____

4. a.
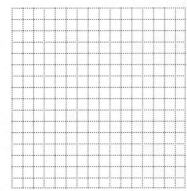

5. Find an equation for the image of $y = x^2 - 2x + 5$ under $R_{\pi/6}$ about the origin.

_____

6. $\frac{(x-1)^2}{25} + \frac{(y+2)^2}{16} = 1$

   b. _____

1. a.

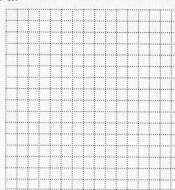

7. What type of geometric figure is a degenerate ellipse? Describe how it is formed from the intersection of a cone and a plane.

   _____

   _____

8. Consider the hyperbola $\frac{x^2}{25} - \frac{y^2}{64} = -1$.

   a. Find equations for its asymptotes.   **8. a.** _____

   b. Find equations for its symmetry lines.   **b.** _____

In 9–11, describe the graph of the relation represented by the given equation.

9. $3x^2 - 2xy + y^2 + 4x - 2y + 5 = 0$ **9.** _____

10. $x^2 - 7xy - 2y^2 - 3x + 5y + 4 = 0$ **10.** _____

11. $x^2 - 4xy + 4y^2 - 8x - 16y - 5 = 0$ **11.** _____

12. *True or false.* The graph of $\frac{x^2}{4} - \frac{y^2}{4} = 1$ is a rectangular hyperbola. Justify your answer.

   _____

13. Rewrite $\frac{(x-3)^2}{2} - \frac{(y+1)^2}{3} = 1$ in the general   **13.** _____
   form of a quadratic relation in two variables.

14. The comet Hale-Bopp travels in an elliptical orbit with   **14.** _____
   the sun at one focus. Given that the orbit's closest
   distance to the center of the sun is 85 million miles
   and its farthest distance is 23.25 billion miles, what
   is the distance from the sun to the orbit's second focus?

Check all your work carefully.

Functions, Statistics, and Trigonometry © Scott Foresman Addison Wesley

CHAPTER 12 TEST, Form B

1. Draw an ellipse for which the distance between the foci is 24 and the focal constant is 26.

1. a.

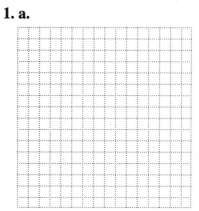

2. Find an equation for the hyperbola with foci (6, 0) and (-6, 0) and focal constant 10.

2. _____

In 35, a quadratic relation is given. a. Graph the equation. b. Give the coordinates for the foci of the curve.

3. $\frac{x^2}{25} - \frac{y^2}{9} = 1$

3. a.

b. _____

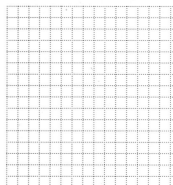

4. $\frac{x^2}{64} + \frac{y^2}{144} = 1$

4. a.

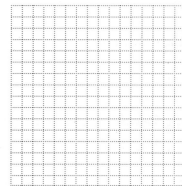

b. _____

5. Find an equation for the image of $y = x^2 - 6x + 2$ under $R_{\pi/4}$ about the origin.

_____

6. $\dfrac{(x + 1)^2}{16} + \dfrac{(y - 2)^2}{4} = 1$

5. a.

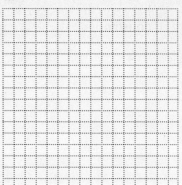

b. _____

7. What type of geometric figure is a degenerate hyperbola?
   Describe how it is formed from the intersection of a cone and a plane.

   _____

   _____

8. Consider the hyperbola $\dfrac{(x - 7)^2}{49} - \dfrac{(y - 6)^2}{144} = 1$.

   a. Find equations for its asymptotes.   **8. a.** _____

   b. Find equations for its symmetry lines.   **b.** _____

In 9–11, describe the graph of the relation represented by the given equation.

9. $x^2 + 2xy + y^2 - 2x - 2y - 5 = 0$ **9.** _____

10. $2x^2 - 3xy + 4y^2 + x + y - 15 = 0$ **10.** _____

11. $x^2 - 5xy - 3y^2 + 2x - y - 1 = 0$ **11.** _____

12. *True or false.* The graph of $\dfrac{x^2}{4} - y^2 = 1$ is a rectangular hyperbola. Justify your answer.

   _____

13. Rewrite $\dfrac{(x + 2)^2}{5} - \dfrac{(y - 1)^2}{2} = 1$ in the general   **13.** _____
    form of a quadratic relation in two variables.

14. The comet Encke travels in an elliptical orbit with   **14.** _____
    the sun at one focus. Given that the major axis of
    the orbit is 4.42 a.u. and the minor axis is 2.35 a.u.,
    what is the closest distance the comet gets to the sun?

Check all your work carefully.

Functions, Statistics, and Trigonometry © Scott Foresman Addison Wesley

CHAPTER 12 TEST, Form C

1. State as many facts as you can about the ellipse that is graphed at the right.

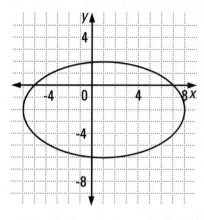

2. How are the graphs of the following equations alike? different? State as many likenesses and differences as you can.

   i. $\dfrac{x^2}{100} - \dfrac{y^2}{81} = 1$ **ii.** $\dfrac{y^2}{100} - \dfrac{x^2}{81} = 1$

3. The figure at the right is a cone of two nappes. The dashed line is its axis. Explain the importance of the angle measure k in determining the conic sections.

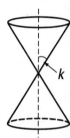

4. Write an equation in standard form for an ellipse whose center is the origin. Then rewrite it in the general form of a quadratic relation in two variables. Last find an equation for its image under a rotation of 45° about the origin and graph the image on the axes at the right.

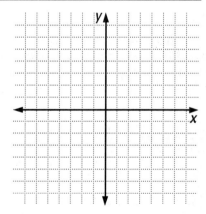

Functions, Statistics, and Trigonometry © Scott Foresman Addison Wesley

CHAPTER 12 TEST, Form D

The Conic Cereal Company is planning to produce a new cereal, which will be packaged in cylindrical canisters. To promote the cereal, the company is holding a contest for the best design of a label for the canister. When you enter the contest, your receive the sketch at the right. It gives the size of the canister and shows three ellipses that must be part of the design, two in the front and one in the back.

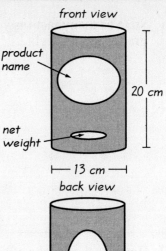

front view

product name

net weight

20 cm

13 cm

back view

ingredients list

a. Consider the *product name* ellipse in the sketch at the right. What do you think should be the length of its major axis? of its minor axis? Choose measures that are whole numbers of centimeters.

b. On the grid below, sketch a graph of the *product name* ellipse as you specified in part **a.** Use the origin of the axes as the center of the ellipse. Let one grid unit represent one centimeter.

c. Refer to your ellipse from part **b.**

   i. What is its focal constant?   **ii.** What are its foci?

   iii. Give an equation for the ellipse in standard form.

   vi. Give an equation for the ellipse in the general form of a quadratic relation in two variables.

d. Suppose the grid below represents the label. Explain why it is not correct for the center of the *product name* ellipse to be the origin.

e. Choose a more appropriate point as the center of the *product name* ellipse and sketch it in this new location. Then repeat steps **i** to **iv** of part **c** for the new ellipse.

f. Select appropriate sizes and locations for the *net weight* and *ingredients list* ellipses. Give equations for each ellipse both in standard form and in the general form of a quadratic relation in two variables.

g. Create an original label design to enter in the contest. You may add other shapes to the three required ellipses, provided that each additional shape is a conic section or part of one. Submit your design on grid paper and provide equations for all the shapes you suggest.

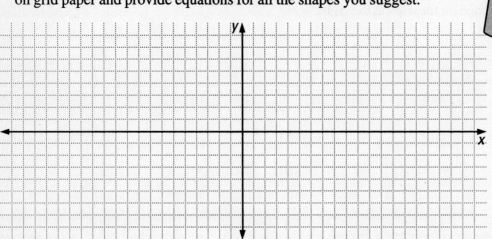

Name _____

CHAPTER 12 TEST, Cumulative Form

1. Determine the coordinates of the foci of
   the hyperbola $\frac{x^2}{5} - \frac{y^2}{2} = 1$.

   1. _____

2. Draw a graph of the ellipse with foci
   at (0, 5) and (0, -1), and focal
   constant 10.

   2. a.

   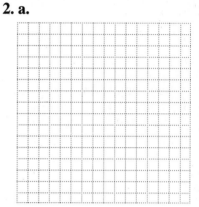

3. Rewrite the expression $\cos \frac{\pi}{11} \sin \frac{\pi}{12} + \sin \frac{\pi}{11} \cos \frac{\pi}{12}$
   as the sine of a single argument.

   3. _____

4. Give an equation for the image of the
   hyperbola $xy = -8$ under $R_{-\pi/4}$.

   4. _____

5. Assume that the ratio of the births of boys
   to girls is 51:49. What is the probability that
   a family with 4 children has at least 2 boys?

   5. _____

6. Give an equation for the hyperbola with
   foci (0, 5) and (0, -5) and focal constant 8.

   6. _____

7. Given $\ln a = 0.2030$, $\ln b = 1.5628$, and
   $\ln c = -2.103$, evaluate $\ln \frac{a^2 b}{c}$.

   7. _____

8. Below is a matrix of currency exchange rates for July 29, 1997.

	U.S. (dollars)	France (Franc)	Spain (Peseta)
1 U.S. Dollar =	1	6.2185	155.550
1 French Franc =	0.1608	1	25.0080
1 Spanish Peseta =	0.006429	0.03999	1

Suppose you were traveling through Spain, and France, and you had with you in cash 152 U.S. dollars, 520 French francs, and 1830 Spanish pesetas. Write a matrix equation giving the total value of your cash in each of the four different currencies.

9. If $f(x) = \sin x$ and $g(x) = \dfrac{1}{\sqrt{1-x}}$, give an expression for $g(f(x))$ and describe the domain of $g \circ f$.

10. *Multiple choice.* Which figure cannot result from the intersection of a plane and one nappe of a cone?
    (a) circle　　　　(b) point
    (c) hyperbola　　(d) parabola

    10. _____

11. What kind of conic section is the graph of the quadratic relation

    $3x^2 + 4xy + 2y^2 - 5x + y + 3 = 0$?

    11. _____

12. Determine equations for the asymptotes of the hyperbola $\dfrac{(y-2)^2}{25} - \dfrac{(x+1)^2}{16} = 1$.

    12. _____

13. Use an automatic grapher to estimate the smallest real zero of $f(x) = x^5 - 5x^3 + 4x^2 + 3x - 8$ to the nearest tenth.

    13. _____

Functions, Statistics, and Trigonometry © Scott Foresman Addison Wesley

14. Given $\sin A = \frac{3}{5}$, $\cos B = \frac{5}{13}$, find $\sin 2A$.

14. _____

15. Rewrite $\dfrac{(x-2)^2}{4} + \dfrac{(y-\frac{3}{2})^2}{3} = 1$ in the general form of a quadratic relation in two variables.

15. _____

16. Consider the following system of equations.

$$\begin{cases} 3x - y = 2 \\ x + 4y = 18 \end{cases}$$

a. Represent the system by a matrix equation.

16. a. _____

b. Find the solution to the system.

b. _____

Check all your work carefully.

1. Fill in the table at the right with exact values, whenever they are defined. Write undefined if there is no value.

θ	sec θ	csc θ	cot θ
630°	_____	_____	_____
$\frac{5\pi}{4}$	_____	_____	_____
-420°	_____	_____	_____

2. Identify the domain and range of the function with equation $y = \csc x$.

2. _____

_____

3. *Multiple choice.* Which equation is graphed at the right?

   (a) $f(x) = 2 \sec \left(\frac{x - \pi}{2}\right)$

   (b) $g(x) = 2 \csc \left(2x - \frac{\pi}{2}\right)$

   (c) $h(x) = 2 \sec \left(2x + \frac{\pi}{2}\right)$

   (d) $k(x) = 2 \sec \left(2x - \frac{\pi}{2}\right)$

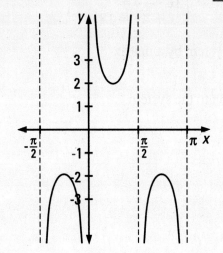

3. _____

4. **a.** *Multiple choice.* Use an automatic grapher to decide which expression could possibly complete $(\csc^2\theta + \sec^2\theta)\sin 2\theta = \underline{\ ?\ }$ to make it an identity.

4. a. _____

   (a) $\sec 2\theta$ (b) $4 \csc 2\theta$ (c) $\sec^2\theta - \csc^2\theta$

   b. Prove that your equation from part **a** is an identity.

   c. State any restrictions on the identity from part **a**.

_____

Functions, Statistics, and Trigonometry © Scott Foresman Addison Wesley

Name _____

QUIZ

In 1 and 2, plot each point on the polar grid at the right. Be sure to label each point with the appropriate letter.

1., 2.

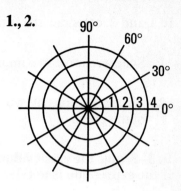

1. $P = \left[-2, \frac{\pi}{6}\right]$

2. $Q = [3, 630°]$

In 3 and 4, find the rectangular coordinates of each point.

3. $[4, 225°]$

3. _____

4. $\left[-\sqrt{3}, \frac{\pi}{3}\right]$

4. _____

5. Find two different pairs of polar coordinates for the point $(-1, -\sqrt{3})$.

5. _____

6. Given that the point $[a, \alpha]$ lies on the graph of the polar equation $r = \sin 3\theta$, prove that the point $\left[-a, \alpha + \frac{\pi}{3}\right]$ lies on the same graph.

_____

_____

7. *Multiple choice.* Which polar equation is graphed at the right?

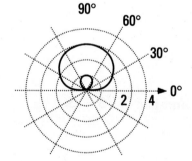

(a) $r = 2 \sin \theta - 2$

(b) $r = 2 \sin \theta - 1$

(c) $r = 2 \cos \theta - 2$

(d) $r = 2 \cos \theta - 1$

7. _____

8. Fill in the blanks in the following table.

$a + bi$ form	trigonometric form	polar form
$2 - 2\sqrt{3}\,i$		
	$6(\cos 225° + i \sin 225°)$	
		$\left[10, \frac{5\pi}{6}\right]$

CHAPTER 13 TEST, Form A

In 1 and 2, consider the function f with $f(x) = \csc x$.

1. State a relative maximum of f.

   1. _____

2. Write equations of two asymptotes of the graph of f.

   2. _____

In 3–5, give the exact value for the expression. If the expression is not defined, write "undefined."

3. $\csc(-540°)$

   3. _____

4. $\cot\left(\frac{2\pi}{3}\right)$

   4. _____

5. $\sec\left(-\frac{\pi}{4}\right)$

   5. _____

6. **a.** Determine the singularities of the function g with $g(x) = \frac{x-2}{\ln(x-1)}$.

   6. a. _____

   b. Are the singularities found in part **a** removable or nonremovable?

   b. _____

7. Compute the rectangular coordinates of $\left[\sqrt{2}, -\frac{\pi}{4}\right]$.

   7. _____

8. *Multiple choice.* Which polar coordinates represent the same point as $\left[-3, \frac{3\pi}{5}\right]$?

   8. _____

   (a) $\left[3, -\frac{4\pi}{5}\right]$ (b) $\left[3, -\frac{6\pi}{5}\right]$

   (c) $\left[3, -\frac{\pi}{5}\right]$ (d) $\left[3, -\frac{14\pi}{5}\right]$

In 9 and 10, write the complex number $-3\sqrt{3} + 3i$ in the given form.

9. polar coordinate form

   9. _____

10. trigonometric form

    10. _____

Functions, Statistics, and Trigonometry © Scott Foresman Addison Wesley

11. Find polar coordinates for three different points that lie on the graph of the equation $r = 2 \cos 8\theta$.

11. _____

12. Let $U = -1 + 2i$, $V = 3 - i$, and $M = 0$.

   a. Calculate $U + V$.

12. a. _____

   b. Plot M, U, V, and $U + V$ on the complex plane.

   b. _____

   c. Prove that M, U, V, and $U + V$ are the vertices of a parallelogram.

_____

_____

_____

_____

_____

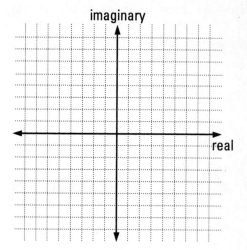

13. Graph the equation $r = 4 \sin\left(\frac{\theta}{2}\right)$ in the polar coordinate system over the domain $0 \le \theta \le 2\pi$.

13.

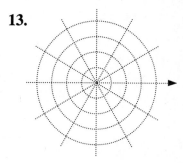

In 14 and 15, let $z_1 = 2(\cos 54° + i \sin 54°)$ and $z_2 = 5(\cos 100° + i \sin 100°)$
Express each answer in trigonometric form.

14. $z_1 z_2$

14. _____

15. $\frac{z_1}{z_2}$

15. _____

16. Express the complex number $(\sqrt{3} - i)^5$ in trigonometric form.

16. _____

17. Find the 4 fourth roots of
$81\left(\cos\frac{2\pi}{5} + i\sin\frac{2\pi}{5}\right)$.

17. _____

_____

_____

_____

18. a. *Multiple choice.* Use an automatic grapher to decide which expression could possibly complete the equation $\cot\theta + \tan\theta = \underline{\quad?\quad}$ to make it an identity.

18. a. _____

    (a) $(\cot\theta + \tan\theta)^2$

    (b) $\cot^2\theta + \tan^2\theta$

    (c) $2\csc 2\theta$

b. Prove that your equation from part **a** is an identity.

c. State any restrictions on the identity found in part **a**.

_____

Check all your work carefully.

Functions, Statistics, and Trigonometry © Scott Foresman Addison Wesley

CHAPTER 13 TEST, Form B

In 1 and 2, consider the function f with $f(x) = \sec x$.

1. What is the period of f?

1. _____

2. Write equations of two asymptotes of the graph of f.

2. _____

In 3–5, give the exact value for the expression. If the expression is not defined, write "undefined."

3. $\sec\left(\frac{\pi}{3}\right)$

3. _____

4. $\csc\left(\frac{5\pi}{4}\right)$

4. _____

5. $\cot(-1080°)$

5. _____

6. **a.** Determine the singularities of the function h with $h(t) = \dfrac{t + 3}{t^2 + t - 6}$.

6. a. _____

   b. Are the singularities found in part **a** removable or nonremovable?

   b. _____

7. Compute the rectangular coordinates of $\left[\sqrt{3}, -\frac{\pi}{6}\right]$.

7. _____

8. *Multiple choice.* Which polar coordinates represent the same point as $\left[7, -\frac{2\pi}{5}\right]$?

8. _____

   (a) $\left[-7, \frac{3\pi}{5}\right]$ (b) $\left[-7, \frac{2\pi}{5}\right]$

   (c) $\left[7, -\frac{13\pi}{5}\right]$ (c) $\left[7, \frac{13\pi}{5}\right]$

In 9 and 10, write the complex number $2 - 2\sqrt{3}i$ in the given form.

9. polar coordinate form

9. _____

10. trigonometric form

10. _____

11. Find polar coordinates for three different points that lie on the graph of the equation $r = 2 \sin 8\theta$.

11. _____

12. Let $U = 2 - i$, $V = -3 - i$, and $M = 0$.

   a. Calculate $U + V$.

12. a. _____

   b. Plot M, U, V, and $U + V$ on the complex plane.

   b.

   c. Prove that M, U, V, and $U + V$ are the vertices of a parallelogram.

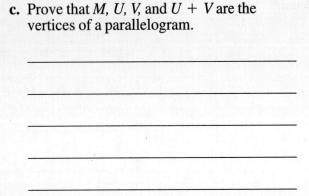

_____

_____

_____

_____

_____

13. Graph the equation $r = 4 \cos\left(\frac{\theta}{2}\right)$ in the polar coordinate system over the domain $0 \le \theta \le 2\pi$.

13.

In 14 and 15, let $z_1 = 4(\cos 76° + i \sin 76°)$ and $z_2 = 10(\cos 110° + i \sin 110°)$. **Express each answer in trigonometric form.**

14. $z_1 z_2$

14. _____

15. $\frac{z_1}{z_2}$

15. _____

16. Express the complex number $(-1 + \sqrt{3}i)^5$ in trigonometric form.

16. _____

Functions, Statistics, and Trigonometry © Scott Foresman Addison Wesley

17. Find the 4 fourth roots of
    $256\left(\cos\frac{2\pi}{7} + i\sin\frac{2\pi}{7}\right).$

17. _____

   _____

   _____

   _____

18. **a.** *Multiple choice.* Use an automatic grapher
    to decide which expression could possibly
    complete the equation $\csc^2\theta + \sec^2\theta = \underline{\quad?\quad}$
    to make it an identity.

18. **a.** _____

   (a) $(\cot\theta - \tan\theta)^2$

   (b) $\cot^2\theta - \tan^2\theta$

   (c) $\csc^2\theta \sec^2\theta$

   b. Prove that your equation from part **a** is an identity.

   c. State any restrictions on the identity found in part **a**.

   _____

Check all your work carefully.

CHAPTER 13 TEST, Form C

1. Write a question about $\triangle ABC$ that you can answer using one of the reciprocal trigonometric functions. Show how to use that function to answer the question.

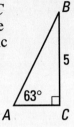

2. State two trigonometric identities that involve the cotangent function. Explain how to use an automatic grapher to test the identities. Then prove each identity, taking care to state any restrictions on its domain.

3. The circle graphed on the polar coordinate system at the right is symmetric with respect to the polar axis. Give a polar equation for the circle. Now choose a point of the circle *that does not lie on the axis.* Give polar coordinates and rectangular coordinates for this point.

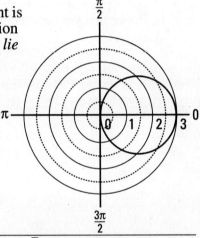

4. State as many facts as you can about the complex number $-5 + 2i$. Be sure to include information about its geometric representation(s) and about different forms.

5. Let $z = \frac{1}{2} + \frac{\sqrt{3}}{2} i$. Identify a computation involving z that can be performed using DeMoivre's Theorem. Explain why the theorem makes the computation easier than it might otherwise be. Then perform the computation. Show all your work.

Functions, Statistics, and Trigonometry © Scott Foresman Addison Wesley

CHAPTER 13 TEST, Form D

A friend who has not studied polar coordinates noticed the graphs of polar equations in your textbook and was intrigued by them. Since your friend knows rectangular coordinates, a natural question was how the polar coordinate system compares to the rectangular coordinate system. As a means of explaining, consider these two coordinate systems.

A.

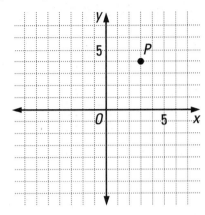

B.

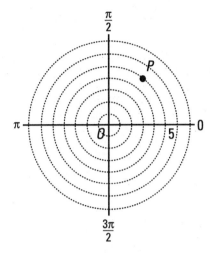

a. Compare grid A and grid B for your friend.
  i. What similarities are there? List as many as you can.
  ii. What differences are there? Again, list as many as you can.

b. Now compare the graphs of some simple equations.
  i. In the rectangular coordinate system, what type of figure is the graph of $x = 1$? of $y = 1$?
  ii. In the polar coordinate system, what type of figure is the graph of $r = 1$? of $\theta = 1$?

c. Consider a graph that is a circle.
  i. In the rectangular coordinate system, what type of equation is associated with it?
  ii. In the polar coordinate system, what type of equation is associated with it?

d. What other common types of graphs have you studied:
  i. in the rectangular coordinate system?
  ii. in the polar coordinate system?

e. Suppose that most students in your school have not yet studied the polar coordinate system. Write an article titled *Coordinates – Not just for Squares!* for your school newspaper. The purpose of the article is to inform these students about the polar coordinate system. You know that most of them have studied the rectangular coordinate system, so the article should focus on a comparison of the two systems, perhaps pointing out what you see as some advantages and disadvantages of each. Be sure that your article includes at least one graph of a polar equation.

CHAPTER 13 TEST, Cumulative Form

In 1 and 2, consider the equation $\dfrac{\csc x \sec x}{\cot x - \tan x} = \sec 2x$.

1. Prove that the equation is an identity.

2. State any restrictions on the identity.

2. _____

3. Consider the hyperbola with the equation $25x^2 - 4y^2 = 100$. Find each of the following.

   a. the coordinates of its vertices

3. a. _____

   b. the coordinates of its foci

     b. _____

   c. equations for its asymptotes

     c. _____

4. Convert $\left[4, \frac{3\pi}{4}\right]$ from polar to rectangular coordinates.

4. _____

5. Convert $\left(-\sqrt{3}, -1\right)$ from rectangular to polar coordinates.

5. _____

6. Consider a bacteria population which doubles in size every 6.5 hr. If the population at time $t = 0$ hr is 300 bacteria, how many are there at time $t = 96$ hr?

6. _____

7. Construct a graph of the equation $r = 2\cos\theta$ in the polar coordinate system.

7.

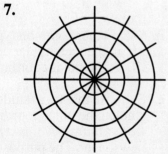

8. Give an equation of the image of the parabola $y = x^2 + 2$ after it is rotated by $\frac{\pi}{2}$ around the origin.

8. _____

Functions, Statistics, and Trigonometry © Scott Foresman Addison Wesley

9. Given that $z_1 = 9(\cos 230° + i \sin 230°)$ and $z_2 = 3(\cos 170° + i \sin 170°)$, express $\frac{z_1}{z_2}$ in both trigonometric and $a + bi$ forms.

9. _____

10. **a.** If a fair coin is tossed 16 times, what is the expected number of heads?

10. **a.** _____

b. What is the probability of getting exactly the expected number of heads?

b. _____

11. Find all solutions to the equation $x^3 = -27$.

11. _____

12. Draw a graph of the ellipse with equation $9(x + 1)^2 + 25(y - 2)^2 = 225$. Label the endpoints of the major and minor axes with their coordinates.

12.

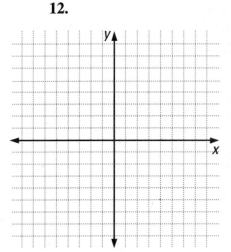

13. A 24-foot ladder is placed against a building so that it forms an angle θ with the ground. Given that the ground is perfectly flat and that $\sec θ = 3$, find each of the following, to the nearest tenth of a foot.

a. the distance from the bottom of the ladder to the building

13. **a.** _____

b. the height of the top of the ladder above the ground

b. _____

14. Given that $f(x) = \sec x$, $g(x) = \frac{x^2 - 1}{x^2}$, and $h = g \circ f$, find and simplify $h(x)$.

14. _____

15. *Multiple choice.* Which is the matrix product $\begin{bmatrix} \cos A & -\sin A \\ \sin A & \cos A \end{bmatrix} \cdot \begin{bmatrix} \cos B & \sin B \\ \sin B & -\cos B \end{bmatrix}$?

(a) $\begin{bmatrix} \cos (A - B) & \sin (A + B) \\ \sin (A + B) & -\cos (A - B) \end{bmatrix}$

(b) $\begin{bmatrix} \cos (A + B) & \sin (A + B) \\ \sin (A + B) & -\cos (A + B) \end{bmatrix}$

(c) $\begin{bmatrix} \sin (A + B) & \cos (A + B) \\ \cos (A + B) & -\sin (A + B) \end{bmatrix}$

(d) $\begin{bmatrix} \sin (A - B) & \cos (A + B) \\ \cos (A + B) & -\sin (B - A) \end{bmatrix}$

15. _____

16. State the domain and range of the function f with
$f(x) = 2 \sec \left(x - \frac{\pi}{2} \right)$.

16. _____

_____

17. An ice cream parlor serves 31 different flavors. If Gina decides she wants a cup with 3 different flavors topped with either sprinkles, nuts, or chocolate sauce, how many possible combinations does she have to choose from?

17. _____

18. The distribution of students among the four classes of a high school is given in the following table.

18. _____

Class	Freshman	Sophomore	Junior	Senior
No. Students	550	450	350	300

Suppose that you are to present the data in a circle graph. What should be the central angle of the sector corresponding to the Freshman class? Give your answer in radians.

In 19 and 20, decide whether the equation represents a parabola, ellipse, hyperbola, degenerate parabola, degenerate ellipse, or degenerate hyperbola.

19. $x^2 - 4x + y^2 - 6y + 13 = 0$

19. _____

20. $4x^2 - 9y^2 = 0$

20. _____

Check all your work carefully.

COMPREHENSIVE TEST, CHAPTERS 1-13

1. What type of function best models periodic motion?

    (a) linear   (b) circular

    (c) exponential   (d) power

1. _____

2. Refer to the bar chart at the right, which shows the number of students in each grade at a high school. If the data are to be displayed in a pie chart, what should be the measure of the central angle of the sector for the 12th grade?

    (a) 94°   (b) 80°

    (c) 45°   (d) 120°

2. _____

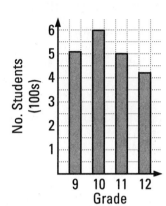

In 3–5, refer to the stem plot at the right, which lists the daily wages w_i (in dollars) of the employees of a small company.

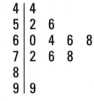

```
4 | 4
5 | 2  6
6 | 0  4  6  8
7 | 2  6  8
8 |
9 | 9
```

3. Which expression represents the mean *weekly* wage, if the employees work 5 days a week?

    (a) $11\sum_{i=1}^{5} w_i$ (b) $5\sum_{i=1}^{11} w_i$

    (c) $\frac{11}{5}\sum_{i=1}^{5} w_i$ (d) $\frac{5}{11}\sum_{i=1}^{11} w_i$

3. _____

4. What is the five-number summary for the daily wages?

    (a) 34, 52, 60, 72, 99   (b) 44, 56, 66, 76, 99

    (c) 44, 56, 68, 78, 99   (d) 34, 56, 99, 68, 78

4. _____

5. What is the standard deviation of the daily wages?

    (a) $1.51   (b) $80.21   (c) $14.78   (d) $101.54

5. _____

6. Which of the following is a possible equation for a line of fit for the data shown in the scatterplot at the right?

    (a) $y = 90$ (b) $y = 0.25x + 105$

    (c) $x = 60$ (d) $y = -0.25x + 105$

6. _____

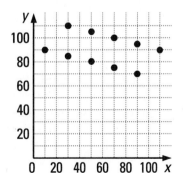

7. Suppose a ball is thrown vertically from the top of an 80-ft high building. How much longer would it take for the ball to hit the ground if it were thrown upward with an initial speed of 64 ft/sec than if it were thrown downward with the same speed? Recall that Newton's equation for height as a function of time is

   $h = -\frac{1}{2} gt^2 + vt + h_0$, where $g = 32\text{ft/sec}^2$, and that an upward velocity is positive and a downward velocity is negative.

   (a) 5 sec   (b) 1 sec   (c) 6 sec   (d) 4 sec

   7. _____

8. A truck rental agency's charges for a certain type of truck are $30 for up to four hours and $20 for each additional four-hour period or part thereof. Which of the following equations represents the cost c in dollars of renting a truck for h hours, where $h > 0$?

   (a) $c = 30 + 20\lceil \frac{h}{4} \rceil$ (b) $c = 30 + 20\lfloor \frac{h-4}{4} \rfloor$

   (c) $c = 30 + 20\lceil \frac{h-4}{4} \rceil$ (d) $c = 30 + 20\lceil 4h \rceil$

   8. _____

9. Suppose $y = f(x)$. If S maps each point (x, y) in the plane to $(2x, 5y)$, what is the equation for the image of the graph of $y = f(x)$?

   (a) $\frac{y}{5} = f(\frac{x}{2})$ (b) $5y = f(\frac{x}{2})$

   (c) $y = 2f(5x)$ (d) $y = 5f(2x)$

   9. _____

10. A savings account that earns 3.5% interest, compounded continuously, is opened with an initial deposit of $500. If no withdrawals or additional deposits are made, which of the following equations gives the balance B in the account n years after it was opened?

    (a) $B = (500e^{.035})^n$ (b) $B = 500e^{.035n}$

    (c) $B = 500e^{1.035n}$ (d) $B = (500e^{1.035})^n$

    10. _____

11. If $f(x) = \tan x + \cot x$ and $g(x) = \frac{2}{x}$, what is $(g \circ f)(\frac{\pi}{4})$?

    (a) $\frac{1}{2}$ (b) 2   (c) $\sqrt{2}$ (d) 1

    11. _____

12. If each element d_i of a data set is tripled and then increased by 5, so that $d_i \to 3d_i + 5$, what is the ratio of the variance of the new data set to that of the old data set?

    (a) 3 : 1   (b) 15 : 1   (c) 9 : 1   (d) 5 : 1

    12. _____

Functions, Statistics, and Trigonometry © Scott Foresman Addison Wesley

13. Which of the following equations is *not* an identity?　　　13. _____

    (a) $\cos(\theta + \pi) = -\sin\left(\frac{\pi}{2} - \theta\right)$

    (b) $\sin(\pi + \theta) = \sin(\pi - \theta)$

    (c) $\cos(2\pi + \theta) = \cos\theta$

    (d) $\tan(-\theta) = -\tan\theta$

14. Which equation corresponds　　　　　　　　　　　　　　14. _____
    to the graph at the right?

    (a) $y = -1 + 2\cos 4x$

    (b) $y = 1 + 2\sin\left(4x - \frac{\pi}{2}\right)$

    (c) $y = 1 + 2\sin\left(4x + \frac{\pi}{2}\right)$

    (d) $y = 1 + 4\sin\left(2x + \frac{\pi}{4}\right)$

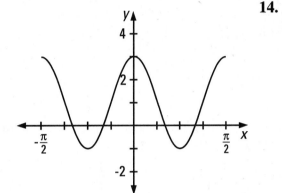

15. Which of the following functions of θ is decreasing　　　15. _____
    on the interval $\frac{3\pi}{2} < \theta < 2\pi$?

    (a) $f(\theta) = \sin\theta$　　　　　　(b) $g(\theta) = \cos\theta$

    (c) $h(\theta) = \sin\left(\theta - \frac{\pi}{2}\right)$　　　(d) $k(\theta) = \tan\theta$

16. What is the value of $\cos\left(\text{Arccos}\left(-\frac{1}{2}\right)\right)$?　　　16. _____

    (a) $\frac{1}{2}$　　　　　　　　　　　(b) $-\frac{1}{2}$

    (c) $-\frac{\sqrt{3}}{2}$　　　　　　　　　(d) $\frac{\sqrt{3}}{2}$

17. What is the set of *all* solutions of the equation $\sin^2 x = \frac{1}{2}$?　　　17. _____

    (a) $\{x : x = \frac{\pi}{4} + 2\pi n, \text{ for all integers } n\}$

    (b) $\{x : x = \frac{\pi}{4}n, \text{ for all integers } n\}$

    (c) $\{x : x = \frac{\pi}{4} + \pi n, \text{ for all integers } n\}$

    (d) $\{x : x = \frac{\pi}{4} + \frac{\pi}{2}n, \text{ for all integers } n\}$

18. In $\triangle ABC$, $b = 13$, m$\angle A = 35°$, and m$\angle B = 21°$.　　　18. _____
    Approximate the value of c.

    (a) 21　　　(b) 6　　　(c) 30　　　(d) 19

19. An 18 foot ladder is placed against a building so that its base is x feet from the wall. Find an expression for the angle θ that the ladder makes with the ground.

    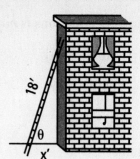

    19. _____

    (a) $\theta = \text{Arctan}\left(\sqrt{1 - \frac{324}{x^2}}\right)$

    (b) $\theta = \sin^{-1}\left(\sqrt{1 - \frac{x^2}{324}}\right)$

    (c) $\theta = \text{Arccos}\left(\frac{x}{\sqrt{324 + x^2}}\right)$

    (d) $\theta = \text{Arcsin}\left(\sqrt{\frac{324 - x^2}{324 + x^2}}\right)$

20. If $2\log_b x - \log_b y = \log_b z$, find an equation not involving logarithms that expresses z in terms of x and y.

    20. _____

    (a) $z = 2x - y$ (b) $2 = \frac{2x}{y}$ (c) $z = \frac{x^2}{y}$

    (d) Can't be determined without knowledge of the base b.

21. If $\log_b a = 7$ and $\log_b c = 3.5$, what is $\log_c a$?

    21. _____

    (a) 2   (b) 0.5   (c) 1   (d) 0.25

22. The functions f and g are defined for all nonnegative real values of x by the equations $f(x) = x^3$ and $g(x) = x^5$. For what values of x is $f(x) \geq g(x)$?

    22. _____

    (a) $0 \leq x \leq 1$ (b) $x \geq 1$

    (c) $x \leq 1$ (d) $0 < x < 1$

23. Recall that the volume V of a sphere of radius r is given by $V = \frac{4}{3}\pi r^3$. Which of the following numbers is closest to the radius in inches of a sphere with a volume of 4,000 in³?

    23. _____

    (a) 30   (b) 15   (c) 10   (d) 25

24. If you were to guess on all 50 multiple-choice questions of this test (each question has 4 choices), approximately what is the probability that you would get 90% or more correct?

    24. _____

    (a) .007   (b) .09

    (c) 4.2×10^{-22} (d) 9.5×10^{-16}

Functions, Statistics, and Trigonometry © Scott Foresman Addison Wesley

25. Sandra and Roberta together have read 100 books. Sandra has read 65 of these books, and Roberta has read 40 of them. How many books have been read by both?

    (a) 5   (b) 25   (c) 40

    (d) cannot be determined from the given information

25. _____

26. Each permutation of the letters in the word BATCH is written on a slip of paper and placed in a bowl. One of the slips is drawn at random from the bowl. What is the probability that the letter T will appear in the last position?

    (a) $\frac{1}{5}$ (b) $\frac{1}{24}$ (c) $\frac{1}{120}$ (d) $\frac{5}{24}$

26. _____

27. A fair six-sided die is tossed twice. Let A be the event that the first number is odd and B be the event that the product of the two numbers is even. How are the two events related?

    (a) They are complementary.   (b) They are independent.

    (c) They are dependent.   (d) They are mutually exclusive.

27. _____

28. Which of the following expressions has the same value as

$$_nC_0 4^n + {}_nC_1 4^{n-1}\left(\tfrac{1}{3}\right) + {}_nC_2 4^{n-2}\left(\tfrac{1}{3}\right)^2 + \cdots + {}_nC_{n-1} 4\left(\tfrac{1}{3}\right)^{n-1} + {}_nC_n\left(\tfrac{1}{3}\right)^n?$$

    (a) $\left(\frac{4}{3}\right)^n$ (b) $\left(4\tfrac{1}{3}\right)^n$

    (c) $\frac{4^n}{3}$ (d) 7^n

28. _____

29. How many different five-card hands can be drawn from a deck of 52 cards?

    (a) $\frac{52!}{5!}$ (b) $\frac{52!}{47!}$ (c) $\frac{52!}{5!47!}$ (d) $\frac{5!47!}{52!}$

29. _____

30. Evaluate $\displaystyle\lim_{n\to\infty}\sum_{i=1}^{n}\left(\frac{2}{5^i}\right)$.

    (a) $\frac{2}{5}$ (b) $\frac{1}{2}$ (c) $\frac{8}{5}$ (d) $\frac{5}{4}$

30. _____

31. What is the sum of the integers from 200 through 400?

    (a) 60,300   (b) 120,200

    (c) 20,100   (d) 80,200

31. _____

32. Given that $y = f(x)$, where f is a polynomial function, determine the degree of f from the following table.

32. _____

x	-2	-1	0	1	2	3
y	-15	-4	-1	0	5	20

  (a) 4   (b) 3   (c) 2   (d) Cannot be determined.

33. Suppose f is a polynomial function of degree 5 with real coefficients. If the leading coefficient is 2 and the roots of the equation $f(x) = 0$ include 5, 3, -2i, and i, which of the following could be an expression for $f(x)$?

33. _____

  (a) $f(x) = 2(x + 5)(x^2 - 6x + 13)(x^2 + 1)$

  (b) $f(x) = 2(x - 5)(x^2 - 6x - 13)(x^2 + 1)$

  (c) $f(x) = 2(x - 5)(x^2 - 6x + 13)(x^2 + 1)$

  (d) $f(x) = 2(x - 5)(x^2 - 6x + 13)(x^2 - 1)$

34. Determine the remainder when $2x^4 + x^3 - 13x^2 + 8x + 11$ is divided by $x - 2$.

34. _____

  (a) $r(x) = 11$ (b) $r(x) = -4$

  (c) $r(x) = 15$ (d) $r(x) = -49$

35. What percent of data with a normal distribution falls within 1 standard deviation of the mean?

35. _____

  (a) 50%   (b) 34%   (c) 96%   (d) 68%

36. Given that $P(z \leq a) = 0.7$, where z is a normally distributed random variable with mean $m = 0$ and standard deviation $s = 1$, what is $P(|z| \geq a)$?

36. _____

  (a) 0.3   (b) 0.4   (c) 0.21   (d) 0.6

37. Suppose that a population mean is being estimated through sampling. Which of the following will decrease the margin of error for the estimate?

37. _____

  (a) increasing the sample size   (b) increasing the confidence level

  (c) decreasing the sample size   (d) not sampling randomly

38. One-half of one percent of the bolts manufactured by a certain factory are defective. To the nearest integer, find the mean and standard deviation for the number of defective bolts in a shipment of 10,000 bolts from this factory.

38. _____

  (a) $m = 500, s = 50$ (b) $m = 50, s = 50$

  (c) $m = 7, s = 50$ (d) $m = 50, s = 7$

Functions, Statistics, and Trigonometry © Scott Foresman Addison Wesley

39. Which matrix represents R_{120}?   39. _____

(a) $\begin{bmatrix} -\frac{1}{2} & -\frac{\sqrt{3}}{2} \\ \frac{\sqrt{3}}{2} & -\frac{1}{2} \end{bmatrix}$ (b) $\begin{bmatrix} -\frac{\sqrt{3}}{2} & -\frac{1}{2} \\ \frac{1}{2} & -\frac{\sqrt{3}}{2} \end{bmatrix}$

(c) $\begin{bmatrix} \frac{1}{2} & \frac{\sqrt{3}}{2} \\ -\frac{\sqrt{3}}{2} & \frac{1}{2} \end{bmatrix}$ (d) $\begin{bmatrix} \frac{\sqrt{3}}{2} & \frac{1}{2} \\ \frac{1}{2} & \frac{\sqrt{3}}{2} \end{bmatrix}$

40. Given that $\sin \theta = 0.8$, what is $\cos 2\theta$?   40. _____

(a) 0.28   (b) -0.96

(c) 1.2   (d) -0.28

41. Find $\begin{bmatrix} 3 & -2 \\ -5 & 4 \end{bmatrix}^{-1}$.   41. _____

(a) $\begin{bmatrix} 2 & 2.5 \\ 1 & 1.5 \end{bmatrix}$ (b) $\begin{bmatrix} 3 & 3 \\ 4 & 4 \end{bmatrix}$

(c) $\begin{bmatrix} 2 & 1 \\ 2.5 & 1.5 \end{bmatrix}$ (d) $\begin{bmatrix} 1 & 2 \\ 1.5 & 2.5 \end{bmatrix}$

42. Which matrix represents the composite transformation of $r_y \circ R_{225}$?   42. _____

(a) $\begin{bmatrix} \frac{\sqrt{2}}{2} & -\frac{\sqrt{2}}{2} \\ -\frac{\sqrt{2}}{2} & -\frac{\sqrt{2}}{2} \end{bmatrix}$ (b) $\begin{bmatrix} -\frac{\sqrt{2}}{2} & -\frac{\sqrt{2}}{2} \\ -\frac{\sqrt{2}}{2} & -\frac{\sqrt{2}}{2} \end{bmatrix}$

(c) $\begin{bmatrix} -\frac{\sqrt{2}}{2} & \frac{\sqrt{2}}{2} \\ \frac{\sqrt{2}}{2} & \frac{\sqrt{2}}{2} \end{bmatrix}$ (d) $\begin{bmatrix} \frac{\sqrt{2}}{2} & \frac{\sqrt{2}}{2} \\ \frac{\sqrt{2}}{2} & -\frac{\sqrt{2}}{2} \end{bmatrix}$

43. What are the foci of the hyperbola with the equation $\frac{x^2}{16} - \frac{2}{9} = 1$?   43. _____

(a) (5, 0) and (-5, 0)   (b) (4, 0) and (-4, 0)

(c) (3, 0) and (-3, 0)   (d) (0, 5) and (0, -5)

44. Find an equation for the ellipse with center (0, 0), major axis of length 12, and minor axis of length 10.   44. _____

(a) $\frac{x^2}{36} + \frac{y^2}{25} = 1$ (b) $\frac{x^2}{144} + \frac{y^2}{100} = 1$

(c) $\frac{x^2}{36} - \frac{y^2}{25} = 1$ (d) $\frac{x^2}{6} + \frac{y^2}{5} = 1$

45. What type of graph corresponds to the equation $x^2 + 6xy + 8^2 = 0$?   **45.** _____

    (a) a circle   (b) a hyperbola

    (c) a pair of lines   (d) a parabola

46. Find the equations of the asymptotes of the hyperbola   **46.** _____
$\frac{(x + 1)^2}{49} - \frac{(y - 2)^2}{25} = 1$.

    (a) $y - 2 = \pm\frac{5}{7}(x + 1)$ (b) $y + 2 = \pm\frac{7}{5}(x + 1)$

    (c) $y - 2 = \pm\frac{5}{7}(x - 1)$ (d) $y - 2 = \pm\frac{7}{2}(x - 1)$

47. Which of the following equations is an identity?   **47.** _____

    (a) $\csc 2\theta - \csc \theta = \csc \theta$

    (b) $\csc \theta \cot \theta = \sin \theta$

    (c) $\csc \theta \cos \theta = 1$

    (d) $\cot \theta - \tan \theta = 2 \cot 2\theta$

48. Which equation that has the polar graph shown at the right?   **48.** _____

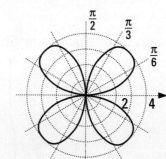

    (a) $r = 4 \cos 2\theta$

    (b) $r = 4 \sin 2\theta$

    (c) $r = 4 \sin 4\theta$

    (d) $r = 4 \sin 3\theta$

49. Write the complex number $2 + 2\sqrt{3}\, i$ in trigonometric form.   **49.** _____

    (a) $4\left(\cos \frac{\pi}{6} + i \sin \frac{\pi}{6}\right)$ (b) $\frac{1}{2}\left(\cos \frac{\pi}{3} + i \sin \frac{\pi}{3}\right)$

    (c) $4\left(\cos \frac{\pi}{3} + i \sin \frac{\pi}{3}\right)$ (d) $-4\left(\cos \frac{\pi}{3} + i \sin \frac{\pi}{3}\right)$

50. Express the quotient $\frac{5 - 2i}{3 + 2i}$ in $a + bi$ form.   **50.** _____

    (a) $\frac{11}{13} + \frac{4}{13} i$ (b) $\frac{11}{13} - \frac{16}{13} i$

    (c) $\frac{11}{5} - \frac{16}{5} i$ (d) $\frac{11}{13} + \frac{16}{13} i$

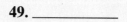

Check all your work carefully.

Functions, Statistics, and Trigonometry © Scott Foresman Addison Wesley

Answers and Evaluation Guides*

Quiz   **Lessons 1-1 Through 1-3**

1. 28.2%
2. ≈ 9.3
3. Brazil
4. 110°
5. Footnote 1 indicates that the totals include data for companies in other countries not shown.
6. a. 6 years
   b. 7.5 years
7. a. 13
   b. the mean age in years of the people on the bus
8. the mean
9. $14,500
10. $24,450
11. five states

Quiz   **Lessons 1-4 Through 1-6**

1. a. 1950 and 2000
   b. about 71,400,000 people per year
2. about 16,100,000 people per year
3. a. i. 0
      ii. 4
      iii. 4
   b. 11, 12, and 24
4. 96th percentile
5. min, Q_1
6. about twice as many
7. 10 million $\leq x <$ 20 million
8. four airports

Chapter 1 Test, Form A

1. a. 0.5%
   b. the number of raisins per cookie
   c. Any bag that has been opened cannot be sold.
2. a. 10
   b. 72
   c. 73
3. 200
4. a. 14 times
   b. 3
   c. 3.14
5. Jill's data have the greater spread. Sample justification: The population variance and standard deviation for Jill's data are slightly greater than the corresponding measures for Jack's data. (Jack's data: $\sigma^2 \approx 2.959$, $\sigma \approx 1.720$; Jill's data: $\sigma^2 \approx 2.980$, $\sigma \approx 1.726$)
6. about 836,000 female high school graduates
7. In 1995, 61.9% of all high school graduates enrolled in college.
8. Sample: The percent of female high school graduates who enrolled in college increased from 1960 through 1990, but decreased slightly from 1990 to 1995.

9. a. bar graph
   b. Line graph: The data do not involve two numerical variables. Dotplot: There are too many students, so the display would require too many dots.
10. 108°
11. (a)
12. (d)
13. (j)
14. (i)
15. (f)
16. a. $1.5 million
    b. summer, fall
17. false.
18. a. 41
    b. 25%
19. a. i. 38.5 billion
       ii. 50 billion
       iii. 77.5 billion
    b. 147 billion, 168 billion
    c. 75th percentile
    d. See below.

19. d.
Twenty Largest United States Corporations

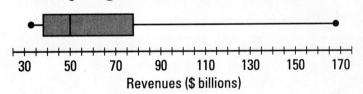

Revenues ($ billions)

Functions, Statistics, and Trigonometry © Scott Foresman Addison Wesley

ANSWERS

*Evaluation Guides for Chapter Test, Forms C and D, are on pages 215–240.

Chapter 1 Test, Form B

1. a. 0.6%
   b. the butterfat content of a quart of ice cream
   c. Any quart that has been opened cannot be sold.
2. a. 11
   b. 86
   c. 86
3. at least 216
4. a. 15
   b. 3
   c. 3.33
5. Jack's data have the greater spread. Sample justification: The population variance and standard deviation for Jack's data are slightly greater than the corresponding measures for Jill's data. (Jack's data: $\sigma^2 \approx 3.307$, $\sigma \approx 1.818$; Jill's data: $\sigma^2 \approx 3.289$, $\sigma \approx 1.814$)
6. about 110,038,000 workers
7. In 1985, 18.0% of the United States labor force were union members.
8. Sample: The percent of the United States labor force who are union members decreased from 1945 to 1995.

9. a. bar graph
   b. Line graph: The data do not involve two numerical variables. Dotplot: There are too many residents, so the display would require too many dots.
10. $\approx 123°$
11. (a)
12. (c)
13. (j)
14. (h)
15. (f)
16. a. $3 million
    b. winter
17. true
18. a. 28
    b. 50%
19. a. i. 0.655 million
       ii. 0.905 million
       iii. 1.335 million
    b. 2.73 million, 3.45 million, 7.33 million
    c. 60th percentile
    d. See below.

19. d.

Twenty United States Cities with the Greatest Populations

Population (millions)

1. a. 41.5
   b. 41.5
   c. 5.5
2. all real numbers greater than or equal to 5.5
3. a. domain: {2, 4, 5, 10}; range: {-1, 0, 7}
   b. true
   c. true
4. a. {x: -5 $\leq x \leq$ 5}
   b. {y: -5 $\leq y \leq$ 2}
   c. No. Explanations may vary. Sample: The graph fails the vertical-line test for a function. That is, a vertical line with an x-intercept anywhere between -5 and 5 will intercept the graph in two points.
5. a. $\approx(-0.97)$
   b. (c)
6. a. $y = 689.58x - 50{,}355.83$
   b. about $22,050 million
   c. extrapolation
7. a. $y = 699.90x - 51{,}318.91$
   b. about $117.35 million
   c. ≈ 0.999
   d. The center of gravity: is (88.6, 10,691.8). When $x = 88.6$, the value of $699.90x - 51{,}318.91$ is 10,692.23. Considering that the numbers in the regression equation are rounded, 10,692.23 and 10,691.8 round to the same number. So it is reasonable to believe that the coordinates of the center of gravity satisfy the regression equation, and thus that the regression line passes through the center of gravity.

1. exponential growth
2. neither
3. exponential decay
4. exponential growth
5. (d)
6. a. $c = (30.2)(0.879^h)$
   b. about 30.2 mg/dl
   c. about 6.4 mg/dl
7. (c)
8. a. 52.8 m
   b. 25 s
   c. 125 m
   d. 1.6 m/s^2

Chapter 2 Test, Form A

1. a. domain: {-1, 0, 1};
   range: {-1, 0}
   b. It is not a function.
   One value of x, namely
   0, is paired with two
   different values of y,
   0 and -1.
2. a. domain:
   {x: $0 \leq x \leq 4$}; range:
   {y: $-1 \leq y \leq 1$}
   b. It is a function because
   it passes the vertical-
   line test for a function.
   That is, any vertical
   line intersects the
   graph no more than
   once.
3. a.

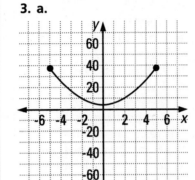

   b. {y: $y \geq \frac{14}{3}$}
   c. There are no x-
   intercepts.
4. a. $\approx 35.1\%$
   b. about 218 billion

5. a. g
   b. (0, 1)
   c. They are reflection
   images of each other
   over the y-axis.
6. a. 1
   b. 0.5
   c. 1
7. B, D, A, C
8. a. 72
   b. $m = 12 \lfloor \frac{d}{2.99} \rfloor$
   c. See below.
9. (a)
10. a. $h = -4.9t^2 + 10,000$
    b. about 45.18 s
11. (a)
12. a. $y = 0.85x - 3.82$
    b. 69.5%, 108.3%
    c. 2030; A value greater
    than 100% is
    impossible.
13. a. $y = 0.007x^2 + 0.98x +$
    11.82
    b. $\approx 83.2\%$
    c. -2.3%
14. The residual for the linear
    model are positive at
    both ends, indicating that
    a better model can be
    found. The residuals for
    the quadratic model fall
    within a horizontal band
    centered around zero, so
    the quadratic model is a
    good fit.

8. c.

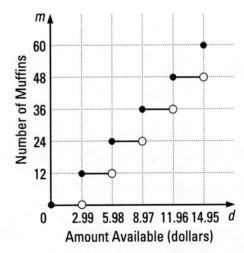

ANSWERS

Chapter 2 Test, Form B

1. a. domain: {-2, -1, 0, 4}; range: (0, 2, 4, 5}
   b. It is a function because, for all ordered pairs (x, y), each value of x is paired with exactly one value of y.
2. a. domain: all real numbers; range: $\{y: y \le -10 \text{ or } y \ge 10\}$
   b. It is not a function because it fails the vertical-line test for a function. That is, any vertical line will intercept the graph in two points.
3. a.

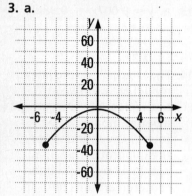

   b. $\left\{y: y \le -\frac{9}{4}\right\}$
   c. There are no x-intercepts.
4. a. ≈36.4%
   b. about 2.64 billion
5. a. f
   b. (0, 1)

8. c.

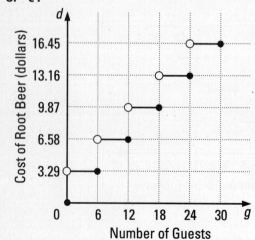

Cost of Root Beer (dollars) vs. Number of Guests

---

c. As x increases, $f(x)$ approaches 0 and $g(x)$ increases without bound. As x decreases, $g(x)$ approaches 0 and $f(x)$ increases without bound.

6. a. 0.75
   b. 2
   c. 1
7. C, B, D, A
8. a. $13.16
   b. $d = 3.29 \left\lceil \frac{g}{6} \right\rceil$
   c. See below.
9. (d)
10. a. $h = -4.9t^2 + 25t$
    b. about 5.1 s
11. (d)
12. a. $y = 0.19x - 1.42$
    b. ≈ 16.2%
    c. -1.5%
13. a. $y = 0.0025x^2 + 0.62x + 3.07$
    b. 15.9%, 110.5%
    c. 2120; A value greater than 100% is impossible.
14. The residuals for the linear model are positive at both ends, indicating that a better model can be found. The residuals for the quadratic model fall within a horizontal band centered around zero, so the quadratic model is a good fit.

Chapter 2 Test
Cumulative Form

1. (c)
2. a. 23 students
   b. 12 students
   c. 73
3. a. 7
   b. -5
   c. -35
4. a. between 35 births per thousand persons and 45 births per thousand
   b. No. According to the $1.5 \times$ IQR criterion, the birth rate would have to be greater than 60 births per thousand persons in order to be an outlier.
5. a. about $1785
   b. food, clothing
6. a. miscellaneous
   b. a child 15–17 years of age
7. a. $\{x: x \le -10 \text{ or } x \ge 10\}$
   b. all real numbers
   c. It is not a function because it fails the vertical-line test for a function. That is, many vertical lines will intercept the graph in two points.
8. false
9. a. about 105 billion shares
   b. i. about -3.6 billion shares   ii. about 14.2 billion shares
   c. exponential model; It yields the lesser residual for the data for 1996.
10. a. i. about 2.9×10^{17} shares   ii. about 2.78 trillion shares
    b. extrapolations
    c. quadratic model; It gives the more reasonable prediction for the year 2100.
11. a. $y = 4.39x + 12.11$
    b. about 130.6 years
12. a. about 193.74 mg
    b. $200(0.9687)^y$ mg

ANSWERS

Quiz — Lessons 3-1 Through 3-3

1. $x = 3, y = 1$
2. a. $p(x) = \dfrac{1}{x^2}$
   b. $T: (x, y) \rightarrow (x - 1, y + 4)$
3. a. $y = (3.2)^{x+4} + 3$
   b. The graph of g is translated 4 units to the left and 3 units up.
4. a. 176.5 lb
   b. 15.6 lb
   c. 174.5 lb
   d. 49.0 lb
   e. 189.0 lb
5. $(11, -10)$
6. $y = \sqrt{x - 2} + 3$

Quiz — Lessons 3-4 Through 3-6

1. even function; $f(-x) = |(-x)^3| = |-(x^3)| = |x^3| = f(x)$
2. When $x = 1$, $g(-x) = g(-1) = -2$, and $g(x) = g(1) = 0$. Since $g(-x) \neq g(x)$, the function g is not an even function. When $x = 1$, $g(-x) = g(-1) = 2$, and $-g(x) = -g(1) = -0 = 0$. Since $g(-x) \neq -g(x)$, the function g is not an odd function.
3. a. $x = 0$
   b. $x = -2.5$
4. a. $y = 4(3.2)^{3x}$
   b. The graph is shrunk horizontally by a factor of $\frac{1}{3}$ and stretched vertically by a factor of 4.
5. 1, -.4, 1.4
6. true
7.

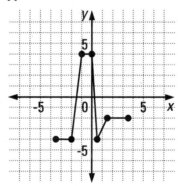

8. a. mean: 1; standard deviation: ≈ 0.7266
   b. all are divided by the mean.

Chapter 3 Test, Form A

1. $f(-x) = 4(-x)^3 - 3(-x) = -4x^3 + 3x = -(4x^3 - 3x) = -f(x)$; Since $f(-x) = -f(x)$, f is by definition an odd function.
2. $T: (x, y) \rightarrow (x + 2, y + 4)$
3. a. $y = \dfrac{1}{x - 2} - 3$
   b. The inverse is a function
4. a. $\{(3, -5), (2, -3), (7, -1), (3, 0)\}$
   b. The inverse is not a function.
5. $-\dfrac{1}{5}$
6. $-\dfrac{7}{3}$
7. $y = \dfrac{1}{-x - 2} = -\dfrac{1}{x + 2}$
8. $\{x: x \neq -2\}$
9. false
10. true
11. An item with a z-score of 1.2 is 1.2 standard deviations greater than the mean.
12. $x = 10, y = 0$
13. σ^2
14. (a)
15. a. mile: $-\frac{1}{4} = -0.25$; long jump: $\frac{7}{12} \approx 0.58$
    b. the mile
16. $y = (x + 2)^3 + 4$
17.

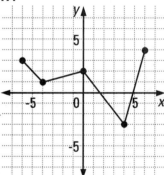

18. a. 91 mrem
    b. 46 mrem
    c. 169 mrem
    d. 155 mrem

19. Neither. The graph is not symmetric with respect to the y-axis, so it does not represent an even function. The graph is not symmetric with respect to the origin, so it does not represent an odd function.

20. the inverse-square function, $y = \frac{1}{x^2}$

21. The graph is symmetric with respect to the y-axis.

22. (b)

23. No. Explanations may vary. Sample: The graph of g fails the horizontal-line test. That is, any horizontal line with a y-intercept greater than 0 will intersect the graph of g in two points, so the inverse of g is not a function.

1. $f(-x) = 4(-x)^2 - 3 = 4x^2 - 3 = f(x)$; Since $f(-x) = f(x)$, f is by definition an even function.

2. $S: (x, y) \to \left(\frac{1}{3}x, 4y\right)$

3. a. $y = \frac{7}{5(x + 2)}$
   b. The inverse is a function.

4. a. {(-1, 0), (1, 1), (2, 2), (3, 3), (5, 4)}
   b. The inverse is a function.

5. 2

6. $5 - \sqrt{5}$

7. $2\sqrt{7 - x}$

8. {x: x ≤ 7}

9. true

10. false

11. An item with a z-score of -0.5 is 0.5 standard deviations less than the mean.

12. x-intercepts; -12, 3, 24; y-intercept: 1

13. $a^2\sigma^2$

14. (d)

15. a. Patricia: -1.7; Maria: ≈ (-1.52)
    b. Patricia

16. $y = (x - 2)^3 - 4$

17.

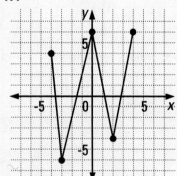

18. a. 208 psi
    b. 4 psi
    c. 233 psi
    d. 40 psi

19. Even. The graph is symmetric with respect to the y-axis, so it represents an even function.

20. the hyperbola function, $y = \frac{1}{x}$

21. The graph is symmetric with respect to the origin.

22. (c)

23. Yes. Explanations may vary. Sample: The graph of g passes the horizontal-line test. That is, any horizontal line intersects the graph of g no more than once, so the inverse of g is a function.

Functions, Statistics, and Trigonometry © Scott Foresman Addison Wesley

**Chapter 3 Test,
Cumulative Form**

1. exponential growth function
2. $y = 0$
3. $y = (.3)(2.5)^{x+1} + 3$
4. $y = \frac{-1.5}{x}$
5. odd function; $g(-x) = \frac{-1.5}{-x} = \frac{1.5}{x} = -\left(\frac{-1.5}{x}\right) = -f(x)$
6. $S: (x, y) \to (x, -1.5y)$
7. $y = x$
8. a.

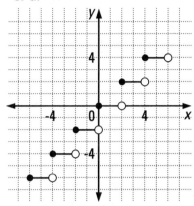

   b. Answers may vary. Samples: -2, 0, 4
9. a. 45
   b. 10
10. -1.5
11. mean: 82; standard deviation: 8
12. (c)
13. 0
14. $\frac{1}{2}$
15. $\{x: x < 0 \text{ or } x \geq 1\}$
16. a. 9
   b. $n = \left\lceil \frac{p}{32} \right\rceil$
17. the mean

18. a. 8th grade: min = 24, $Q_1 = 45$, med = 53, $Q_3 = 58.5$, max = 82; 9th grade: min = 14, $Q_1 = 55$, med = 63, $Q_3 = 76$, max = 97
   b. 8th grade: 24, 82; 9th grade: 14
   c. See below.
19. a. mean: 50.6875; standard deviation: ≈ 14.87
   b. mean: ≈ 61.89; standard deviation: ≈ 19.53
   c. The 8th grader. The z-score for 65 is $\approx .96$, while the z-score for 74 is $\approx .62$.
20. $758.97
21. a. $y = 0.0367x^2 + 0.95x - 1.25$
   b. ≈ -36.4 billion kilowatt-hours
22. a. $y = 5.68x - 114.23$
   b. The center of gravity is (69.6, 281.2). When $x = 69.6$, the value of $5.68x - 114.23$ is 281.098, which is close to 281.2. The numbers in the equation are rounded, so it is reasonable to believe that (69.6, 281.2) satisfies the regression equation, and thus that the regression line passes through the center of gravity.

**Comprehensive Test,
Chapters 1–3**

1. (b)
2. (d)
3. (b)
4. (c)
5. (a)
6. (b)
7. (c)
8. (d)
9. (b)
10. (b)
11. (b)
12. (c)
13. (d)
14. (c)
15. (a)
16. (a)
17. (a)
18. (b)
19. (a)
20. (c)
21. (a)
22. (b)
23. (b)
24. (a)
25. (a)

ANSWERS

18. c.

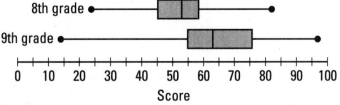

Quiz — Lessons 4-1 Through 4-3

1.

Equivalent Measures of Rotations

Deg.	Rad. (exact)	Rad. (10ths)	Rev.
144°	$\frac{4\pi}{5}$	2.5	0.4
-240°	$-\frac{4\pi}{3}$	-4.2	$-\frac{2}{3}$
1116°	$\frac{31\pi}{5}$	19.5	3.1
732°	$\frac{61\pi}{15}$	12.8	$\frac{61}{30}$

2. about 241 miles
3. 36°
4. 792 inches
5.

Exact Values of Trigonometric Ratios

θ	$\sin\theta$	$\cos\theta$	$\tan\theta$
135°	$\frac{\sqrt{2}}{2}$	$-\frac{\sqrt{2}}{2}$	-1
$\frac{3\pi}{2}$	-1	0	undefined
7π	0	-1	0
450°	1	0	undefined

Quiz — Lessons 4-4 Through 4-6

1. a. 0.47
   b. 0.47
   c. -0.47
   d. -0.47
2. a. Opposites Theorem
   b. Complements Theorem
   c. Periodicity Theorem
3. a. $-\frac{\sqrt{3}}{2}$
   b. $\frac{\sqrt{3}}{2}$
   c. 1
   d. $\frac{1}{2}$
4. a. Answers will vary. Samples: $\frac{\pi}{2}, \frac{3\pi}{2}$
   b. the set of all real numbers
   c. The graph is symmetric with respect to the origin.
5. $g(-x) = \cos(-x)$; by the Opposites Theorem, $\cos(-x) = \cos x$; $\cos x = g(x)$. Thus, by the Transitive Property of Equality, $g(-x) = g(x)$; therefore, g is by definition an even function.

Chapter 4 Test, Form A

1. $-\frac{7\pi}{3}$
2. 105°
3. $\frac{\pi}{15}$ radians
4. ≈ 70.69 square inches
5. about 3220 kilometers
6. $-\frac{\sqrt{2}}{2}$
7. $\sqrt{3}$
8. $\approx (-0.7265)$
9. a. the set of all real numbers
   b. $\{y: 0 \leq y \leq 4\}$
   c. 2
   d. $\frac{2\pi}{5}$
   e. $-\frac{\pi}{15}$
   f. 2
10. $0 < \theta < \frac{\pi}{2}$ and $\pi < \theta < \frac{3\pi}{2}$
11. $-b$
12. $-a$
13. $f(x) = \cos x$; Justifications may vary. Sample: The x-intercepts of the graph over the interval shown are $-\frac{7\pi}{2}, -\frac{9\pi}{2}$, and $-\frac{11\pi}{2}$, which are odd integral multiples of $\frac{\pi}{2}$. This is a characteristic of the graph of the cosine function.
14. a. 2
    b. 2
    c. π
    d. -2

Functions, Statistics, and Trigonometry © Scott Foresman Addison Wesley

15. $\sin(\pi - \theta) = \sin \theta$
(Supplements
Theorem); $\sin \theta = \cos\left(\frac{\pi}{2} - \theta\right)$
(Complements
Theorem); $\sin(\pi - \theta) = \cos\left(\frac{\pi}{2} - \theta\right)$ (Transitive
Property of Equality)

16. $\frac{9\sqrt{10}}{20}$

17. $y = \tan\left(2x - \frac{\pi}{4}\right)$

18. (b)

19. a. $\frac{2}{\pi}$

  b. 0 s; $\frac{\pi}{4}$ s, or $\approx .79$ s;
  $\frac{\pi}{2}$ s, or ≈ 1.57 s

20. (c)

21. ≈ 29.14 m

Chapter 4 Test, Form B

1. $\frac{22\pi}{5}$ radians

2. $\approx 114.592°$

3. $\frac{4\pi}{5}$ radians

4. ≈ 11.00 square
centimeters

5. about 2167 kilometers

6. $\frac{\sqrt{3}}{3}$

7. $\frac{1}{2}$

8. ≈ 0.9511

9. a. the set of all real
numbers

  b. $\{y: -10 \leq y \leq -2\}$

  c. 4

  d. 1

  e. $\frac{1}{\pi}$

  f. -6

10. $0 < \theta < \frac{\pi}{2}$ and
$\frac{3\pi}{2} < \theta < 2\pi$

11. -c

12. -d

13. $g(x) = \sin x$;
Justifications may vary.
Sample: The
x-intercepts of the
graph over the interval
shown are
$\frac{14\pi}{2} = 7\pi$, $\frac{16\pi}{2} = 8\pi$,
and $\frac{18\pi}{2} = 9\pi$,
which are integral
multiples of π. This is a
characteristic of the
graph of the sine
function.

14. a. $\frac{1}{2}$

  b. 2

  c. $-\frac{\pi}{4}$

  d. 1

15. $\sin\left(\frac{\pi}{2} - \theta\right) = \cos \theta$
(Complements Theorem);
$\cos \theta = \cos(-\theta)$
(Opposites Theorem);
$\sin\left(\frac{\pi}{2} - \theta\right) = \cos(-\theta)$
(Transitive Property
of Equality)

16. $-\frac{\sqrt{15}}{15}$

17. $y = 3 \sin\left(3x - \frac{3\pi}{2}\right)$

18. (c)

19. a. $\frac{1}{4}$

  b. 0 s, 2s, 4s

20. (b)

21. ≈ 4.68 m

ANSWERS

ANSWERS

Chapter 4 Test, Cumulative Form

1. a. about 54.5%
   b. $40 < x \le 60$
2. (c)
3. $\frac{9\pi}{5}$ radians
4. 810°
5. 1
6. $\frac{\sqrt{3}}{2}$
7. $\frac{13\pi}{4}$
8. a. Opposites Theorem
   b. Complements Theorem
   c. Half-Turn Theorem
9. a. $n = m^2 - m + 5$
   b. 137 sit-ups
10. a. $\frac{2\sqrt{2}}{3}, -\frac{2\sqrt{2}}{3}$
    b. $\frac{\sqrt{2}}{4}, -\frac{\sqrt{2}}{4}$
11. Answers may vary. Sample: $y = 3\sin(2x + \pi)$
12. a. $y = x^2$
    b. $T: (x, y) \to (x + 3, y + 5)$
    c. $x = 3$
13. a. $r = 1{,}000{,}000(1.07)^{n-1}$
    b. $\approx \$1{,}310{,}800$
14. a. $155
    b. $21
15. a. Answers may vary. Sample:

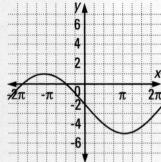

    b. i. 3   ii. 4π
16. $1 - \frac{\pi}{4}$

17. a. $y = \tan\left(x - \frac{\pi}{4}\right)$
    b. the set of all real numbers
18. By the Inverse Function Theorem, if two functions f and g are inverse functions, then $f(g(x)) = x$. For the two given functions f and g, $f(g(x)) = 2\left(\frac{1}{2}x - 7\right) + 7 = x - 7$. Therefore, f and g are not inverse functions.

Quiz   Lessons 5-1 Through 5-3

1. 2
2. $\approx 26.6°$
3. ≈ 4.9
4. $\frac{2\pi}{3}$ radians
5. $\frac{\pi}{2}$ radians
6. $\frac{2\pi}{3}$ radians
7. a. 4.6075°
   b. about 51 ft
8. Neither. Justifications may vary. Sample: The graph of $y = \cos^{-1}x$ is not symmetric with respect to the y-axis, so it does not represent an even function. The graph is not symmetric with respect to the origin, so it does not represent an odd function.
9. By the Law of Cosines, $13^2 = 5^2 + 12^2 - 2(5)(12)\cos\theta$. So $120\cos\theta = 25 + 144 - 169 = 0$. Therefore the triangle is a right triangle.

Quiz   Lessons 5-4 Through 5-6

1. $\frac{\pi}{3}$ radians
2. $-\frac{\pi}{4}$ radians
3. $\frac{\pi}{5}$ radians
4. ≈ 12.4
5. $\approx 54.9°, \approx 125.1°$
6. ≈ 16.1 mm^2
7. Odd. Justifications may vary. Sample: The graph of $y = \tan^{-1}x$ is symmetric with respect to the origin, so it represents an odd function.
8. a. about 24.6 mi
   b. about 23.8 mi

Functions, Statistics, and Trigonometry © Scott Foresman Addison Wesley

198

Chapter 5 Test, Form A

1. $\approx .245$
2. $\frac{5\sqrt{74}}{74}$
3. $\frac{7}{5}$
4. a. $\frac{5\sqrt{74}}{74}$
   b. $\approx 36°$
5. $\frac{\pi}{6}$
6. $-\frac{\pi}{4}$
7. $0 \le \theta \le \pi$
8. a. $y = \tan^{-1}x$
   b. $y = -\frac{\pi}{2}, y = \frac{\pi}{2}$
9. ≈ 6.1
10. about 6 feet 8 inches
11. about 2700 square feet
12. 257 feet
13. a. $h = 6 - 5\cos\theta$
    b. about 1.9 meters
14. .5 s, ≈ 2.7 s
15. $\approx 59.9°$, $\approx 120.1°$
16. ≈ 2.134 radians,
    ≈ 5.275 radians
17. $\theta = \frac{\pi}{6} + 2\pi n$ or

    $\theta = \frac{11\pi}{6} + 2\pi n$, for all
    integers n
18. a. 90°
    b. 35 squre units
19. By the Law of Cosines, in
    any $\triangle ABC$, $c^2 = a^2 +$
    $b^2 - 2ab\cos C$. Let $\triangle ABC$
    be a right triangle, with
    $\angle C$ the right angle. Then
    $\cos C = \cos 90° = 0$. It
    follows that $c^2 = a^2 +$
    $b^2 - 2ab(0) = a^2 + b^2$.
    This is the Pythagorean
    Theorem.

Chapter 5 Test, Form B

1. $\approx .264$
2. $\frac{2\sqrt{13}}{13}$
3. $\frac{2}{3}$
4. a. $\frac{2\sqrt{13}}{13}$
   b. $\approx 56°$
5. $\frac{\pi}{4}$
6. $-\frac{\pi}{3}$
7. $-\frac{\pi}{2} < \theta < \frac{\pi}{2}$.
8. The graph is symmetric
   with respect to the origin.
9. $\approx 6.6°$
10. about 1 foot 8 inches.
11. about 3300 square feet
12. 56 feet
13. a. $h = 4.75 - 4\cos\theta$
    b. about 1.1 meters
14. ≈ 1.9 s, ≈ 3.8 s
15. $\approx 34.0°$
16. ≈ 3.508 radians,
    ≈ 5.917 radians
17. $\theta = \frac{\pi}{6} + \pi n$, for all

    integers n
18. a. 90°
    b. 10 units
19. Since $\angle ACB$ and $\angle ACD$
    are supplementary,
    $m\angle ACB = (180 - n)°$.
    By the SAS Area Formula
    for a Triangle, the area of
    $\triangle ABC$ is $\frac{1}{2}xy \sin n°$, and
    the area of $\triangle ACD$ is
    $\frac{1}{2}xy \sin (180 - n)°$. By
    the Supplements
    Theorem, $\sin (\pi - \theta) =$
    $\sin \theta$. Therefore, by the
    Substitution Property, the
    area of $\triangle ACD$ is
    $\frac{1}{2}xy \sin \theta$. So $\triangle ABC$ and
    $\triangle ACD$ are equal in area.

Chapter 5 Test, Cumulative Form

1. $\frac{4\pi}{3}$ radians
2. $\approx 14.3°$
3. $\approx 219°$, $\approx 321°$
4. $r = \left\lceil \frac{27n}{500} \right\rceil$
5. $\approx 77°$
6. False. Justifications may
   vary. Sample: Suppose
   $A = \frac{\pi}{2}$ and $B = \pi$. Then
   $\sin A = 1$, $\sin B = 0$, and
   $\sin A > \sin B$. But
   $\frac{\pi}{2} < \pi$, so $A < B$.
7. (iii), (iv)
8. about 46 nautical miles
9. $y = (x + 5)^3 + 7$
10. 1
11. about 220 miles
12. a. $\{x: x \ne \frac{\pi}{6} + \pi n$, for all
       integers $n\}$
    b. the set of all real
       numbers.
13. $\theta \approx .464 + \pi n$, for all
    integers n
14. $\approx 19°$
15. $\frac{4}{3}$ s, $\frac{8}{3}$ s
16. a. $\frac{7}{6}$
    b. $y = \frac{1}{x^2 - x} + 1$, or
       $y = \frac{x^2 - x + 1}{x^2 - x} + 1$
17. 2.25
18. (c)
19. a. 23.5
    b. 12 months
    c. $T =$
       $23.5 \sin\left(\frac{n - 3}{\frac{6}{\pi}}\right) + 54.5$
       if amplitude, period,
       and phase shift are
       estimated) or $T =$
       $23.41 \sin (.51n - 1.62)$
       $+ 54.28$ (if using a
       statistics utility)

ANSWERS

Quiz Lessons 6-1 Through 6-3

1. $-7, 7$
2. 1
3. $\frac{1}{5}$
4. 4
5. a. $\frac{64\pi}{3}$ cm^3
6. a. $x^{\frac{7}{3}}$
   b. all real numbers
7. a. .032 moles/liter
   b. ≈ 4.3
8. a. $\{x: 0 < x < 1\}$
   b. $\{x: x > 1\}$
9. 4
10. $\frac{1}{4}$

Quiz Lessons 6-4 Through 6-6

1. ≈ 194
2. $\approx (-1.139)$
3. The account paying 6.25% annual interest compounded continuously is a better investment; $5000 invested at 6.3% compounded twice a year would grow to $5000\left(1 + \frac{.063}{2}\right)^2 =$ $5319.96; $5000 invested at 6.25% compounded continuously would grow to $5000e^{.0625} =$ $5322.47.
4. a. i. ≈ 868 ii. ≈ 1070
   b. ≈ 1097
5. $a = b^5 c^2$
6. 3
7. (a)
8. $x = \frac{5}{6}$, or $x = .8\overline{3}$
9. $z \approx 1.277$
10. about 15.1 years

Chapter 6 Test, Form A

1. $\frac{3}{2}$
2. $a^{\frac{5}{4}} b^{\frac{1}{4}}$
3. a. $\{x: x \geq 0\}$
   b. $\{y: y \geq 0\}$
4. $f^{-1}(x) = x^{\frac{4}{3}}$
5. $T = \left(\frac{R}{k}\right)^{\frac{1}{4}}$
6. $\log_{20}\left(\frac{b^{\frac{1}{2}}}{c^2}\right)$
7. ≈ 2.77
8. $x = 7776$
9. $n \approx -1.010$
10. ≈ 2.1452
11. ≈ 0.491
12. 114.90
13. about 69 minutes
14. (c)
15. a.

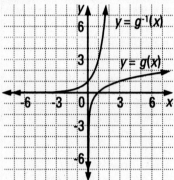

   b. $x = 0$
   c. $y = 3^x$
16. (d)
17. $\frac{1}{6}$
18. 3
19. -5
20. $\ln y = (\ln 1.5)x + \ln 6.3$
21. a. $\log D = .25 \log P + 1.45$
    b. $n = 4, k \approx 28.2$

Chapter 6 Test, Form B

1. $\frac{5}{3}$
2. $m^{\frac{1}{6}} n^{\frac{5}{6}}$
3. a. all real numbers
   b. all real numbers
4. $g^{-1}(x) = x^5$
5. $A = \frac{D^4}{k^4}$
6. $\ln b^3 c^2$
7. ≈ 1.76
8. $x = \frac{1}{9}$
9. $r \approx 3.957$
10. ≈ 2.3456
11. $\approx (-.4168)$
12. 8698.47
13. about 461 minutes
14. (b)
15. a.

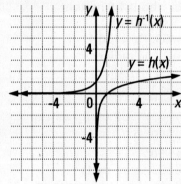

   b. $x = 0$
   c. $h^{-1}(x) = 4^x$
16. (c)
17. $\frac{3}{8}$
18. $\frac{1}{2}$
19. $\frac{1}{3}$
20. $\ln y = (\ln .71)x + \ln 2.5$
21. a. $\log N = .69 \log Y + .996$
    b. $N = 9.9 Y^{.69}$

Chapter 6 Test, Cumulative Form

1. a. min = 36, Q_1 = 63, med = 73, Q_3 = 88, max = 100
   b. There are no outliers.
2. (b)
3. 15
4. -8
5. an odd function
6. No
7. $\frac{3\sqrt{13}}{13}$
8. $\approx 33.7°$
9. ≈ 1.639735
10. ≈ 1.55677
11. about 38.9 days
12. $1527.30
13. $\theta = \frac{\pi}{3} + 2\pi n$, for all integers n, or $\theta = \frac{5\pi}{3} + 2\pi n$, for all integers n
14. $y = e^{3x+5}$
15. ≈ 6.6
16. (c)
17. $\approx 56°$
18. ≈ 49.1
19. $T: (x, y) \rightarrow (x + 5, y - 10)$
20. about 8.7 years
21. $x \approx 2.10$
22. $\theta = \frac{\pi}{6}$
23. true
24. (b)
25. a. $\frac{8}{9}$ radian
    b. 32 inches
26. 343 cubic centimeters
27. False. Justifications may vary. Sample: By the Half-Turn Theorem, for all θ, $\tan(\pi + \theta) = \tan\theta$. By the Supplements Theorem, for all θ, $\tan(\pi - \theta) = -\tan\theta$. Then by the Substitution Property, for all θ, $\tan\theta = -\tan\theta$. Since this statement is false, it follows that the original statement, $\tan(\pi + \theta) = \tan(\pi - \theta)$, also is false.

Comprehensive Test, Chapters 1–6

1. (c)
2. (a)
3. (b)
4. (b)
5. (a)
6. (d)
7. (d)
8. (b)
9. (b)
10. (c)
11. (d)
12. (d)
13. (d)
14. (c)
15. (c)
16. (b)
17. (b)
18. (c)
19. (d)
20. (b)
21. (d)
22. (a)
23. (d)
24. (c)
25. (c)
26. (c)
27. (d)

Quiz   Lessons 7-1 Through 7-3

1. Yes, events A and C and events C and D
2. all ordered pairs (x, y) where either $x = 0$ or $y = 0$ or both
3. $\frac{1}{20}$ or 0.05
4. 75,600,000
5. a. {ACT, ATC, CAT, CTA, TAC, TCA}
   b. $\frac{1}{6}$
6. a. 27
   b. $\frac{1}{27}$

Quiz   Lessons 7-4 Through 7-6

1. 2520
2. Yes; $P(A)$ = .25, $P(B)$ = .44, $P(A \cap B)$ = .11. Since $P(A) \cdot P(B) = .11 = P(A \cap B)$, the events of gene A occurring and gene B occurring are independent.
3. .44
4. $n = 12$
5. 0, 1, 2, 3, 4, 5
6. $\frac{10}{21}$
7. 3

Chapter 7 Test, Form A

1. 0.4
2. a. 16
   b. $\frac{3}{16}$
3. $\frac{1}{4}$
4. 1680
5. 2730
6. a. 720
   b. 24
7. $P(A \cap B) =$
   $P(A) \cdot P(B) \neq 0$. Since
   $P(A \cup B) = P(A) +$
   $P(B) - P(A \cap B)$ and
   $P(A \cap B) \neq 0$, $P(A \cup B) \neq$
   $P(A) + P(B)$
8. $n = 7$
9. mutually exclusive but
   not complementary
10. complementary
11. .28
12. 2160
13. 63,700,992
14. Designs will vary. Sample:
    Simulate a single package
    by tossing a pair of fair
    coins 10 times. If, in the
    10 pairs, no pair of tosses
    results in two tails, count
    it as a package with no
    underweight cookies.
    Repeat the experiment
    100 times.
15. Sample: Use a random
    number generator to
    randomly select n points
    (x, y) such that $0 < x < \frac{\pi}{2}$
    and $0 < y < 1$ and where n
    is large. Determine the
    number of points m such
    that $y < \sin x$. Estimate is
    $\frac{m}{n} \cdot \frac{\pi}{2}$.
16. a. $P(x_i) \geq 0$ for each x_i;
    $x_1 + x_2 + x_3 + x_4 +$
    $x_5 + x_6 + x_7 + x_8 = 1$.
    b. 4.5

Chapter 7 Test, Form B

1. 0.6
2. a. 25
   b. $\frac{6}{25}$
3. $\frac{5}{12}$
4. 720
5. 1320
6. a. 5040
   b. 120
7. Events B and C
8. $n = 9$
9. mutually exclusive but
   not complementary
10. complementary
11. .73
12. 72
13. 655,360,000
14. Sample: .24
15. Use a random number
    generator to randomly
    select n points in the
    rectangular region
    bounded by the lines
    $x = 0$, $x = \frac{\pi}{4}$, $y = 0$, and
    $y = 1$, where n is large.
    Calculate the number m
    of points such that
    $y < \tan x$. Estimate is
    $\frac{m}{n} \cdot \frac{\pi}{4}$.
16. a. $P(x_i) \geq 0$ for each x_i;
    $x_1 + x_2 + x_3 + x_4 +$
    $x_5 + x_6 = 1$.
    b. 4.05

Chapter 7 Test, Cumulative Form

1. $\frac{3}{4}$
2. (b)
3. .55
4. ≈ 5.6
5. $5c^4$
6. 0
7. 2
8. $n = 10$
9. $-\sqrt{8} = -2\sqrt{2}$
10. $t = 50.1$ seconds
11. 10.29
12. a.

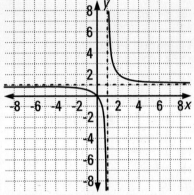

   b. $y = \frac{1}{x}$; $T(x, y) =$
      $(x + 1, y + 1)$
13. $\frac{1}{24}$
14. 1953
15. 40,320
16. 2.98%

Functions, Statistics, and Trigonometry © Scott Foresman Addison Wesley

Quiz — Lessons 8-1 Through 8-3

1. a. 4, 9, 14, 19, 24
   b. arithmetic
2. a. $3, 1, \frac{1}{3}, \frac{1}{9}, \frac{1}{27}$
   b. geometric
3. the fifth year
4. 333rd term
5. 0
6. $-\frac{4}{5}$
7. no limit
8. $405,000
9. 2300
10. 1104

Quiz — Lessons 8-4 Through 8-6

1. $5215
2. 4 cm
3. 2556
4. $\frac{r}{n} \cdot {}_nC_r$

   $= \frac{r}{n} \cdot \frac{n!}{(n-r)!r!}$

   $= \frac{r}{n} \cdot \frac{n(n-1)!}{(n-r)!\, r(r-1)!}$

   $= \frac{(n-1)!}{(n-r)!(r-1)!}$

   $= \frac{(n-1)!}{((n-1)-(r-1))!(r-1)!}$

   $= {}_{n-1}C_{r-1}$
5. converges to 8
6. does not converge
7. 38,760
8. 6750

Chapter 8 Test, Form A

1. 0, 3, 8, 15, 24
2. neither
3. 5321
4. 65
5. converges to 0
6. converges to $\frac{3}{2}$
7. a. $a_n = 187 + (n-1)(-13)$
      $= 200 - 13n,$
      for $n \geq 1$
   b. $\begin{cases} a_1 = 187 \\ a_n = a_{n-1} - 13, \end{cases}$
      for $n \geq 2$
8. a. $g_n = 3(-17)^{n-1}$
      for $n \geq 1$
   b. $\begin{cases} g_1 = 3 \\ g_n = -17g_{n-1}, \end{cases}$
      for $n \geq 2$
9. $16x^4 - 96x^3 + 216x^2 - 216x + 81$
10. $64x^3 + 240x^2y + 300xy^2 + 125y^3$
11. a. 1, 50, 1225
    b. 1225, 50, 1
12. $2^{100} \approx 1.2677 \cdot 10^{30}$
13. converges to 18
14. does not converge
15. true
16. false
17. a. $465
    b. $55,080
18. $\approx$ $3.7 million
19. 53,130
20. 3150
21. ≈ 0.47

Chapter 8 Test, Form B

1. 5, 2.5, 1.25, .625, .3125
2. geometric
3. 3513.9
4. 135.19
5. does not converge
6. converges to $\frac{5}{7}$
7. a. $a_n = 243 + (n-1)(-15)$
      $= 258 - 15n,$
      for $n \geq 1$
   b. $\begin{cases} a_1 = 243 \\ a_n = a_{n-1} - 15, \end{cases}$
      for $n \geq 2$
8. a. $g_n = 5 \cdot 19^{n-1}$
      for $n \geq 1$
   b. $\begin{cases} g_1 = 5 \\ g_n = 19g_{n-1}, \end{cases}$
      for $n \geq 2$
9. $125x^3 - 150x^2 + 60x - 8$
10. $81x^4 + 216x^3y + 216x^2y^2 + 96xy^3 + 16y^4$
11. a. 1, 20, 190, 1140
    b. 1140, 190, 20, 1
12. 9,657,700; 10,400,600; 9,657,700
13. does not converge
14. converges to 77,370
15. false
16. true
17. a. $2,240
    b. $14,560
18. 1630 miles
19. 142,506
20. 8800
21. ≈ 0.075

ANSWERS

Chapter 8 Test, Cumulative Form

1. a. $31,200
   b. $7,200
2. a. $3, 2, \frac{4}{3}, \frac{8}{9}, \frac{16}{27}$
   b. geometric
3. .

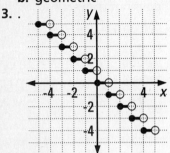

4. period $= \frac{2\pi}{5}$
   amplitude $= 3$
5. $a_n = 5 - (n - 1)15$
   $= 20 - 15n$, for $n \geq 1$
6. ≈ 2.898 or 2.9 ft^2
7. $a^4 - 16a^3 b + 96a^2b^2 - 256ab^3 + 256b^4$
8. $x = 12$
9. 120
10. 5040
11. 1794 hr
12. No
13. $\frac{1}{6}$
14. Yes; $\frac{70}{9}$
15. Sample: Use a calculator's random number generator to generate 20 numbers between 0 and 1. Consider a number less than .7 to be a survival and count the number of survivals. Repeat this experiment 50 times and count the number of times the number of survivals in each experiment is greater than 15. This number divided by 50 is the probability.
16. a. $f^{-1}(x) = \sqrt[3]{x + 5}$
    b. domain: set of all real numbers range: set of all real numbers
17. $\frac{1}{2380}$
18. ≈ 0.078

Quiz — Lessons 9-1 Through 9-3

1. a. $V = 8000x - 360x^2 + 4x^3$
   b. 3
2. a. $A(x) = 1000(1 + x)^3 + 1500(1 + x)^2 + 2000(1 + x) + 2500$
   b. $7479.33
3. -0.8
4. a. Yes
   b. $g(n) = 4n^3 - 3n^2 + 2n + 1$
5. a. 2
   b. -1.5, 0.5, 1.0
   c. $-1.5 < x < 0.5$ and $x > 1$
   d. $x < -1.5$ and $0.5 < x < 1$
   e. $x < -0.75$ and $.75 < x$
   f. $-0.75 < x < .75$

Quiz — Lessons 9-4 Through 9-7

1. $x^3 + 2x^2 - x + 3$
2. -3
3. $(t + 1)(t^2 + t - 1)$
4. $f(x) = (x - 1)\left(x + \frac{1}{2}\right)\left(x - \frac{2}{3}\right)$
5. a. $4 + i$
   b. $5 + 5i$
   c. $.5 - .3i$
6. $3 - \sqrt{2}\, i$
7. $\left(x - \left(\frac{1}{2} + \frac{\sqrt{19}}{2} i\right)\right)$
   $\left(x - \left(\frac{1}{2} - \frac{\sqrt{19}}{2} i\right)\right)$
8. False
9. 7

Chapter 9 Test, Form A

1. $g(x) = x^3 - 2x^2 + x - 4$
2. $q(x) = 2x^3 + x^2 + 3x + 2$, $r(x) = 11$
3. (c)
4. 2.4
5. $(5x - 2)(3x + 4)$
6. $(4m^2 + 3n)(16m^4 - 12m^2n + 9n^2)$
7. a. True
   b. $-i, i, -2, 3$
8. a. 4
   b. 6
9. $5 + i$
10. $0 + i$
11. True
12. 25
13. -1
14. 6
15. 3
16. $V = 1000\pi((r + 8)^2 - r^2) = 16,000\pi r + 64,000\pi$ cm^3

Chapter 9 Test, Form B

1. $g(x) = -x^3 + 5x^2 + x + 5$
2. $q(x) = 3x^3 - 7x^2 + 16x - 36$; $r(x) = 82$
3. (d)
4. -1.2
5. $(3n - 2)(2n + 3)$
6. $(5p - 2q^4)(25p^2 + 10pq^4 + 4q^8)$
7. a. True
   b. $-i, i, -\frac{3}{2}, 2$
8. a. 5
   b. 7
9. $-1 - 3i$
10. $0 + i$
11. False
12. $\sqrt{\frac{1 + \sqrt{13}}{2}} \approx 1.52$
13. $-\frac{1}{3}$
14. 7
15. 3
16. $V = (4 - \pi)r^2\ell + 40r\ell + 100/$cm^3

Functions, Statistics, and Trigonometry © Scott Foresman Addison Wesley

1. False
2. a. 7
   b. 2
   c. 7
3. -1
4. $n = 8$
5. $x = \frac{1}{4} \pm \frac{\sqrt{119}}{4} i$
6. $q(x) = x^2 - x + 1$,
   $r(x) = x - 4$
7. a. $P(x) \geq 0$ for all x;
      $P(1) + P(2) + P(3) +$
      $P(4) + P(5) = 1$
   b. 1.64
8. $\approx .64$ radians or $\approx 36.9°$
9. a. 162
   b. 81.54
10. $-\frac{5}{13} + \frac{12}{13} i$
11. $(m - 3)(3m - 1)(m + 1)$
12. $\approx .146$
13. $\sqrt{3}\, i$
14. a. $2000(1 - x)^4 +$
       $2000(1 - x)^3 +$
       $2000(1 - x)^2 +$
       $2000(1 - x)$
    b. ≈ 7417.7 gallons
15. $833.33376 \approx 833.33$
16. $f^{-1}(x) = \ln x$
17. False
18. $V = 2\pi x^3 + 4\pi x^2 y + 2\pi x y^2$
19. 560
20. $(a + bi)(a - bi) = a^2 - abi +$
    $abi - b^2 i^2 = a^2 + b^2$.
    Since a and b are real
    numbers, $a^2 + b^2$ is a real
    number.

1. (d)
2. (d)
3. (a)
4. (a)
5. (b)
6. (c)
7. (d)
8. (c)
9. (c)
10. (c)
11. (b)
12. (d)
13. (a)
14. (b)
15. (c)
16. (c)
17. (d)
18. (c)
19. (d)
20. (d)
21. (d)
22. (a)
23. (a)
24. (a)
25. (b)

1. a. $B(k) =$
      $_{35}C_k(.8)^k(.2)^{35-k}$
   b. ≈ 0.16649
2. mean $= 28$
   s.d. ≈ 2.366
3. False; the area under
   any binomial distribution
   always equals 1.
4. 0.5
5. a. ≈ 23.3
   b. ≈ 1.87
6. a. H_0: Clare has a free-
      throw percentage of
      at least 90%.
      H_1: Clare has a free-
      throw percentage
      less than 90%.
   b. No; the probability of
      making 16 or fewer
      free throws given a
      90% free-throw
      percentage is ≈ 0.13,
      which is greater than
      0.05. So the null
      hypothesis cannot
      be rejected.

1. (a)
2. false
3. 0.1336
4. a. 0.2860
   b. 0.2140
5. No; $np = 17 \geq 5$ but
   $nq = 3 < 5$
6. about 27%

ANSWERS

Chapter 10 Test, Form A

1.

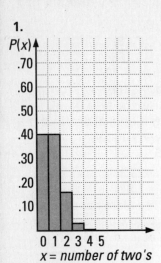

x = number of two's

2. The domain would increase to 100. The range would decrease. The shape would become more symmetric, looking more like a bell-shaped curve.

3. mean = 10
s.d ≈ 2.8

4. (d)

5. 0.1056

6. 0.2417

7. 35,388

8. ≈0.2177

9. 0.8904

10. a. H_0: The coin is fair (the probability that the coin lands heads is 0.5).
H_1: The coin is not fair (the probability that the coin lands heads is not 0.5).
b. No, P(13 or more heads or 2 or fewer heads) = 0.007385 < 0.01, so H_0 can be rejected.

11. true

12. 5%

13. $37,250 ± $637

Chapter 10 Test, Form B

1.

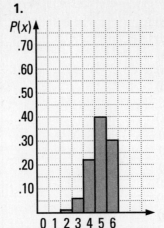

x = number of free throws made

2. The domain stays the same. The range will decrease. The shape becomes symmetric to the mode $x = 3$.

3. mean = 10
variance ≈ 8.3

4. (c)

5. 0.2549

6. 0.7698

7. 242,084

8. 0.7406

9. 0.0548

10. a. H_0: the coin is fair (the probability that the coin lands tails is 0.5).
H_1: The coin is not fair (the probability that the coin lands tails is not 0.5).
b. Yes; P(2 or fewer tails or 12 or more tails) = 0.0129 > 0.01, so the null hypothesis cannot be rejected.

11. ≈(-1, 0.242), ≈(1, 0.242)

12. 97.5%

13. 125.2 watts ±2.05 watts

Chapter 10 Test, Cumulative Form

1. mean = 31.25
s.d. ≈ 4.84

2. 0.3050

3. a. mutually exclusive
b. independent
c. mutually exclusive

4. 0.0228 ≈ 2%

5. 0.4 + 0.8i

6. $g(x) = (x + 2)^4(x - 7)^2(2x - 3)$

7. ≈$78,883

8. 119

9. $y = \dfrac{1}{\sqrt{3}}e^{-x^{\frac{2}{3}}}$

10. mean = 98.2
s.d. ≈ 0.7

11. No; P(guessing 4 or more digits) ≈0.013 > 0.01

12. a. 520 ± 27
b. 800

13. $f(x) = (x - (3 - 2i)) \cdot (x - (3 + 2i))(x - 7) \cdot (x + 1)$

1. $\begin{bmatrix} 38 & 18 & 13 \\ 41 & 23 & 10 \end{bmatrix}$

2. $\begin{bmatrix} 2 & 3 \\ \frac{8}{3} & 4 \end{bmatrix}$

3. 3×4

4. $\begin{bmatrix} \$169,640 \\ \$205,820 \\ \$161,890 \end{bmatrix}$

5. $\begin{bmatrix} 0 & 1 \\ -1 & 0 \end{bmatrix}$

6. $\begin{bmatrix} 7 & 0 \\ 0 & 7 \end{bmatrix}$

7. $\begin{bmatrix} 0 & -1 \\ -1 & 0 \end{bmatrix}$

8. a. $\begin{bmatrix} 0 & 6 & 2 \\ 6 & 4 & 2 \end{bmatrix}$, $\begin{bmatrix} 0 & -6 & -2 \\ -6 & -4 & -2 \end{bmatrix}$

   b. $\begin{bmatrix} -1 & 0 \\ 0 & -1 \end{bmatrix}$

1. $\approx (2,205, -.3715)$

2. (c)

3. $\dfrac{\sqrt{6}}{4} + \dfrac{\sqrt{2}}{4}$

4. $\dfrac{\sqrt{6}}{4} - \dfrac{\sqrt{2}}{4}$

5. 1

6. $\cos\left(x - \frac{\pi}{2}\right) =$
$\cos x \cos\left(\frac{\pi}{2}\right) + \sin x \sin\left(\frac{\pi}{2}\right)$
$= (\cos x)(0) + (\sin x)(1)$
$= \sin x$

7. $-\dfrac{4\sqrt{2}}{9}$

8. $\frac{1}{2}\sqrt{2 + \sqrt{2}}$

Chapter 11 Test, Form A

1. $\begin{bmatrix} 112 \\ -48 \end{bmatrix}$

2. $\begin{bmatrix} 54 & 33 & 33 \\ 24 & 23 & 14 \end{bmatrix}$

3. $\begin{bmatrix} \frac{7}{17} & -\frac{9}{17} \\ -\frac{2}{17} & \frac{5}{12} \end{bmatrix}$

4. No inverse exists.

5. $\dfrac{\sqrt{2}}{4} - \dfrac{\sqrt{6}}{4}$

6. $\dfrac{4\sqrt{21}}{25}$

7. $x = 2\sqrt{3}$ and $x = -2\sqrt{3}$

8. 3×6

9. a. $\begin{bmatrix} 7 & 2 \\ 2 & 3 \end{bmatrix}\begin{bmatrix} x \\ y \end{bmatrix} = \begin{bmatrix} 53 \\ 37 \end{bmatrix}$

   b. $\begin{bmatrix} x \\ y \end{bmatrix} = \begin{bmatrix} 5 \\ 9 \end{bmatrix}$

10. $\begin{bmatrix} .829 & -.559 \\ .559 & .829 \end{bmatrix}$

11. $\begin{bmatrix} 1 & 0 \\ 0 & \frac{1}{4} \end{bmatrix}$

12. a. 272

   b. $\begin{bmatrix} \$32,853,000 \\ \$20,958,000 \\ \$23,438,000 \end{bmatrix}$

13. $\begin{bmatrix} 0 & -1 \\ 1 & 0 \end{bmatrix}$

14. $\begin{bmatrix} 0 & 1 \\ -1 & 0 \end{bmatrix}$

---

15. a. $\begin{bmatrix} -4 & 4 & 4 & -4 \\ 4 & 4 & -4 & -4 \end{bmatrix}$

   b. $\begin{bmatrix} -5 & -7 & 5 & 7 \\ -7 & 5 & 7 & -5 \end{bmatrix}$

   c.

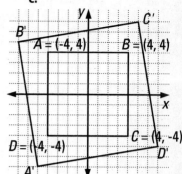

16. a. r_x
   b. r_y
   c. R_{180}

ANSWERS

ANSWERS

Chapter 11 Test, Form B

1. $\begin{bmatrix} 9 \\ 1 \end{bmatrix}$

2. $\begin{bmatrix} 47 & 70 & 41 & -4 \\ 26 & 46 & 15 & -1 \end{bmatrix}$

3. No inverse exists.

4. $\begin{bmatrix} -5 & 8 \\ 2 & -3 \end{bmatrix}$

5. $-\dfrac{\sqrt{2} + \sqrt{6}}{4}$

6. $-\dfrac{3}{8}$

7. $y = 0$

8. 4×7

9. a. $\begin{bmatrix} 7 & 391 \\ 5 & -21 \end{bmatrix} \begin{bmatrix} x \\ y \end{bmatrix} = \begin{bmatrix} 426 \\ 4 \end{bmatrix}$

   b. $\begin{bmatrix} x \\ y \end{bmatrix} = \begin{bmatrix} 5 \\ 1 \end{bmatrix}$

10. $\begin{bmatrix} 0.743 & 0.669 \\ -0.669 & 0.743 \end{bmatrix}$

11. $\begin{bmatrix} \frac{3}{7} & 0 \\ 0 & 1 \end{bmatrix}$

12. $\begin{bmatrix} 15,200 \\ 18,780 \\ 19,710 \end{bmatrix}$

13. $\begin{bmatrix} 0 & 1 \\ -1 & 0 \end{bmatrix}$

14. $\begin{bmatrix} -1 & 0 \\ 0 & -1 \end{bmatrix}$

15. a. $\begin{bmatrix} -3 & 3 & 3 & -3 \\ 3 & 3 & -3 & -3 \end{bmatrix}$

    b. $\begin{bmatrix} 3 & 1 & -3 & -1 \\ -1 & 0 & 1 & 0 \end{bmatrix}$

    c.

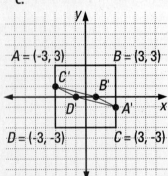

$A = (-3, 3)$ $B = (3, 3)$
$D = (-3, -3)$ $C = (3, -3)$

16. a. $r_y = x$
    b. $r_y = -x$
    c. R_{180}

Chapter 11 Test, Cumulative Form

1. $\dfrac{-\sqrt{2} + \sqrt{6}}{4}$

2. $\begin{bmatrix} -\frac{3}{2} & \frac{7}{2} \\ 1 & -2 \end{bmatrix}$

3. False. A positive slope means the independent and dependent variables have a positive relation which determines the sign of the correlation coefficient.

4. $\begin{bmatrix} -1 & 0 \\ 0 & 1 \end{bmatrix}$

5. 0.0668

6. Yes. $|r| < 1$.
   $S_\infty = \dfrac{27}{2} = 13.5$

7. $\det = 3 \cdot 12 - 4 \cdot 9 = 0$

8. $\begin{bmatrix} \$14.73 \text{ million} \\ \$19.5 \text{ million} \\ \$21.9 \text{ million} \\ \$12.87 \text{ million} \end{bmatrix}$

9. mean = 30, variance = 27

10. $\begin{bmatrix} .9336 & -.3584 \\ .3584 & .9336 \end{bmatrix}$

11.

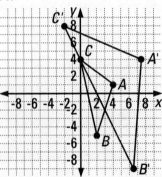

12. $\begin{bmatrix} 7.5 & 6.5 & -2 \\ 4 & -9 & 8 \end{bmatrix}$

13. 8

14. True

15. (c)

16. ≈ 5.492

17. a. 0.3174
    b. 0

18. $\begin{bmatrix} \dfrac{\sqrt{2}}{2} & -\dfrac{\sqrt{2}}{2} \\ -\dfrac{\sqrt{2}}{2} & -\dfrac{\sqrt{2}}{2} \end{bmatrix}$

14. a. German; 1.25; English: 0.8
    b. German test

20. 1995.4 ± 3.7 ml

Functions, Statistics, and Trigonometry © Scott Foresman Addison Wesley

1. a.

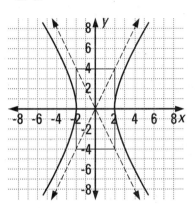

b. $(-3, 6 + \sqrt{7})$

$(-3, 6 - \sqrt{7})$

2. a.

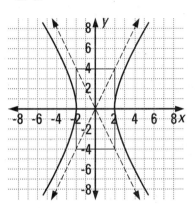

b. $y = 2x, y = -2x$
3. $(-5, 3), (5, -3), (-3, 5)$
4. perihelion ≈ 1.58 a.u.;
aphelion ≈ 5.22 a.u.
5. Yes;
$|\sqrt{(10-7)^2 + (10-6)^2} - \sqrt{(10-5)^2 + (10--2)^2}| =$
$|5 - 13| = 8$

Chapter 12 Test, Form A

1.

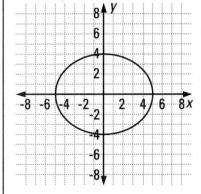

2. $\frac{x^2}{9} - \frac{y^2}{7} = 1$
3. a.

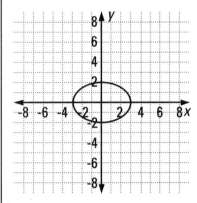

b. $(\sqrt{5}, 0), (-\sqrt{5}, 0)$
4. a.

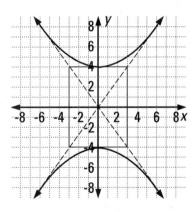

b. $(0, 5), (0, -5)$

---

5. $3x^2 + 2\sqrt{3}xy + y^2 - (4\sqrt{3} - 2)x - (2\sqrt{3} + 4)y + 20 = 0$
6. a.

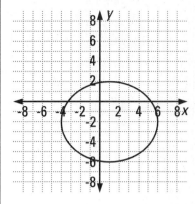

b. $(4, -2), (-2, -2)$
7. A point; the plane intersects the cone at the vertex, making an angle with the cone's axis greater than the angle between the axis and the cone's edge.
8. a. $y = \frac{8}{5}x, y = -\frac{8}{5}x$
b. $x = 0, y = 0$
9. the null set
10. hyperbola
11. parabola
12. True; the asymptotes have equations $y = \pm x$, so they are perpendicular to one another.
13. $3x^2 - 2y^2 - 18x - 4y + 19 = 0$
14. about 23.165 billion miles

ANSWERS

Chapter 12 Test, Form B

1.

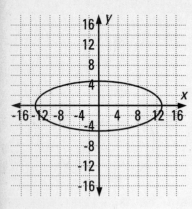

2. $\dfrac{x^2}{25} - \dfrac{y^2}{11} = 1$

3. a.

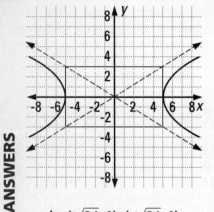

b. $(\sqrt{34}, 0)$, $(-\sqrt{34}, 0)$

4. a.

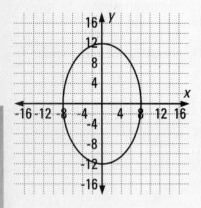

b. $(0, 4\sqrt{5})$, $(0, -4\sqrt{5})$

5. $x^2 + 2xy + y^2 - 5\sqrt{2}x - 7\sqrt{2}y + 4 = 0$

6. a.

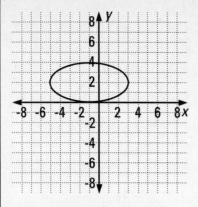

b. $(2\sqrt{3} - 1, 2)$, $(-2\sqrt{3} - 1, 2)$

7. Two intersecting lines; the plane intersects the cone at an angle less than the angle between the cone's axis and edge and the plane passes through the cone's vertex.

8. a. $y = \dfrac{12}{7}x - 6$,

$y = -\dfrac{12}{7}x + 18$

b. $x = 7$, $y = 6$

9. two parallel lines

10. ellipse

11. hyperbola

12. False; the asymptotes are $y = \pm\dfrac{1}{2}x$, which are not perpendicular to one another.

13. $2x^2 - 5y^2 + 8x + 10y - 7 = 0$

14. ≈ 0.34 a.u.

Chapter 12 Test, Cumulative Form

1. $(\sqrt{7}, 0)$, $(-\sqrt{7}, 0)$,

2.

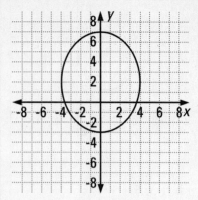

3. $\sin\left(\dfrac{23\pi}{132}\right)$

4. $x^2 - y^2 = -16$

5. ≈ 0.70

6. $\dfrac{y^2}{16} - \dfrac{x^2}{9} = 1$

7. 4.0718

8. See below left.

9. $g(f(x)) = \dfrac{1}{\sqrt{1 - \sin x}}$; the domain is $\{x : x \neq n\pi + \dfrac{\pi}{2},$ where n is any integer$\}$

10. (c)

11. ellipse

12. $y = \dfrac{5}{4}x + \dfrac{13}{4}$,

$y = -\dfrac{5}{4}x + \dfrac{3}{4}$

13. $(-2.4, 0)$

14. $\dfrac{24}{25}$

15. $3x^2 + 4y^2 - 12x - 56y + 196 = 0$

16. a.

$$\begin{bmatrix} 3 & -1 \\ 1 & 4 \end{bmatrix} \begin{bmatrix} x \\ y \end{bmatrix} = \begin{bmatrix} 2 \\ 18 \end{bmatrix}$$

b. $x = 2$, $y = 4$

8. (Cumulative Form)

$[152 \quad 520 \quad 1830] \cdot$

$$\begin{bmatrix} 1 & 6.2185 & 155.550 \\ 0.1608 & 1 & 25.0080 \\ 0.006429 & 0.03999 & 1 \end{bmatrix} =$$

$[247.38 \quad 1538.39 \quad 38477.76]$

ANSWERS

Functions, Statistics, and Trigonometry © Scott Foresman Addison Wesley

Quiz — Lessons 13-1 Through 13-3

1.

θ	sec θ	csc θ	cot θ
630°	und.	-1	0
$\frac{5\pi}{4}$	$-\sqrt{2}$	$-\sqrt{2}$	1
-420°	2	$-\frac{2\sqrt{3}}{3}$	$-\frac{\sqrt{3}}{3}$

2. domain = $\{x: x \neq n\pi$ for all integers $n\}$
range = $\{y: y \geq 1\}$

3. (d)

4. a. (b)

b. $(\csc^2\theta + \sec^2\theta)\sin 2\theta$

$= \left(\frac{1}{\sin^2\theta} + \frac{1}{\cos^2\theta}\right) \cdot$
$2\sin\theta\cos\theta$

$= \frac{\cos^2\theta + \sin^2\theta}{\sin^2\theta\cos^2\theta} \cdot$
$2\sin\theta\cos\theta$

$= \frac{2}{\sin\theta\cos\theta}$

$= \frac{4}{2\sin\theta\cos\theta}$

$= \frac{4}{\sin 2\theta} = 4\csc 2\theta$

c. $\theta \neq \frac{n\pi}{2}$, where n is an integer

8.

$a + bi$ form	trigonometric form	polar form
$2 - 2\sqrt{3}i$	$4\left(\cos\frac{\pi}{3} - i\sin\frac{\pi}{3}\right)$	$\left[4, \frac{-\pi}{3}\right]$
$-3\sqrt{2} - 3\sqrt{2}i$	$6(\cos 225° + i\sin 225°)$	$[6, 225°]$
$-5\sqrt{3} + 5i$	$10\left(\cos\frac{5\pi}{6} + i\sin\frac{5\pi}{6}\right)$	$\left[10, \frac{5\pi}{6}\right]$

Quiz — Lessons 13-4 Through 13-7

1., 2.

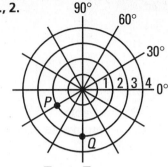

3. $(-2\sqrt{2}, -2\sqrt{2})$

4. $\left(\frac{-\sqrt{3}}{2}, -\frac{3}{2}\right)$

5. $\left(2, \frac{4\pi}{3}\right), \left(-2, \frac{\pi}{3}\right)$

6. $a = \sin 3\alpha$. So

$\sin 3\left(\alpha + \frac{\pi}{3}\right) =$

$\sin(3\alpha + \pi) =$

$-\sin 3\alpha = -a$. So $\left[a, \alpha + \frac{\pi}{3}\right]$
satisfies the equation
$r = \sin 3\theta$ and lies on its graph.

7. (b)

8. See below left.

Chapter 13 Test, Form A

1. -1

2. $x = 0, x = \pi$

3. undefined

4. $-\frac{\sqrt{3}}{3}$

5. $\sqrt{2}$

6. a. $x = 2$
b. removable

7. $(1, -1)$

8. (c)

9. $[6, 150°]$

10. $6(\cos 150° + i\sin 150°)$

11. $[2, 0], \left[-2, \frac{\pi}{8}\right], \left[0, \frac{\pi}{16}\right]$

12. a. $2 + i$

b.

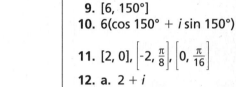

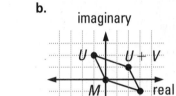

c. slope $\overline{U(U + V)}$
$= -\frac{1}{3} =$ slope $\overline{MV}$.
slope $\overline{UM} = -2 =$
slope $\overline{(U + V)V}$.

Opposite sides are parallel. Therefore it is a parallelogram.

ANSWERS

13.

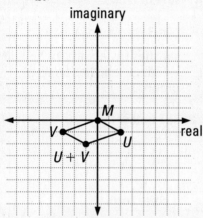

14. $10(\cos 154° + i \sin 154°)$
15. $0.4(\cos 46° - i \sin 46°)$
16. $32(\cos 150° - i \sin 150°)$
17. $3\left(\cos \frac{\pi}{10} + i \sin \frac{\pi}{10}\right)$

$3\left(\cos \frac{3\pi}{5} + i \sin \frac{3\pi}{5}\right)$

$3\left(\cos \frac{11\pi}{10} + i \sin \frac{11\pi}{10}\right)$

$3\left(\cos \frac{8\pi}{5} + i \sin \frac{8\pi}{5}\right)$

18. a. (c)
  b. $\cot \theta + \tan \theta$
  $= \dfrac{\cos \theta}{\sin \theta} + \dfrac{\sin \theta}{\cos \theta}$
  $= \dfrac{\cos^2\theta + \sin^2\theta}{\sin \theta \cos \theta}$
  $= \dfrac{1}{\sin \theta \cos \theta}$
  $= \dfrac{2}{2 \sin \theta \cos \theta} = \dfrac{2}{\sin 2\theta}$
  $= 2 \csc 2\theta$
  c. $\theta \neq \dfrac{n\pi}{2}$, for all integers n

---

1. 2π
2. $x = \frac{\pi}{2}, x = \frac{3\pi}{2}$
3. 2
4. $-\sqrt{2}$
5. undefined
6. a. $t = -3, t = 2$
   b. -3 removable, 2 nonremovable
7. $\left(\frac{3}{2}, -\frac{\sqrt{3}}{2}\right)$
8. (a)
9. $\left[4, -\frac{\pi}{3}\right]$
10. $4\left(\cos \frac{\pi}{3} - i \sin \frac{\pi}{3}\right)$
11. $[0, 0], \left[2, \frac{\pi}{16}\right], \left[-2, -\frac{\pi}{16}\right]$
12. a. $-1 - 2i$
   b.

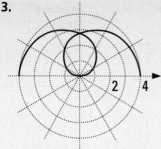

  c. slope $\overline{MU} = -\frac{1}{2}$
   $=$ slope $\overline{V(U + V)}$.
   slope $\overline{VM} = \frac{1}{3}$
   $=$ slope $\overline{(U + V)U}$.

   Opposite sides are parallel. Therefore it is a parallelogram.

13.

14. $40(\cos 186° + i \sin 186°)$
15. $0.4(\cos 34° - i \sin 34°)$
16. $32\left(\cos \frac{10\pi}{3} + i \sin \frac{10\pi}{3}\right)$
17. $4\left(\cos \frac{\pi}{14} + i \sin \frac{\pi}{14}\right)$

$4\left(\cos \frac{4\pi}{7} + i \sin \frac{4\pi}{7}\right)$

$4\left(\cos \frac{15\pi}{4} + i \sin \frac{15\pi}{4}\right)$

$4\left(\cos \frac{11\pi}{7} + i \sin \frac{11\pi}{7}\right)$

18. a. (c)
  b. $\csc^2\theta + \sec^2\theta$
  $= \dfrac{1}{\sin^2\theta} + \dfrac{1}{\cos^2\theta}$
  $= \dfrac{\cos^2\theta + \sin^2\theta}{\sin^2\theta \cos^2\theta}$
  $= \dfrac{1}{\sin^2\theta \cos^2\theta}$
  $= \dfrac{1}{\sin^2\theta} \cdot \dfrac{1}{\cos^2\theta}$
  $= \csc^2\theta \sec^2\theta$
  c. $\theta \neq \dfrac{n\pi}{2}$, for all integers n

Functions, Statistics, and Trigonometry © Scott Foresman Addison Wesley

Chapter 13 Test, Cumulative Form

1. $\dfrac{\csc x \sec x}{\cot x - \tan x}$

$= \dfrac{\csc x \sec x}{\dfrac{\cos x}{\sin x} - \dfrac{\sin x}{\cos x}}$

$= \dfrac{\csc x \sec x}{\dfrac{\cos^2 x - \sin^2 x}{\sin x \cos x}}$

$= \dfrac{\csc x \sec x \sin x \cos x}{\cos^2 x - \sin^2 x}$

$= \dfrac{1}{\cos^2 x - \sin^2 x}$

$= \dfrac{1}{\cos 2x}$

$= \sec 2x.$

2. $x \neq \dfrac{n\pi}{2}$, all integers n

3. a. $(2, 0)$, $(-2, 0)$
   b. $(\sqrt{29}, 0)$, $(-\sqrt{29}, 0)$
   c. $y = \pm\dfrac{5}{2}x$

4. $(-2\sqrt{2})$, $(2\sqrt{2})$

5. $[2, 210°]$ or $\left[2, \dfrac{7\pi}{6}\right]$

6. $\approx 8{,}377{,}274$

7.

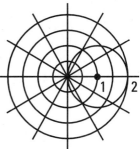

8. $x = -2 - y^2$
9. $3(\cos 60° + i \sin 60°)$
   $\dfrac{3}{2} + \dfrac{3\sqrt{3}}{2}i$

10. a. 8
   b. ≈ 0.196

11. -3, $\dfrac{3}{2} + \dfrac{3\sqrt{3}}{2}i$, $\dfrac{3}{2} - \dfrac{3\sqrt{3}}{2}i$

12.

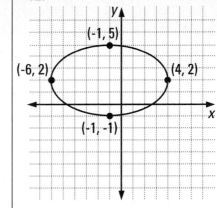

13. a. 8 ft
   b. ≈ 22.6 ft
14. $h(x) = \sin^2 x$
15. (b)
16. domain $= \{x: x \neq n\pi,$
   for all integers $n\}$
   range $= \{y: |y| \geq 2\}$
17. $13{,}485$
18. $\dfrac{2\pi}{3}$
19. degenerate ellipse
20. degenerate hyperbola

Comprehensive Test, Chapters 1-13

1. (b)
2. (b)
3. (d)
4. (b)
5. (c)
6. (d)
7. (d)
8. (c)
9. (a)
10. (b)
11. (d)
12. (c)
13. (b)
14. (c)
15. (c)
16. (b)
17. (d)
18. (c)
19. (b)
20. (c)
21. (a)
22. (a)
23. (c)
24. (c)
25. (a)
26. (a)
27. (c)
28. (b)
29. (c)
30. (b)
31. (a)
32. (b)
33. (c)
34. (c)
35. (c)
36. (d)
37. (a)
38. (d)
39. (a)
40. (d)
41. (c)
42. (a)
43. (a)
44. (a)
45. (c)
46. (a)
47. (d)
48. (b)
49. (c)
50. (b)

ANSWERS

1. Create a single set of data for which the following statements are each true. Justify your answer.

$$\sum_{i=6}^{8} g_i = 63 \qquad \frac{1}{8}\sum_{i=1}^{8} g_i = 19$$

Objectives A, B

☐ Is able to use sigma notation to represent a sum and a mean.
☐ Gives an appropriate set of data. (Sample: 17, 17, 18, 18, 19, 20, 21, 22)
☐ Gives a logical explanation.

2. Explain the difference between a *population* and a *sample*. Then describe a situation in which you might survey a population and a situation in which you might survey a sample.

Objective D

☐ Gives a logical explanation of the difference between a population and a sample.
☐ Gives an appropriate example of a situation in which a population is surveyed.
☐ Gives an appropriate example of a situation in which a sample is surveyed.

---

3. State at least two conclusions that can be drawn from the data in the table below.

United States Population (millions)				
Year	Age in Years			Total
	Under 20	20–64	Over 64	
1930	24.0	34.7	3.3	62.1
1950	25.9	43.1	5.8	74.8
1970	77.0	106.2	20.0	203.2
1990	71.7	145.9	31.1	248.7

Objective E

☐ Is able to interpret data presented in a table.
☐ Draws at least two correct conclusions. (Samples: Over the given intervals, the rate of population growth was greatest from 1950 to 1970. From 1930 to 1990, the percent of the population that is under 20 years of age is generally decreasing, while the percent over 64 years of age is generally increasing.)

4. The box plot and histogram represent the same set of data. What statistical measures can be read from the box plot but not the histogram? from the histogram but not the box plot? from neither?

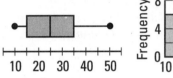

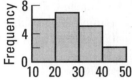

Objectives H, I

☐ Is able to read and interpret a box plot.
☐ Is able to read and interpret a histogram.
☐ Identifies measures that can be read from the box plot alone (Sample: five-number summary)
☐ Identifies measures that can be read from the histogram alone. (Sample: number of data items)
☐ Identifies measures that can be read from neither. (Samples: mean, standard deviation)

---

5. At the right are two students' scores on twelve math tests this year. Use statistical measures to compare and contrast the scores.

What do you think is the most appropriate type of display for these data? Explain your choice. Then draw the display.

Larry		Mary	
85	92	79	79
98	86	77	86
80	88	82	76
85	69	88	84
89	82	74	86
52	78	81	92

Objectives A, C, F, J

☐ Correctly calculates measures of center, spread, variance, and standard deviation for each data set. Samples are as follows.
Larry: range = 46; mean = 82; mode = 85; median = 85; Q_1 = 79; Q_3 = 88.5; $\sigma \approx 11.4$; IQR = 9.5; outlier = 52
Mary: range = 18; mean = 82; modes = 79, 86; median = 81.5; Q_1 = 78; Q_3 = 86; $\sigma \approx 15.1$; IQR = 8; no outliers
☐ Uses the statistical measures to make a meaningful comparison of the scores.
☐ Chooses and appropriate type of display and justifies the choice. (Sample: a back-to-back stemplot)
☐ Correctly draws a display of the data.

EVALUATION GUIDES

Teacher Notes

Objectives A, C, E, F, J

Concepts and Skills This activity requires students to:
- read and interpret information from a table.
- compare data using statistical measures.
- determine the statistical measures and displays most appropriate to a given situation.
- create a poster that utilizes statistical measures and display to convey a message.

Guiding Questions
- Each numerical entry in the table has three parts. What is the meaning of each part?
- If you know the number of data items and their mean, how can you calculate the *sum* of the items?
- In creating a poster, might it be more effective to arrange the data into broader categories? (Sample: *High School Diploma or Less* and *More Than High School Diploma*)

Answers
a. Answers will vary. Sample: The table gives data about income in the U.S. from 1991–1995. It organizes people into categories according to the amount of education they received, and it gives the mean and median income for each category.
b. Yes; ≈ $22,407
c. No. Explanations will vary. Sample: To find the median income for all persons, both male and female, you need to be given all the data items so that you can make a combined list of incomes arranged in increasing or decreasing order.
d. Answers will vary. Sample: The median. It is less likely to be affected by extremely high or low incomes, so it probably is more representative of income for the general population.
e. Answers will vary. Sample: Display the data in a line graph.
f. Answers will vary. Check students' work.

Extension
Have students research other data relating educational attainment to attributes of the population. (Some samples are health insurance coverage and cigarette smoking.) Tell them to compute any significant statistical measures and then create an appropriate display of the data and the measures. Ask them what conclusions, if any, can be drawn from the data.

216

Evaluation

Level | **Standard to be achieved for performance at specified level**

5 The student demonstrates an in-depth understanding of statistical measures and visual data displays studied in the chapter. All calculations, graphs, and displays are accurate and complete. The student prepares a poster that effectively conveys the desired message, and it may be presented imaginatively.

4 The student demonstrates a clear understanding of the statistical measures and visual data displays studied in the chapter. The student performs all necessary calculations and prepares appropriate displays, but they may contain minor errors. The poster effectively utilizes the given data to convey the desired message, but it may lack in some detail.

3 The student demonstrates a fundamental understanding of the statistical measures and displays studied in the chapter, but may need some assistance in making appropriate choices for the given situations. There may be one or more major errors or omissions in the student's calculations or displays. The poster is essentially complete, but it may not convey the desired message as effectively as possible.

2 The student demonstrates some understanding of the statistical measures and displays studied in the chapter, but needs considerable assistance in making appropriate choices for the given situations. Even with help, the student may make several major errors in performing calculations or creating displays, or may omit one or more major steps of a process. The student attempts to prepare a poster, but it lacks cohesion and does not convey the message effectively.

1 The student demonstrates little if any understanding of the statistical measures and displays studied in the chapter. Any attempts to perform calculations or create displays are superfluous or irrelevant. Rather than create an original presentation of data for the poster, the student may simply copy the given table.

Functions, Statistics, and Trigonometry © Scott Foresman Addison Wesley

EVALUATION GUIDES

1. Draw and label a set of coordinate axes. On the axes, sketch the graph of a relation that is *not* a function. State the domain and range of the relation, and explain how you know it is not a function.

Objective J

☐ Is able to interpret properties of relations from graphs.
☐ Sketches an appropriate relation.
☐ Correctly identifies the domain and range.
☐ Gives a logical explanation.

2. Compare $f(x) = x^2$ with $g(x) = 2^x$. How are the functions and their graphs alike? How are they different? State at least two significant likenesses and two significant differences.

Objectives B, D

☐ Is able to describe propoerties of quadratic and exponential functions.
☐ States at least two likenesses, (Sample: Each is defined on the domain of all real numbers.)
☐ States at least two differences. (Sample: The minimum point of the graph of *f* is (0, 0); the graph of *g* has no minimum point.)

3. Give an example of a real-life situation that you can model with a floor function and another situation that you can model with a ceiling function. If possible, use Euler's notation to describe each function. If it is not possible, explain why. Then graph each function on a separate set of coordinate axes.

Objectives A, H, I

☐ Understands the use of Euler's notation.
☐ Recognizes the types of situations that can be modeled by step functions.
☐ Recognizes the characteristics of the graph a step function.
☐ Gives an appropriate floor-function situation.
☐ Gives an appropriate ceiling-function situation.
☐ Gives a logical explanation of the use of Euler's notation.
☐ Correctly graphs each function.

4. The data at the right appear in the *Statistical Abstract of the United States, 1995*. Find a linear model, an exponential model, and a quadratic model for these data. Which model do you think is most appropriate? Explain.

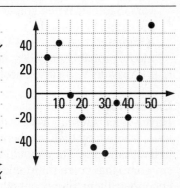

VCRs in U.S. Households	
Year	Millions
1980	1
1985	18
1988	51
1989	58
1990	63
1991	67
1992	69
1993	72
1994	74

Objectives E, F, G

☐ Demonstrates an understanding of linear, exponential, and quadratic models for data.
☐ Finds appropriate models. (Given $x =$ years after 1980 and $V =$ millions of VCRs, models are $V = 5.74x + 0.266$; $V = 2.43(1.34)^x$; and $V = -0.103^x + 7.2^x - 2.73$.)
☐ Identifies the quadratic model as most appropriate *over the given period*.
☐ Gives a logical explanation.

5. At the right are two scatterplots related to a set of data. Explain what they tell you about the data. What conclusions, if any, might you draw about the data?

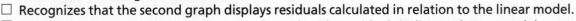

Objectives C, K

☐ Understands properties of regression lines.
☐ Is able to use scatterplots to draw conclusions about models for data.
☐ Recognizes that the first graph displays a set of data and a regression line.
☐ Recognizes that the second graph displays residuals calculated in relation to the linear model.
☐ Draws one or more correct conclusions. (Sample: The residuals indicate a better model probably exists.)

EVALUATION GUIDES

Teacher Notes

Objectives E, F, G, H, I, K

Concepts and Skills This activity requires students to:
- read information from tables.
- understand characteristics of functions.
- recognize when data can and cannot be used to make predictions.
- model situations using linear, exponential, quadratic, and step functions.
- summarize results in graphics and in writing.

Guiding Questions
- How do you use a model to make an estimate or a prediction?
- When several models seem very close to the data, what technique can you use to describe if one is more suitable than the others?

Answers
a. All. Sample explanation: Each can be represented as a set of ordered pairs, (x, y) in which each value of x corresponds to exactly one value of y.

b. The income tax data. Sample explanation: Data are only given for one year, so it is impossible to analyze it to find a trend over time.

c. If x = year after 1970, y = population (1000s):
   i. $y = 8.056x + 330.2$ **ii.** $y = 338.4(1.019)^x$
   iii. $y = 0.1390x^2 + 4.474x + 343.7$

d. **i.** about 370.5 thousand
   ii. about 371.2 thousand
   iii. about 369.5 thousand; The values obtained from all three models are relatively close, so any model provides a reasonable estimate.

e. **i.** about 580.0 thousand
   ii. about 600.0 thousand
   iii. about 615.9 thousand; Answers may vary. Sample: When graphed, the residuals of the exponential model most closely fall into a horizontal band centered around zero, so this model probably provides the best prediction.

f., g. Answers will vary. Check students' work.

Extension
Have students research data about the city or town where they live, or where they might like to live some day. They should try to find data similar to that given for Mapleville, but also encourage them to seek out other categories of data. Have them use their data to make as many predictions as possible about life in the chosen city or town five years from now.

Evaluation

Level	Standard to be achieved for performance at specified level
5	The student demonstrates an in-depth understanding of function concepts and the use of functions as models of data. Models are chosen thoughtfully, and all calculations and graphs are accurate and complete. The student prepares a well-organized set of graphs and a reasonable set of predictions, and they may be presented imaginatively.
4	The student demonstrates a clear understanding of function concepts and the use of functions as models for data. The chosen models are all appropriate, but some calculations and graphic displays may contain minor errors. The set of graphs and the predictions are well-organized and easy to read, but they may lack in some detail.
3	The student demonstrates a fundamental understanding of function concepts and the use of functions as models for data, but may need some asssistance in making appropriate choices for the given situations. There may be one or more major errors or omissions in the student's calculations or graphs. A complete set of graphs and predictions is prepared, but it may be somewhat lacking in focus.
2	The student demonstrates some understanding of function concepts and the use of functions as models for data, but needs considerable assistance in making appropriate choices for the given situations. Even with help, the student may make several major errors in performing calculations or generating graphs, or may omit a major step of the process. The student attempts to prepare a set of graphs and predictions, but it is jumbled and incomplete.
1	The student demonstrates little if any understanding of function concepts and the use of functions as models for data. Even with assistance, any attempts to choose models or graph them are incoherent or irrelevant. Instead of making meaningful predictions, the student may simply restate the given information.

1. Identify a transformation S that stretches the graph of $y = \lceil x \rceil$ vertically and shrinks it horizontally. Give an equation for the image of the graph under the transformation.

Objectives C, D

☐ Understands the Graph Scale-Change Theorem.
☐ Understands the effect of a scale change on a function and its graph.
☐ Gives an appropriate transformation. (Sample: $S: (x, y) \rightarrow (0.5x, 3y)$)
☐ Gives a correct equation. (Sample for the transformation S given above: $y = 3\lceil 2x \rceil$)

2. Kioko says that, if a parent function is even, then the function represented by a translation of its graph also is even. Is Kioko's statement always, sometimes, or never true? Explain, using graphs to illustrate your response.

Objectives F, J, K

☐ Is able to recognize and graph parent functions.
☐ Understands the Graph Translation Theorem.
☐ Understands the symmetries of graphs.
☐ Describes Kioko's statement as *sometimes true*.
☐ Gives a logical explanation.
☐ Draws appropriate graphs.

3. Let $f(x) = \frac{3}{x}$. Identify a function g such that $(f \circ g)(1) = 1$. What is $(g \circ f)(1)$? Give a formula for $f \circ g$ and a formula for $g \circ f$. What are the domain and range of $f \circ g$? What are the domain and range of $g \circ f$.

Objectives A, G

☐ Is able to find values of composites of functions.
☐ Understands properties of composites.
☐ Identifies an appropriate function g. (Sample: $g(x) = x + 2$)
☐ Correctly evaluates $(g \circ f)(1)$. (Sample: When $g(x) = x + 2$, $(g \circ f)(1) = 5$.)
☐ Gives correct formulas for the composites. (Sample: When $g(x) = x + 2$, $(f \circ g)(x) = \frac{3}{x + 2}$ and $(g \circ f)(x) = \frac{3}{x} + 2$)
☐ Correctly identifies the domains and ranges.

4. A set of data is transformed by a translation. Then the same set of data is transformed by a scale change. Compare the effects of these transformations on the measures of center and spread. How are they alike? different? Give examples to justify your response.

Objectives E, I

☐ Understands the effects of translations and scale changes on measures of center and spread.
☐ Is able to use translations and scale changes to analyze data.
☐ Describes a significant likeness. (Sample: Both transformations change the measures of center.)
☐ Describes a significant difference. (Sample: Scale changes change the measures of spread, but translations do not.
☐ Gives appropriate examples.

5. The diagram at the right is supposed to appear in a lesson about functions, but someone lost the caption. What do you think the diagram is meant to illustrate? Label the graphs and write an appropriate caption.

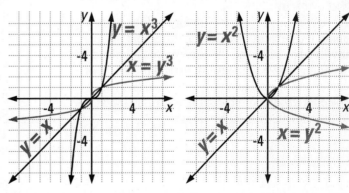

Objectives B, G, M

☐ Is able to find inverses of functions.
☐ Is able to identify properties of inverses.
☐ Is able to graph inverses.
☐ Recognizes that the figures show one function whose inverse is a function ($y = x^3$) and another function whose inverse is not a function ($y = x^2$).
☐ Labels the graphs correctly. (See sample labels on diagram.)
☐ Writes an appropriate caption.

Functions, Statistics, and Trigonometry © Scott Foresman Addison Wesley

EVALUATION GUIDES

Teacher Notes

Objectives A, B, C, D, J

Concepts and Skills This activity requires students to:
- read information from text and a table.
- find algebraic models for sets of data.
- find formulas and values of inverses and composites of functions.
- create an informative poster using functions and graphs to illustrate the desired message.

Guiding Questions
- When the reaction time is 1.5 seconds, what is the value of n? [$n = 2$]
- What is the stopping distance for a speed of 40 km/h? [18.740 m]
- What message(s) will you try to convey with your poster? [Samples: Don't drink and drive. Avoid excessive speed.]

Answers
a. i. $f(x) - .2085x$ **ii.** Check students' graphs.   **iii.** $p(x) = x$.
b. i. $T: (x, y) \rightarrow (x, 2y)$ **ii.** scale change   **iii.** Check students' graphs. The graph of f is stretched horizontally.   **iv.** $q(x) = x$
c. i. $h(x) = \frac{1}{.2085}x$, or $h(x) \approx 4.7962x$ **ii.** They are inverse functions.   **iii.** $r(x) = x$
d. i. $j(x) = 3.28x$ **ii.** $(j \circ f)(x) = .68388x$ **iii.** You use $(j \circ f)(x)$ to compute reaction distance in feet given a speed in kilometers per hour.
e. $k(x) = .2085x + .0065x^2$
f. Check students' work.

Extension
Have students research data for the fifty states about the percent of traffic fatalities that involved alcohol and the percent that involved speeding. Have them use statistical measures of center and spread to analyze the data and use z-scores to compare the statistics for their state to the statistics for other states.

Evaluation

Standard to be achieved for
Level   **performance at specified level**

5   The student demonstrates and in-depth understanding of functions, inverses, composites, and their application to the given situation. All calculations, equations, and graphs are accurate and complete. The student creates a well-organized poster that conveys the desired message effectively, and may present thoughtful conclusions, beyond those prompted by the questions in the activity.

4   The student demonstrates a clear understanding of functions, inverses, composites, and their application to the given situation. The student performs appropriate calculations and develops the required equations and graphs, but they may contain minor errors. The poster is well organized and informative, but it may lack in some detail.

3   The student demonstrates a fundamental understanding of functions, inverses, and composites, but may need some assistance in applying the concepts to the given situation. There may be one or more major errors or omissions in calculations, equations, or graphs. The poster is essentially complete, but it may be somewhat disorganized.

2   The student demonstrates some understanding of functions, inverses, composites, but needs considerable assistance in understanding their application to the given situation. Even with help, there may be several major errors in the student's calculations, equations, or graphs. The student attempts to create a poster, but it is jumbled and does not effectively convey the desired message.

1   The student demonstrates little if any understanding of functions, inverses, composites, and their application to the given situation. Even with assistance, any attempts to perform calculations or to develop equations or graphs are superficial or irrelevant. Rather than create an informative poster, the student may simply copy the given data.

Functions, Statistics, and Trigonometry © Scott Foresman Addison Wesley

EVALUATION GUIDES

220

1. Choose any rotation of magnitude greater than one full turn and less than $1\frac{1}{4}$ turns. Specify a direction of rotation, and draw a picture to illustrate the rotation. Then give the measure of the angle of rotation as a number of revolutions, a number of degrees, and a number of radians.

Objective A

☐ Understands relationships among revolution, degree, and radian measures of a rotation.

☐ Identifies an appropriate rotation and direction. (Sample: one and one-sixth turns clockwise)

☐ Draws an appropriate picture.

☐ Gives correct measures for the chosen rotation. (Sample [for the above rotation]: $1\frac{1}{6}$ revolutions clockwise, -420°, $-\frac{7\pi}{3}$ radians)

2. In circle P, Kelly found the area of the shaded region to be 3240 m² by applying the Circular Sector Area Formula as follows.

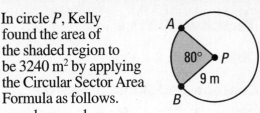

$$A = \tfrac{1}{2}\theta r^2 = \tfrac{1}{2}(80)(9)^2$$

However, Kelly realized that the area of the entire circle is only about 250 m². Identify the error in Kelly's work and correct it.

Objective B

☐ Is able to find the area of a sector of a circle.

☐ Recognizes that θ must be measured in radians in order to apply the formula.

☐ Finds the correct area. (18π m², or ≈ 56.5 m²)

---

3. Choose one of these theorems: Opposites Theorem, Supplements Theorem, Complements Theorem, Half-Turn Theorem. State the theorem. Then show how you can use the unit circle to show that it is true.

Objectives D, E, J

☐ Understands the concept of the unit circle.

☐ Understands the definitions of sin, cos and tan.

☐ Is able to apply theorems about sines, cosines, and tangents.

☐ Makes a correct statement of one theorem.

☐ Uses the unit circle to demonstrate the theorem.

4. Suppose you are asked *What is cos (-150°)?* and *What is cos (-151°)?* How is answering the first question similar to answering the second? How is it different? Name as many similarities and differences as you can.

Objective C

☐ Is able to find sines, cosines, and tangents of angles.

☐ Identifies one or more similarities. (Sample: Both values can be approximated using a calculator.)

☐ Identifies one or more differences. (Sample: The value cos (-150°) can be found exactly.)

---

5. The functions f and g, graphed at the right, are a parent circular function and its image under a transformation. Identify the parent function and the transformation. Then make a table in which you compare f and g by listing as many properties of each as you can.

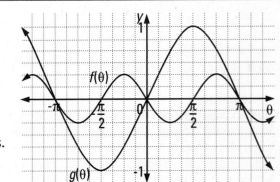

Objectives F, K, M

☐ Is able to identify properties of circular functions.

☐ Is able to interpret graphs of parent circular functions.

☐ Is able to state equations for graphs of circular functions.

☐ Recognizes that g is the parent function. ($g(x) = \sin x$)

☐ Correctly identifies the transformation that maps g to f. ($T: (x, y) \rightarrow \left(\frac{1}{2}x - \frac{\pi}{2}, \frac{1}{3}y\right)$)

☐ Lists several properties of g. (Samples: amplitude 1, period 2π, phase shift 0, vertical shift 0)

☐ Lists several properties of f. (Samples: amplitude $\frac{1}{3}$, period π, phase shift $\frac{\pi}{2}$, vertical shift 0)

EVALUATION GUIDES

Teacher Notes

Objectives F, I, J, L

Concepts and Skills This activity requires students to:
- read information from text and graphics.
- identify points on a unit circle.
- use circular functions to model periodic phenomena.
- identify properties of circular functions.
- graph transformation images of circular functions.
- summarize results in a written set of instructions.

Guiding Questions
- What is the measure of the angle formed by $\overline{AB}$ and the y-axis when $t = 5$? [30°, or $\frac{\pi}{6}$ radians]
- How can you assure that the numbers identifying the address are integers? [Use the floor function or the ceiling function.]

Answers

a. p: $0, \frac{1}{2}, \frac{\sqrt{3}}{2}, 1, \frac{\sqrt{3}}{2}, \frac{1}{2}, 0, -\frac{1}{2}, -\frac{\sqrt{3}}{2}, -1, -\frac{\sqrt{3}}{2}, -\frac{1}{2}, 0$; q: $1, \frac{\sqrt{3}}{2}, \frac{1}{2}, 0, -\frac{1}{2}, -\frac{\sqrt{3}}{2}, -1, -\frac{\sqrt{3}}{2}, -\frac{1}{2}, 0, \frac{1}{2}, \frac{\sqrt{3}}{2}, 1$

b. (iii)

c. $p - \sin\left(\frac{\pi}{30}t\right) + 2$

d. $p = 5\sin\left(\frac{\pi}{30}\right)$

e. Answers will vary. Sample: $q - \cos\left(\frac{\pi}{30}t\right)$

f. Answers will vary. Samples (using the equation given in part **e**): **d.** $p = \cos\left(\frac{\pi}{30}\right) + 3$; **e.** $p = 5\cos\left(\frac{\pi}{30}\right)$

g., h. Check students' work.

Extension
Have students write a similar set of equations to simulate the movement of the tip of the minute hand of the stopwatch (the hand within the smaller dial). Have them research other common resolutions for computer screens and modify all their equations to accommodate these resolutions. To check the effectiveness of the equations, have students research how to use the parametric graphing mode of an automatic grapher.

Evaluation

Level	Standard to be achieved for performance at specified level
5	The student demonstrates an in-depth understanding of circular functions and their application to the given situation. All questions are answered accurately and completely. The student prepares a thorough, well-organized set of instructions, and it may be presented imaginatively. The student may offer additional insights.
4	The student demonstrates a clear understanding of circular functions and their application to the given situation. The student completes the table of values, chooses appropriate equations, and renders suitable graphs, but the work may contain minor errors. The instructions are well-organized and easy to read, but they may lack in some detail.
3	The student demonstrates a fundamental understanding of circular functions, but may need some assistance in applying the concepts to the given situation. There may be one or more major errors or omissions in the student's calculations, equations, or graphs. The instructions are essentially complete, but they may be somewhat unstructured and difficult to follow.
2	The student demonstrates some understanding of circular functions, but needs considerable assistance in understanding their application to the given situation. Even with help, the student may make several major errors in completing the table, writing equations, or rendering graphs. The student attempts to prepare a set of instructions, but it is incomplete and lacks focus.
1	The student demonstrates little if any understanding of circular functions and their application to the given situation. Even with assistance, any attempts to complete the table, write equations, or prepare graphs are cursory or irrelevant. Rather than write a set of instructions, the students may simply copy or restate the given information.

EVALUATION GUIDES

Functions, Statistics, and Trigonometry © Scott Foresman Addison Wesley

1. On grid paper, draw two different right triangles ABC in which $\angle C$ is the right angle and $\tan B = .8$. Then find the following measures in each triangle: AC, BC, AB, $\sin A$, $\cos A$, $\sin B$, $\cos B$, $m\angle A$, $m\angle B$.

Objectives A, C

☐ Is able to find sines, cosines, and tangents.
☐ Is able to use trigonometry to find angles.
☐ Draws two appropriate triangles.
☐ Gives correct measures for each triangle.
Samples: $AC = 8$, $BC = 10$, $AB \approx 12.8$, $\sin A = \cos B \approx .625$, $\sin B = \cos A \approx .781$, $m\angle A \approx 38.7°$, $m\angle B \approx 51.3°$; and $AC = 4$, $BC = 5$, $AB \approx 6.4$, all other measures identical.
☐ Gives appropriate justifications.

2. In $\triangle RST$, $m\angle T = 52.1°$ and $s = 7$. Give a length t that leads to a unique $\triangle RST$. Then use the given measures and your length t to find $m\angle R$, $m\angle S$, the length r, and the area of $\triangle RST$.

Objectives C, E

☐ Is able to use trigonometry to find measures of angles, lengths, and areas.
☐ Demonstrates an understanding of the Law of Sines.
☐ Chooses an appropriate length t. (Sample: any $t > 7$)
☐ Gives correct measures based on the chosen length. (Sample: If $t = 8$, then $m\angle R \approx 84.2°$, $m\angle S \approx 43.7°$, $r \approx 10.1$, area ≈ 27.9 sq. units)
☐ Gives appropriate justifications.

3. All the following are true statements.
$$\cos\frac{\pi}{3} = .5 \quad \cos\frac{5\pi}{3} = .5 \quad \cos\frac{7\pi}{6} = .5$$
However, the unique value of $\cos^{-1}(.5)$ is $\frac{\pi}{3}$. Explain how this is possible. Then describe a similar situation involving sines.

Objectives B, F

☐ Can evaluate inverse trigonometric functions.
☐ Understands properties of inverse trigonometric functions.
☐ Gives a logical explanation.
☐ Gives a similar situation using sines. (Sample: $\sin 0 = \sin 2\pi = \sin 4\pi = 0$, but $\sin^{-1}0 = 0$).

4. The following equation can be used to model the average monthly temperature T for Cleveland, Ohio, in degrees Fahrenheit, where n is the month after January.
$$T = 23.78 \sin(.49n - 1.51) + 48.16$$
Write a problem that you can solve using this equation. Show how to solve your problem.

Objectives D, I

☐ Is able to solve trigonometric equations.
☐ Is able to apply a trigonometric equation to a real phenomenon.
☐ Writes and appropriate problem.
☐ Gives a correct solution to the problem.

5. Josh drew the diagram at the right as a summary of the inverse trigonometric functions, but he forgot to label the graphs.

Are Josh's graphs accurate? Do they give a *good* representation of the functions? Explain your reasoning. Modify any graphs that you think are inaccurate or inadequate. Then label the graphs with appropriate equations.

Inverse Trigonometric Functions

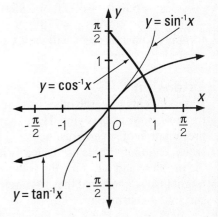

Objectives F, J

☐ Understands properties of inverse trigonometric functions.
☐ Is able to identify graphs of inverse trigonometric functions.
☐ Recognizes that the graphs are accurate in the chosen intervals.
☐ Recognizes that the graph of $y = \cos^{-1}x$ should be extended over the interval $0 \le y \le \pi$, and correctly extends the graph.
☐ Correctly labels the graphs. (See labels on diagram.)

Functions, Statistics, and Trigonometry © Scott Foresman Addison Wesley

Teacher Notes

Objectives A, B, C, D, E, H

Concepts and Skills This activity requires students to:
- read information from text and diagrams.
- find lengths and angle measures using ruler, protractor, and the scale of a drawing.
- find lengths and areas using trigonometry.
- interpret the Laws of Sines and Cosines.
- investigate accuracy and precision in measurement.
- summarize results in a written report.

Materials

- protractor and customary ruler.

Guiding Questions

- How can you find the area of the triangular plot of land using just the given measures?
- How can you use techniques for finding the area of a triangle to help you find the area of the larger plot of land?
- What is the relationship between square feet and square yards?

Answers

a. Yes. The measures satisfy the ASA condition.
b. angle: 104°; sides: ≈ 119.9 yd, ≈ 180.9 yd; area: ≈ 2.2 acres.
c. angle: 104°; sides: ≈ 124.9 yd, ≈ 184.4 yd; area: ≈ 2.4 acres.
d. angle: 102°; sides: ≈ 122.7 yd, ≈ 182.3 yd; area: ≈ 2.3 acres.
e. part **b**: \$176,000; part **c**: \$192,000; part **d**: \$184,000; A difference in area of .1 acre gives a difference in sale price of \$8000.
f. angles: $\approx 94°$, $\approx 59°$, $\approx 103°$, $\approx 104°$; sides: ≈ 550 ft, ≈ 600 ft, ≈ 288 ft, ≈ 425 ft; diagonals: ≈ 568 ft, ≈ 718 ft; area: ≈ 4.6 acres. Other answers will vary. Check students' work.

Extension

Have students research other uses of trigonometry in surveying. Have them prepare a presentation of several distinct situations in which trigonometry is used, clearly identifying the problem and outlining the solution. You might also suggest that they research types of surveying instruments.

Evaluation

Level	Standard to be achieved for performance at specified level
5	The student demonstrates an in-depth understanding of the Laws of Sines and Cosines and their application to the given situations. All calculations are accurate and complete. The student prepares a well-organized report that describes the dimensions of the property in detail and thoughtfully probes the issues of accuracy and precision. The student may offer additional insights.
4	The student demonstrates a clear understanding of the Laws of Sines and Cosines and their applications to the given situations. All questions are answered thoughtfully, but responses may reflect minor errors in calculations. The report contains sound recommendations and is well-organized, but it may lack in some detail.
3	The student demonstrates a fundamental understanding of the Laws of Sines and Cosines, but may need some assistance in applying them to the given situations. There may be one or more major errors or omissions in the student's responses to the questions posed. The report is essentially complete, but it may be somewhat disorganized.
2	The student demonstrates some understanding of the Laws of Sines and Cosines, but needs considerable assistance in understanding their application to the given situations. Even with help, the student may make several major errors in answering the questions posed, or may omit one or more major steps of a process. The student attempts to prepare a report, but it is incomplete and lacks focus.
1	The student demonstrates little if any understanding of the Law of Sines and Cosines and their application to the given situations. Even with assistance, any attempts to answer the questions posed are superficial or irrelevant. Rather than write a report, the student may simply restate the given information or copy the given diagrams.

Functions, Statistics, and Trigonometry © Scott Foresman Addison Wesley

1. a. Consider the expression $a^{\frac{b}{c}}$. Give integral values of the variables *other than 0 or 1* for which it is possible to evaluate the expression without using a calculator. Show how to evaluate the expression.

  b. Repeat part **a** for the expression $\log_m n$.

  c. Repeat part **a** for the expression $\ln e^x$.

Objectives A, C

☐ Is able to evaluate $b^{\frac{m}{n}}$ for $b > 0$.
☐ Is able to evaluate logarithms.
☐ Gives appropriate values for $a^{\frac{b}{c}}$. (Sample: When $a = 8$, $b = 2$, and $c = 3$, $a^{\frac{b}{c}} = 4$.)
☐ Gives appropriate values for $\log_m n$. (Sample: When $m = 3$ and $n = 81$, $\log_m n = 4$.)
☐ Gives an appropriate value for $\ln e^x$. (Sample: For any integer x, $\ln e^x = x$.)

2. Elena solved $5^n = 24$ as shown at the right. Explain how you can tell without calculating that $n \approx 34.34$ is an unreasonable solution. Then correct Elena's error(s) and give the correct solution.

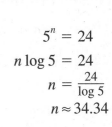

$$5^n = 24$$
$$n \log 5 = 24$$
$$n = \frac{24}{\log 5}$$
$$n \approx 34.34$$

Objective B

☐ Is able to solve exponential equations.
☐ Explains why the answer is unreasonable. (Sample: $5^2 = 25$, so n should be less than 2.)
☐ Identifies Elena's error. (Elena did not take the log of both sides of the equation.)
☐ Gives the correct solution. ($n \approx 1.97$)

3. Using the properties of logarithms, write four expressions involving logarithms that are equivalent to $\log_b 36$. In each case, identify the property of logarithms that you applied.

Objective E

☐ Demonstrates an understanding of the properties of logarithms.
☐ Gives four appropriate expressions. (Samples: $\log_b 4 + \log_b 9$, $\log_b 72 - \log_b 2$, $2 \log_b 6$, $\log 36 \div \log b$)
☐ Correctly identifies the properties used. (Samples [for the expressions given above]: Logarithm of a Product Theorem, Logarithm of a Quotient Theorem, Logarithm of a Power Theorem, Change of Base Theorem)

4. Using the coordinate axes below, draw a figure that illustrates this statement: *In general, the logarithm function with base b is the inverse of the exponential function with base b.* Then write a brief description of the figure you drew.

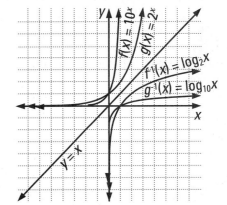

Objectives I, J

☐ Is able to graph logarithm functions.
☐ Is able to interpret graphs of logarithm functions.
☐ Draws an appropriate figure. (See sample on axes above.)
☐ Gives an appropriate description. (Sample: The graph of $y = \log_{10} x$ is the reflection image of the graph of $y = 10^x$ across the line $y = x$; and the graph of $y = \log_2 x$ is the reflection image of the graph of $y = 2^x$ across the line $y = x$; so each pair of functions are inverses.)

Teacher Notes

Objectives B, E, G, H

Concepts and Skills This activity requires students to:
- read information from a table and text.
- solve exponential equations.
- use properties of logarithms.
- use exponential and logarithmic models for data.
- solve problems arising from a logarithmic model.
- make decisions based on real-life experiences.
- summarize results in a written report.

Materials
- statistics utility

Guiding Questions
- When using the exponential model, how is predicting an amount for a given year different from predicting a year for a given amount?
- To plan the financing of a college education, would you consider the most expensive option, the least expensive, or something in between?
- What is a reasonable amount of money you might invest now? What is a reasonable amount of money you might borrow in twenty years?
- How much interest might you earn on a savings account? a certificate of deposit? a different type of investment?
- How much interest might you pay on a loan?

Answers
a. i. $y = 702.71(1.067)^x$
ii. $\log y = 0.28x + 2.85$
iii. In part **ii,** the relationship involving the data as transformed by logarithms is nearly linear, with $r \approx .996$. So the exponential model for the original data is very good.
b. i. about $7738 **ii.** 2007-08
c. i. $13,634.25   **ii.** about 28.9 years
d. i. 556 months, or 46 years, 4 months
ii. $51,200
e. Answers will vary. Check students' work.

Extension
Have students use the given formula to derive the Monthly Payment and Amount of Loan formulas:

$$a = \frac{Pr(1 + r)^n}{(1 + r)^n - 1} \qquad P = \frac{a[(1 + r)^n - 1]}{r(1 + r)^n}$$

Have students discuss how they might use these formulas in developing their financial plans.

226

Evaluation

Level	Standard to be achieved for performance at specified level
5	The student demonstrates an in-depth understanding of exponents and logarithms and their application to the given situation. All questions are answered thoughtfully, and all calculations are accurate. The student's plan is reasonable and is presented in a well-organized manner. The student may offer additional insights or explore other financing options.
4	The student demonstrates a clear understanding of exponents and logarithms. The student applies appropriate methods in answering the questions posed, but there may be minor errors in calculations. The student develops a reasonable plan and summarizes it in a report that is well-organized and easy to read, but the report may lack in some detail.
3	The student demonstrates a fundamental understanding of exponents and logarithms, but may need some assistance in applying the concepts to the given situation. The student answers all the questions posed, but may make one or more major errors or omit an important step of a process. The student develops a plan that is essentially sound, but the presentation may be disorganized and difficult to follow.
2	The student demonstrates some understanding of exponents and logarithms, but needs considerable assistance in applying the concepts to the given situation. Even with help, the student may make several major errors or may omit critical steps of a process. The student attempts to develop a financial plan, but it is somewhat unreasonable, and the presentation is jumbled and incomplete.
1	The student demonstrates little if any understanding of exponents and logarithms and their application to the given situation. Even with assistance, any attempts to address the tasks at hand are superficial or irrelevant. Instead of developing a plan, the student may simply copy or restate the given situations.

1. Each regular *octahedral* die at the right is fair and has eight faces numbered 1, 2, 3, 4, 5, 6, 7, 8. Describe an experiment related to the two dice and list the sample space. Then describe four events—E_1, E_2, E_3, and E_4—that satisfy the following conditions.

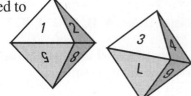

$P(E_1) = 0 \quad P(E_2) = .5 \quad P(E_3) = 1 \quad .5 < P(E_4) < 1$

Objectives A, B, E

☐ Is able to list sample spaces and events for probabilistic experiments.
☐ Is able to compute probabilities.
☐ Is able to use properties of probabilities.
☐ Describes an appropriate experiment. (Sample: rolling the dice and finding the sum of the top numbers)
☐ Gives the correct sample space. (Sample [for the experiment described above]): 2, 3, 4, . . . , 16
☐ Identifies three appropriate events. (Sample [for the experiment described above]: E_1: sum of dice = 1; E_2: sum of dice is an odd number; E_3: sum of dice < 20; E_4: sum of dice > 2)

---

2. You and a friend are studying factorials together, and your friend asks why you can't write $(n - 5)! = n! - 5!$. How would you explain?

Objective D

☐ Is able to evaluate expressions using factorials.
☐ Gives a logical explanation. (Sample: As a counterexample, let $n = 6$. Then $(n - 5)! = (6 - 5)! = 1! = 1$. However, $n! - 5! = 6! - 5! = 720 - 120 = 600$.)

3. Draw a spinner that has the probability distribution shown below. Then give the expected value of one spin of your spinner.

x	1	2	3	4	5	6
$P(x)$	$\frac{1}{8}$	$\frac{1}{8}$	$\frac{1}{4}$	$\frac{1}{8}$	$\frac{1}{8}$	$\frac{1}{4}$

Objective L

☐ Is able to interpret a probability distribution.
☐ Draws an appropriate spinner. (See above.)
☐ Gives the correct expected value. (3.75)

---

4. At the right is shown an intersection of two streets. An engineer needs to find probabilities for all possible paths of a car entering this intersection from the south. Which events should the engineer consider? Characterize the events you identify as: complementary, mutually exclusive, dependent, or independent.

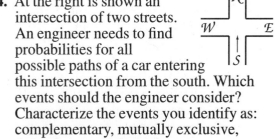

Objectives F, H

☐ Is able to determine if events are mutually exclusive, independent, or complementary.
☐ Is able to apply probabilities to real situations.
☐ Identifies an appropriate set of events. (turn right, turn left, drive straight)
☐ Chooses correct terms for the events. (mutually exclusive, dependent)
☐ Gives a logical explanation.

5. For their next test, a math class may choose:

  (i) *n* multiple-choice items, with each item having choices A, B, C, and D; or

  (ii) an equal number *n* of "matching" items, with each item in column A matching to exactly one of *n* items in column B.

The students believe they have a better chance of correctly guessing all the answers with option (ii). Do you agree or do you disagree? Explain your answer.

Objectives C, I

☐ Is able to find the number of ways of selecting or arranging objects.
☐ Is able to use counting principles and theorems in real situations.
☐ Recognizes that the number of ways to answer the test is 4^n in option (i) and $n!$ in option (ii).
☐ Recognizes that option (ii) is better if $n < 9$, but option (i) is better if $n \geq 9$.

EVALUATION GUIDES

Teacher Notes

Objectives A, B, E, H, J, K, L

Concepts and Skills This activity requires students to:
- list sample spaces for probabilistic events.
- compute probabilities and use their properties.
- apply probabilities to real situations.
- Construct and interpret probability distributions.
- design and conduct simulations.
- create an original game and describe it in a detailed presentation.

Guiding Questions
- In making a probability distribution for the game shown, why is it not sufficient to just list the outcomes *Win* and *Lose*?
- How might you adjust the given game to make it more likely to raise money for charity?

Answers
a. {(1, 1), (1, 2), (1, 3), (1, 4), (1, 15), (2, 1), (2, 2), (2, 3), (2, 4), (2, 15), (3, 1), (3, 2), (3, 3), (3, 4), (3, 15), (4, 1), (4, 2), (4, 3), (4, 4), (4, 15), (15, 1), (15, 2), (15, 3), (15, 4), (15, 15)}

b. i. $\frac{1}{25}$ ii. 0   iii. $\frac{1}{25}$ iv. $\frac{20}{25}$

c.

x	\$0	\$1	\$2	\$3	\$4	\$15
$P(x)$	$\frac{4}{5}$	$\frac{1}{25}$	$\frac{1}{25}$	$\frac{1}{25}$	$\frac{1}{25}$	$\frac{1}{25}$

d. \$1

e. No. Explanations may vary. Sample: If player's expected value on a \$1 play is \$1, then the school probably will only break even on the game and have no money to donate to charity.

f. Simulations will vary. Sample: On a graphics calculator, use the expression INT(25*rand) + 1 to randomly generate the integers from 1 to 25, representing the 25 outcomes in the sample space. Results of the simulations may vary.

g. Answers will vary. Check students' work.

Extension
Obtain the rules of the game or games that comprise a state or regional lottery. Have students compute the probability of winning and the expected value of a ticket. If possible, have them research historical statistics on how much money the lottery has raised, how much has been paid out in prizes, and how the remaining moneys have been distributed.

Evaluation

Level	Standard to be achieved for performance at specified level
5	The student demonstrates an in-depth understanding of probability and its application to the given situation. All questions are answered thoughtfully and thoroughly, and all calculations are accurate. The student creates a viable game, prepares an effective presentation, and may offer additional insights gleaned from the activity.
4	The student demonstrates a clear understanding of probability. All tasks are approached via appropriate methods, but the student may make minor errors in calculations. The student creates a viable, enjoyable game. The presentation is well-organized and easy to read, though it may lack in some detail.
3	The student demonstrates a fundamental understanding of probability, but may need some assistance in answering the questions posed. Though the student has a general sense of appropriate methods to use in approaching the given tasks, the work may contain a major error, or a major step of a process may be omitted. The student creates an appropriate game and prepares a presentation, but it may be somewhat jumbled or lacking in focus.
2	The student demonstrates some understanding of probability, but needs considerable assistance in understanding its application to the given situation. Even with this assistance, the student may make several major errors or omit one or more major steps of a process. The student attempts to create an original game and to prepare a presentation, but the results are disorganized and incomplete.
1	The student demonstrates little if any understanding of probability and its application to the given situation. Even with assistance, any attempts to answer the questions posed are cursory or irrelevant. Rather than create an original game, the student may simply copy the one presented in the introduction to the activity.

Functions, Statistics, and Trigonometry © Scott Foresman Addison Wesley

1. Give the first five terms of a geometric sequence. Explain how you know it is geometric. Then write explicit and recursive formulas for the sequence. Show how to find the 10th term using one of the formulas.

Objectives A, B, E

☐ Recognizes geometric sequences.

☐ Is able to find terms of a sequence from an explicit or recursive formula.

☐ Is able to find explicit and recursive formulas for the nth term of a sequence.

☐ Gives the first five terms of an appropriate sequence. (Sample: 8, 4, 2, 1, .5)

☐ Explains why the sequence is geometric.

☐ Gives a correct explicit formula. (Sample [for the given sequence]: $g_n = g_1(.5)^{n-1}$)

☐ Gives a correct recursive formula. (Sample [for the given sequence]: $g_1 = 8$ and $g_n = .5g_{n-1}$)

☐ Correctly determines the tenth term. (Sample [for the given sequence]: $g_{10} = .015626$)

2. Calculate the partial sum S_8 for each series below. Then compare the series. How are they alike? different? State as many likenesses and differences as you can.

   (i) $\frac{2}{3} + \frac{4}{3} + \frac{6}{3} + \frac{8}{3} + \frac{10}{4} + \cdots$

   (ii) $\frac{2}{3} + \frac{4}{3} + \frac{8}{3} + \frac{16}{3} + \frac{32}{3} + \cdots$

   (iii) $\frac{2}{3} + \frac{4}{9} + \frac{8}{27} + \frac{16}{81} + \frac{32}{243} + \cdots$

Objectives C, G

☐ Can evaluate arithmetic and geometric series.

☐ Can tell whether an infinite series converges.

☐ Gives correct partial sums. (The sums are: (i) 24 (ii) 170 (iii) $\frac{12{,}610}{6561} = 1\frac{6049}{6561} \approx 1.92196$)

☐ States at least one likeness. (Samples: Each series is infinite. The first term of each is $\frac{2}{3}$.)

☐ States at least one difference. (Samples: Series (i) is arithmetic, (ii) and (iii) are geometric, Series (iii) converges, (i) and (ii) do not.)

3. a. What is the meaning of $\lim\limits_{n \to \infty} \left(\frac{1-n}{2-n}\right)$?

   b. Maria says the value of this expression is $\frac{1}{2}$. If you agree, justify her statement. If you disagree, find the correct value.

Objective F

☐ Is able to determine limits of certain sequences.

☐ Gives an appropriate meaning. (Sample: the number that $\frac{1-n}{2-n}$ approaches as n increases.)

☐ Recognizes that Maria's statement is incorrect.

☐ Demonstrates that 1 is the correct limit.

4. Based on your study of Pascal's Triangle in this chapter, make a list of as many facts as you can that lead directly from this statement: *The 5th term in the 30th row of Pascal's Triangle is 27,405.*

Objectives D, L

☐ Locates numerical properties in Pascal's Triangle.

☐ Understands the relationship between binomial expansions and Pascal's Triangle.

☐ Makes a comprehensive list of facts. (Samples: The 27th term in this row is 27,405. The 5th term in the expansion of $(a + b)^{30}$ is $27{,}405\, a^{26}b^4$.)

5. Write a mathematical statement that describes the relationship between $_nP_r$ and $_nC_r$. For what values of n and r is your statement true?

Objective H

☐ Is able to state identities using combinations.

☐ Writes an appropriate statement. (Samples: $_nP_r = r! \,_nC_r;\ _nC_r = \frac{1}{r!}\,_nP_r;\ _nP_r > _nC_r$)

☐ Correctly identifies the values of n and r. (positive integers n and r, with $n \geq r$)

6. Thinking about a die, write a probability problem whose answer is $_{10}C_2 \left(\frac{1}{6}\right)^2\left(\frac{5}{6}\right)^8$. Show how to solve your problem.

Objective K

☐ Is able to determine probabilities in situations involving binomial experiments.

☐ Writes an appropriate problem. (Sample: A fair six-sided die is rolled ten times. What is the probability that 1 appears on top exactly twice?)

☐ Shows a correct solution to the problem.

Teacher Notes

Objectives A, B, C, E, G, I

Concepts and Skills This activity requires students to:
- determine if a sequence is arithmetic or geometric.
- find explicit and recursive formulas for the nth term of an arithmetic or geometric sequence.
- find terms of sequences from formulas.
- evaluate finite arithmetic or geometric series.
- find the limit of an infinite geometric series.
- relate sequences and series to geometric iterations.

Guiding Questions
- What is the formula for the area of an equilateral triangle with side of length s?
$$\left(A = \frac{\sqrt{3}}{4} s^2\right)$$
- When a segment joins the midpoints of two sides of a triangle, how is that segment related to the third side? (It is parallel to the third side, and its length is half the length of the third side.)

Answers
a. **i.** $1, 4, 7, 10$ **ii.** arithmetic **iii.** $a_n = 3n - 2$
    iv. $a_1 = 1; a_n = a_{n-1} + 3, n \geq 2$ **v.** 28

b. **i.** $\dfrac{\sqrt{3}}{4}, \dfrac{\sqrt{3}}{16}, \dfrac{\sqrt{3}}{64}, \dfrac{\sqrt{3}}{256}$ **ii.** geometric

    iii. $g_n = \dfrac{\sqrt{3}}{4^n}$ **iv.** $g_1 = \dfrac{\sqrt{3}}{4};$

    $g_n = \dfrac{g_{n-1}}{4}, n \geq 2$ **v.** $\dfrac{\sqrt{3}}{1048.576}$

c. **i.** $3, 1.5, .75, .375$ **ii.** geometric
    iii. $a_n = 3(.5)^{n-1}$ **iv.** $a_1 = 3; a_n = .5a_{n-1},$
    $n \geq 2$ **v.** $.005859375$

d. **i.** $3 + 1.5 + .75 + \cdots + .005859375$

    ii. $S_{10} = \dfrac{3(1 - .5^{10})}{1 - .5} = 5.994140625$

    iii. $S_\infty = \dfrac{3}{1 - .5} = 6$

e. The length is 1. Explanations will vary. Samples: The length is the sum of the geometric series $.5 + .25 + .125 + .0625 + \ldots$. The length is one-sixth the sum found in question **iii** of part **d**.

f. Answers will vary. Check students' work.

Extension
A "spiral" on the coordinate plane follows this path: $(0, 0) \to (0, 16) \to (27, 16) \to (27, 8) \to (18, 8) \to (18, 12) \to (21, 12) \to (21, 10) \to \ldots$ Have students determine what point this spiral approaches. $[(20.5, 10.\overline{6})]$. Then have them create and specify their own original spirals.

Functions, Statistics, and Trigonometry © Scott Foresman Addison Wesley

EVALUATION GUIDES

Evaluation

Level	Standard to be achieved for performance at specified level
5	The student demonstrates an in-depth understanding of sequences and series and their manifestations in geometric figures. All questions are answered thoughtfully, and all calculations are accurate. The independent analysis of a figure is comprehensive; the figure may be a complex original creation, and it may be rendered imaginatively.
4	The student demonstrates a clear understanding of sequences and series and their manifestations in geometric figures. The student's responses to the questions posed are reasonable, but may contain minor errors. The student draws an appropriate geometric figure and prepares a logical, well-organized analysis, but it may lack in some detail.
3	The student demonstrates a fundamental understanding of sequences and series, but may need some assistance in perceiving their manifestations in geometric figures. Responses to the questions may contain one or more major errors, or a major step of a process may be omitted. The independent analysis is essentially complete, but it may be somewhat disorganized and lack significant insight.
2	The student demonstrates some understanding of sequences and series, but needs considerable assistance in perceiving their manifestations in geometric figures. Even with help, the student may make several major errors, or may omit major steps of a process. The student attempts to prepare an independent analysis of a geometric figure, but the report is incomplete and lacks focus.
1	The student demonstrates little if any understanding of sequences and series and their manifestations in geometric figures. Even with assistance, any attempts to answer the questions posed are superficial or irrelevant. Rather than draw an appropriate figure, the student may simply copy the given figures, or may draw a figure that is trivial.

1. Your friend is studying geometry and has learned the formula $V = \ell wh$ for finding the volume of a right rectangular prism. So your friend says it is hard to understand how a polynomial *with more than one term* might represent the volume of a right rectangular prism. Explain to your friend why this is possible. Include an illustration.

Objective J

☐ Is able to represent three-dimensional figures with polynomials.

☐ Gives an appropriate example. (Sample: If the length, width, and height of the right rectangular prism at the right are each increased by x, the volume of the new prism is $x^3 + 9x^2 + 26x + 24$.)

2. Give two polynomial functions, one of odd degree and one even, each with one zero equal to -3 and another zero of multiplicity 2. Sketch a graph of each function and label all its extrema, giving the value and identifying it as a maximum value, a minimum value, a relative maximum, or a relative minimum.

Objectives B, F, G, K

☐ Is able to apply the vocabulary of polynomials.

☐ Is able to apply the Factor Theorem.

☐ Is able to find extrema of polynomial functions.

☐ Is able to relate properties of polynomial functions and their graphs.

☐ Identifies two appropriate functions. (Samples: $f(x) = (x + 3)(x - 1)^2$, $g(x) = x(x + 3)(x - 1)^2$)

☐ Correctly graphs each function.

☐ Correctly labels all extrema.

3. Using the quadratic regression feature of a calculator, a student found the following model for the data below:

$y = 11.5x^2 - 47.5x + 49.5$

Explain how you know this is not the best model. Show how to find a better model.

x	1	2	3	4	5	6	7	8
y	3	8	21	48	95	168	273	416

Objective A

☐ Is able to use finite differences to determine an equation for a polynomial function given data.

☐ Gives a logical explanation. (Sample: The constant third difference is 6, so an exact cubic model exists.)

☐ Gives the cubic model. ($y = x^3 - 2x^2 + 4x$)

4. In this chapter, it is said that the procedure for dividing polynomials is similar to the procedure for dividing integers. List as many similarities as you can. Give examples.

Objectives C, G

☐ Demonstrates an ability to divide polynomials.

☐ Understands the Remainder Theorem.

☐ Lists two or more similarities. (Samples: When a division does not "come out even," the result is expressed as a quotient and a remainder. The Remainder Theorem can be used to predict whether certain polynomial divisions come out even, just as divisibility tests can be used to make predictions about certain integer divisions.)

☐ Gives appropriate examples.

5. a. Is the sum of two complex numbers *always, sometimes,* or *never* complex? Give examples to illustrate your answer.

   b. Repeat part **a**, this time analyzing the product of two complex numbers.

Objective E

☐ Is able to perform operations with complex numbers.

☐ States that the sum is *sometimes* complex.

☐ States that the product is *sometimes* complex.

☐ Gives appropriate examples.

6. Joy says that the solution of $(n - 2)^3 = 0$ is the same as the solution of $n^3 - 8 = 0$. Do you agree or disagree? If you agree, justify your response. If you disagree, show how the solutions of the two equations differ.

Objective D

☐ Is able to solve polynomial equations using the Factor Theorem and differences of powers.

☐ Recognizes that Joy's statement is incorrect.

☐ Gives a logical explanation. (Sample: The root of $(n - 2)^3 = 0$ is 2, with multiplicity 3. The roots of $n^3 - 8 = 0$ are 2, $-1 + i\sqrt{3}$, and $-1 - i\sqrt{3}$.)

Teacher Notes

Objectives B, D, F, K

Concepts and Skills This activity requires students to:
- apply the vocabulary of polynomials.
- find zeros and extrema of polynomial functions.
- factor polynomials and solve polynomial equations using the Factor Theorem.
- relate properties of polynomial functions and their graphs.
- conduct an original mathematical investigation.
- summarize results in a written report.

Guiding Questions
- How do you determine whether a function is even, odd, or neither?
- How do you determine whether the inverse of a function is a function?

Answers
a. **i.** -2, with multiplicity 2, and -5 **ii.** no maximum or minimum, relative maximum of 4, relative minimum of 0 **iii.** Neither. Explanations will vary. **iv.** No. Explanations will vary.
b. **i.** (-3, 2) **ii.** $T: (x, y) \rightarrow (x + 3, y - 2)$ **iii.** $f'(x) = x^3 - 3x$
c. **i.** $-\sqrt{3}, 0, \sqrt{3}$ **ii.** no maximum minimum, relative maximum of 2, relative minimum of -2 **iii.** Odd. Explanations will vary. **iv.** No. Explanations will vary.
d. **i.** No. **ii.** Yes
e. Justifications will vary. Samples are given.
   i. True: $p(-x) = (-x)^3 - k(-x) = -x^3 + kx$; $-p(x) = -(x^3 - kx) = -x^3 + kx$; since $p(-x) = -p(x)$, p is an odd function. **ii.** True: $x^3 - kx = 0 \rightarrow x(x^2 - k) = 0$ $\rightarrow x(x) + \sqrt{k})(x - \sqrt{k}) = 0 \rightarrow x = 0$ or $x = -\sqrt{k}$ or $x = \sqrt{k}$ **iii.** True: The graph of the function fails the horizontal-line test, so the inverse is not a function.
f. Answers may vary. Samples: Any function of this form is an odd function; has zeros 0, $-i\sqrt{k}$, and $i\sqrt{k}$; and has an inverse that is a function
g. Answers will vary.

Extension
Have students prepare a display that demonstrates how polynomial functions are related to other types of functions they have studied in this course.

Evaluation

Level	Standard to be achieved for performance at specified level
5	The student demonstrates an in-depth understanding of polynomial functions. Responses to all the questions posed are accurate and complete. The student prepares a thoughtful, well-organized report that thoroughly investigates the chosen aspect of polynomial functions, and may offer insights that extend considerably beyond the properties of polynomial functions studied in the chapter.
4	The student demonstrates a clear understanding of polynomial functions. The student uses appropriate strategies in replying to the questions posed, but some responses may contain minor errors. The report examines a meaningful aspect of polynomial functions and is well-organized, but it may lack in some detail.
3	The student demonstrates a fundamental understanding of polynomial functions, but may need some assistance in responding to the questions posed. There may be one or more major errors in the student's work, or a major step of a process may be omitted. The report examines an appropriate aspect of polynomial functions and is essentially complete, but it may be somewhat disorganized.
2	The student demonstrates some understanding of polynomial functions, but needs considerable assistance in responding to the questions posed. Even with this help, the responses may contain several major errors, or the student may omit one or more major steps of a process. The student attempts to prepare a report, but it is jumbled and incomplete.
1	The student demonstrates little if any understanding of polynomial functions. Even with assistance, any attempts to respond to the questions posed are nonsensical or irrelevant. Rather than write an original report, the student may simply copy the given graphs or restate the given investigation.

EVALUATION GUIDES

1. In baseball, "success" for a batter is getting a hit when at bat. Choose a number of times at-bat n and a reasonable nonzero probability of success p. (Average major league batters have a success of about 27% in one season.) Draw a binomial probability distribution for your choices. Show how to find the mean and standard deviation of the distribution. What is the meaning of these statistics.

Objective A, E, I

☐ Can graph a binomial probability distribution and calculate its mean and standard deviation.

☐ Is able to solve probability problems using a binomial distribution.

☐ Draws a correct graph for the chosen n and p.

☐ Gives the correct mean and standard deviation.

☐ Gives a logical interpretation.

2. A six-sided die that came with a new board game has a visible defect, and you suspect the die is not fair. Describe a binomial experiment you might conduct to test whether it is fair. Explain how you can use a binomial distribution to evaluate your experiment.

Objectives F

☐ Understands the process of using binomial distributions to test hypotheses.

☐ Describes an experiment. (Sample: Let success be "1", and failure be any other number. Record the number of times n that 1 appears in 120 rolls).

☐ Gives a logical explanation. (Sample: Let H_0 be: *The probability of 1 is $\frac{1}{6}$*. Decide on a significance level, such as .05. Find the probability of an outcome that is at least as far from H_0 as n and evaluate it in terms of the significance level.)

3. An equation of the curve graphed at the right is: $y = \frac{1}{\sqrt{2\pi}} e^{-z^2/2}$. Label the vertical and horizontal scales of the axes. Then state as many facts as you can about the curve and what it represents.

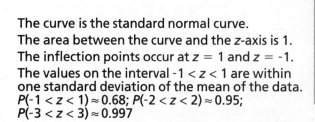

Objective B, D, J

☐ Recognizes properties of normal distributions.

☐ Is able to graph and interpret normal distributions.

☐ Is able to use the standard Normal Distribution to find probabilities.

☐ Correctly labels the scales of the axes. (See figure.)

☐ States several significant facts (See list at right.)

The curve is the standard normal curve.
The area between the curve and the z-axis is 1.
The inflection points occur at $z = 1$ and $z = -1$.
The values on the interval $-1 < z < 1$ are within one standard deviation of the mean of the data.
$P(-1 < z < 1) \approx 0.68$; $P(-2 < z < 2) \approx 0.95$;
$P(-3 < z < 3) \approx 0.997$

4. The average life of a certain type of light bulb is said to be 3000 h, with a standard deviation of 250 h. Explain how a consumer interest group can use the Central Limit Theorem to verify this claim.

Objective G

☐ Is able to apply the Central Limit Theorem.

☐ Gives a logical explanation. (Sample: The group can test several samples of size n, with $n \geq 30$. If the claim is true, the distribution of sample means should have a mean of ≈ 3000 h and a standard deviation of $\approx (250 \div \sqrt{n})$h.)

5. Using the Standard Normal Distribution Table, Joe found $P(z < 1.28) \approx .8997$ and $P(z < 1.29) \approx .9015$. He concluded that the z-score 1.28 corresponds to a 90% confidence level. Do you agree? Why or why not?

Objective H

☐ Understands confidence intervals.

☐ Recognizes that Joe's conclusion is incorrect.

☐ Gives a logical explanation. (Sample: The table values indicate that $\approx 90\%$ of the area under the standard normal curve is to the left of $z \approx 1.28$ A 90% confidence level requires parameters for the 90% of the area centered at the mean.)

Teacher Notes

Objectives D, H, J

Concepts and Skills This activity requires students to:
- find measures of center and variance for a data set.
- use properties of normal distributions.
- interpret normal distributions.
- apply confidence intervals to real-world problems.
- present results in a written report.

Guiding Questions
- What are the characteristics of a normal distribution?
- How might you utilize the Central Limit Theorem in your recommendations?

Answers
a. i. 16.02 **ii.** 16.02 **iii.** 16.019, 16.020, 16.022, and 16.033 **iv.** ≈0.04

b.

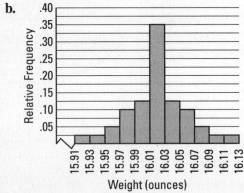

c. Samples: It is symmetric about the mean; ≈68% of the data lies within one standard deviation of the mean, ≈95% within two standard deviations, ≈99.7% within three standard deviations.

d. Check students' drawings. **i.** Sample: The curve somewhat resembles the bell shape of the normal curve. However, it seems to have inflection points at points other than $s = -1$ and $s = 1$. **ii.** Decrease the size of the intervals.

e. Answers will vary Sample: For a 95% confidence level, 15.94 oz $\leq \mu \leq$ 16.10 oz.

f. Answers will vary. Check students' work.

Extension
Have students research skewed distributions. Have them generate a set of sample package weights that would have a skewed distribution, and ask them what inferences they might draw from this sample.

Evaluation

Level	Standard to be achieved for performance at specified level
5	The student demonstrates an in-depth understanding of normal distributions and statistical reasoning and their application to the given situation. All calculations and graphs are accurate and complete. The student presents a sound set of recommendations, clearly recognizing both the power and limitations of the techniques involved.
4	The student demonstrates a clear understanding of normal distributions and statistical reasoning. The student performs appropriate calculations and draws suitable graphs, but the work may contain minor errors. The set of recommendations is reasonable, but the presentation may lack in some detail.
3	The student demonstrates a fundamental understanding of normal distributions and statistical reasoning, but may need some assistance in applying the concepts to the given situation. There may be one or more major errors in calculations or graphs, or a major step of a process may be omitted. The recommendations are essentially sound, but not all critical aspects have been considered.
2	The student demonstrates some understanding of normal distributions and statistical reasoning, but needs considerable assistance in understanding their application to the given situations. Even with help, the student may make several major errors in calculating statistics or drawing graphs, or may omit major steps of a process. The student attempts to make recommendations, but not all are appropriate, and the presentation is jumbled.
1	The student demonstrates little if any understanding of normal distributions and statistical reasoning and their application to the given situation. Even with assistance, any attempts to calculate statistics or draw graphs are superficial or irrelevant. Rather than make a set of recommendations, the student may simply copy theorems presented in the text.

EVALUATION GUIDES

1. a. Identify two matrices, *A* and *B*, for which *AB* and *BA* both exist. Find *AB* and *BA*.

   b. Identify two matrices, *A* and *B*, for which *AB* exists, but *BA* does not. Justify your answer.

Objectives A, D

☐ Demonstrates an ability to multiply matrices.

☐ Can apply properties of matrix multiplication.

☐ Gives appropriate choices for part **a**. (Sample: $A = \begin{bmatrix} 1 & 2 \\ 3 & 4 \end{bmatrix}$; $B = \begin{bmatrix} 1 & 2 \\ 1 & 2 \end{bmatrix}$; $AB = \begin{bmatrix} 3 & 6 \\ 7 & 14 \end{bmatrix}$; $BA = \begin{bmatrix} 7 & 10 \\ 7 & 10 \end{bmatrix}$

☐ Gives appropriate choices for part **b**. (Sample: $A = [1, 2]$; $B = \begin{bmatrix} 1 & 2 \\ 3 & 4 \end{bmatrix}$; $AB = [7 \quad 10]$

☐ Logically explains why *BA* does not exist.

2. Below is an unfinished exercise. What is the goal of the exercise? For each numbered step of the exercise, write a sentence explaining what was done in that step. Then complete the exercise, continuing to number each step and writing a sentence that explains it.

1. $\begin{cases} 2x - 3y = 7 \\ 3x + y = 5 \end{cases}$ 2. $\begin{bmatrix} 2 & -3 \\ 3 & 1 \end{bmatrix}\begin{bmatrix} x \\ y \end{bmatrix} = \begin{bmatrix} 7 \\ 5 \end{bmatrix}$

3. $\begin{bmatrix} 2 & -3 \\ 3 & 1 \end{bmatrix}^{-1}\begin{bmatrix} 2 & -3 \\ 3 & 1 \end{bmatrix}\begin{bmatrix} x \\ y \end{bmatrix} = \begin{bmatrix} 2 & -3 \\ 3 & 1 \end{bmatrix}^{-1}\begin{bmatrix} 7 \\ 5 \end{bmatrix} \cdots$

Objectives B, C

☐ Is able to use matrices to solve linear systems.

☐ Is able to find the inverse of a 2 × 2 matrix.

☐ Correctly completes the exercise.

☐ Writes appropriate explanations for all steps.

3. Choose a real-world situation and show how a matrix can be used to organize information related to it. Use real data if it is available, or create a reasonable set of fictional data. Write a question you can answer using the matrix. Give the answer to your question.

Objective F

☐ Is able to use a matrix to organize information.

☐ Gives an organized matrix of data.

☐ Writes a reasonable question.

☐ Gives the correct answer to the question.

4. Use only the exact values of sin 30°, cos 30°, sin 45°, cos 45°, sin 60°, and cos 60°. From these, obtain several other exact values of sin θ and cos θ for 0° < θ < 180°. Show your work.

Objective E

☐ Is able to apply the Addition Formulas and Double Angle Formulas.

☐ Gives several exact values. (Samples: $\frac{\sqrt{6} - \sqrt{2}}{4}$ = sin 15° = cos 75° = sin 105° = -cos 165°)

5. Write a matrix for △*ABC* at the right. Then choose **a.** a reflection, **b.** a rotation, **c.** a scale change, and **d.** a composite of transformations so that each of the four images of △*ABC* under the transformations lies in a different quadrant from the others. Write a matrix for each transformation and show how to use it to find the image.

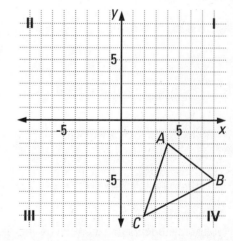

Objectives G, H, I

☐ Can represent reflections, rotations, and scale changes as matrices.

☐ Can represent composites of transformations as matrix products.

☐ Can find the image of a figure under a transformation using a matrix.

☐ Gives a correct matrix to represent △*ABC*.

☐ Selects four appropriate transformations. (Sample: **a.** r_x (quadrant I) **b.** R_{180} (quadrant II) **c.** $S_{1, .5}$ (quadrant IV) **d.** $R_{90} \circ R_{y=x}$ (quadrant III))

☐ Writes a correct matrix for each transformation.

☐ Finds the correct image under each transformation using matrices.

EVALUATION GUIDES

Teacher Notes

Objectives A, G, H, I

Concepts and Skills This activity requires students to:
- represent reflections, rotations, size/scale changes, and composites of transformations as matrices.
- use a matrix to find a transformation image.
- create an animation of a geometric figure and use matrices to describe it.

Guiding Questions
- Where should you position the triangle in stage 1 to achieve stage 8?
- In part **c**, what should be the relationship between the matrix for the transformation in **i** and the matrix for the composite of transformations in **ii**?

Answers
a. Answers will vary. Sample: $\begin{bmatrix} 0 & 0 & 6 \\ 0 & 24 & 6 \end{bmatrix}$

b. i. Reflect it across the line $y = x$. **ii.** Answers may vary. Sample: Rotate it 270°, then reflect that image across the x-axis.

c. i. $r_{y=x} = \begin{bmatrix} 0 & 1 \\ 1 & 0 \end{bmatrix}; \begin{bmatrix} 0 & 1 \\ 1 & 0 \end{bmatrix} \cdot \begin{bmatrix} 0 & 0 & 6 \\ 0 & 24 & 6 \end{bmatrix} =$
$\begin{bmatrix} 0 & 24 & 6 \\ 0 & 0 & 6 \end{bmatrix}$ **ii.** Sample (for the composite given in part **b**): $R_{270} = \begin{bmatrix} 0 & 1 \\ -1 & 0 \end{bmatrix}; r_x = \begin{bmatrix} 1 & 0 \\ 0 & -1 \end{bmatrix};$
$r_x \circ R_{270} = \begin{bmatrix} 0 & 1 \\ 1 & 0 \end{bmatrix};$ Then proceed as in part **i**.

d. reflection across the x-axis; $r_x = \begin{bmatrix} 1 & 0 \\ 0 & -1 \end{bmatrix};$
$\begin{bmatrix} 1 & 0 \\ 0 & -1 \end{bmatrix} \cdot \begin{bmatrix} 0 & 24 & 6 \\ 0 & 0 & 6 \end{bmatrix} = \begin{bmatrix} 0 & 24 & 6 \\ 0 & 0 & -6 \end{bmatrix}$

e. Samples: stage 3 to 4: $r_y \circ R_{270}$; 4 to 5: R_{180}; 5 to 6: $r_x \circ R_{90}$; 6 to 7: r_x; 7 to 8: $r_{y=x}$; Check students' matrices and multiplications.

f. $R_{180} = \begin{bmatrix} -1 & 0 \\ 0 & -1 \end{bmatrix}$

g. Answers will vary. Check students' work.

Extension
Remind students that a *tessellation* is a covering of a plane with nonoverlapping congruent regions and no holes. Have them create an animation of a tessellation that might be proposed as the company "signature." Then have them write the matrix multiplications that will produce the animation.

Evaluation

Level	Standard to be achieved for performance at specified level
5	The student demonstrates an in-depth understanding of matrices and their application to geometric figures and transformations. All calculations are accurate and complete. The student creates an attractive, appropriate animation, and may present it imaginatively. The student may offer additional insights.
4	The student demonstrates a clear understanding of matrices and matrix multiplication. Appropriate methods are used in specifying geometric figures and performing transformations, but there may be minor errors in the calculations involved. The student creates an appropriate animation, but the presentation may lack in some detail.
3	The student demonstrates a fundamental understanding of matrices and matrix multiplication, but may need some assistance in applying the concepts to the given geometric figures and transformations. There may be one or more major errors in the student's calculations, or a major step of a process may be omitted. The student creates a suitable animation, but the presentation may be disorganized and difficult to read.
2	The student demonstrates some understanding of matrices and matrix multiplication, but needs considerable assistance in applying the concepts to transformations. Even with help, the student may make several major errors in calculations or may omit one or more major steps of a process. The student attempts to create a suitable animation, but the presentation is jumbled and incomplete.
1	The student demonstrates little if any understanding of matrices and their application to geometric figures and transformations. Even with assistance, any attempts to write matrices or to perform matrix multiplications are frivolous or irrelevant. Rather than create a new animation, the student may simply copy the given drawings.

1. State as many facts as you can about the ellipse that is graphed at the right.

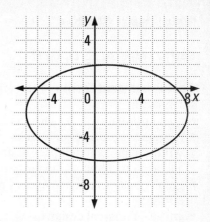

Objectives D, H

☐ Is able to state and apply properties of ellipses to draw or describe them.

☐ Is able to use graph transformation images of parent ellipses.

☐ States several significant facts, such as:
The endpoints of the axes are (8, -2), (-6, -2), (1, -6), (1, 2)
The foci are (1 + √33, -2) and (1 − √33, -2). The focal constant is 14. The length of the minor axis is 8.
An equation of the ellipse is $\frac{(x-1)^2}{49} + \frac{(y+2)^2}{16} = 1$.

---

2. How are the graphs of the following equations alike? different? State as many likenesses and differences as you can.

i. $\frac{x^2}{100} - \frac{y^2}{81} = 1$ **ii.** $\frac{y^2}{100} - \frac{x^2}{81} = 1$

Objectives A, G

☐ Is able to use properties of hyperbolas to write equations describing them.

☐ Is able to identify graphs of hyperbolas with equations in their standard form.

☐ States several significant likenesses, such as:
Each is a hyperbola with center (0, 0) and focal constant 10. Each is the image of the other after reflection across the line $y = x$.

☐ States several differences, such as: The asymptotes of **i** are $y = \pm\frac{9}{10}x$; of **ii** are $y = \pm\frac{10}{9}x$. The vertices of **i** are (±10. 0); of **ii** are (0, ±10). The foci of **i** are (√181, 0), (-√181, 0); of **ii** are (0, √181), (0, -√181).

3. The figure at the right is a cone of two nappes. The dashed line is its axis. Explain the importance of the angle measure k in determining the conic sections.

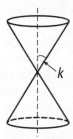

Objective E

☐ Is able to describe the intersections of a plane and a cone of two nappes.

☐ Gives a logical explanation. (Sample: Let θ be the measure of the smallest angle between the axis and a given plane. If $\theta = k$, the intersection of the plane and the cone is a parabola; if $\theta < k$, the intersection is a hyperbola; and if $\theta > k$, the intersection is an ellipse.)

---

4. Write an equation in standard form for an ellipse whose center is the origin. Then rewrite it in the general form of a quadratic relation in two variables. Last find an equation for its image under a rotation of 45° about the origin and graph the image on the axes at the right.

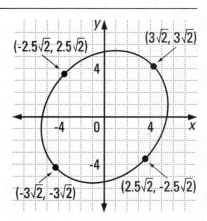

Objectives A, B, C, H

☐ Is able to use properties of ellipses to write equations describing them.

☐ Is able to rewrite equations of conic sections in the general form.

☐ Is able to find equations for and graph rotation images.

☐ Writes an appropriate equation. (Sample: $\frac{x^2}{36} + \frac{y^2}{25} = 1$)

☐ Correctly rewrites the equation in general quadratic form. (For the sample given: $25x^2 + 36y^2 - 900 = 0$)

☐ Gives a correct equation for the rotation image (For the sample given: $122x^2 - 44xy + 122y^2 - 3600 = 0$)

☐ Gives a correct graph of the rotation image. (See figure.)

Teacher Notes

Objectives A, C, D, G, H

Concepts and Skills This activity requires students to:
- read information from a text and a graphic.
- recognize properties of ellipses.
- write equations for ellipses in standard form and as a quadratic relation in two variables.
- graph transformation images of parent ellipses.
- create an original design using conic sections.

Guiding Questions
- How can you use the scale of the sketch to choose an appropriate size and location for the ellipses?
- Which conic sections were used to create the sample designs shown at the bottom of the page?

Answers
a. Samples: major axis 10 cm; minor axis 8 cm.
b. Check students' graphs.
c. Samples (for the ellipse given in part **a**): **i.** 10

   ii. (3, 0), (-3, 0)   **iii.** $\dfrac{x^2}{25} + \dfrac{y^2}{16} = 1$

   iv. $16x^2 + 25y^2 - 400 = 0$

d. Sample: The position of the product name ellipse is above center in the given diagram.
e. Samples (with the center of the ellipse given in part **a** translated to (-10, 3)), **i.** 10

   ii. (-7, 3), (-13, 3) **iii.** $\dfrac{(x + 10)^2}{25} + \dfrac{(y - 3)^2}{16} = 1$

   iv. $16x^2 + 25y^2 + 320x - 150y + 1425 = 0$

f. Samples: *net weight* ellipse — major axis 4, minor axis 2, center (-10, -6), equations

   $\dfrac{(x + 10)^2}{4} + \dfrac{(y + 6)^2}{1} = 1$ and $x^2 + 4y^2 +$

   $20x + 48y + 240 = 0$; *ingredients list* ellipse — major axis 14, minor axis 8,

   center (10, 0), equations $\dfrac{(x - 10)^2}{16} + \dfrac{y^2}{49} = 1$

   and $49x^2 + 16y^2 - 980x + 4116 = 0$
g. Answers will vary. Check students' work.

Extension
Have students find examples of conic sections used as design elements on labels. Have them choose one or more of their favorite designs, draw suitable grids, and write equations that would generate the design(s).

Evaluation

Level	Standard to be achieved for performance at specified level
5	The student demonstrates an in-depth understanding of conic sections and their application to the given situation. All equations are accurate, and all graphs are precise and complete. The student prepares an original design of some complexity, organizing several conic sections into an arrangement that is attractive and imaginative.
4	The student demonstrates a clear understanding of conic sections and their application to the given situation. All equations are of the proper form, and all graphs are suitably located, but there may be minor errors in a computation or in the location of a key point. The student creates an original design that is suitable and attractive, but the presentation may lack in some detail.
3	The student demonstrates a fundamental understanding of conic sections, but may need some assistance in applying them to the given situation. There may be one or more major errors in the student's equations or graphs, or a major step of a process may be omitted. The student's design is essentially complete, but it may be rendered somewhat haphazardly.
2	The student demonstrates some understanding of conic sections, but needs considerable assistance in understanding their application to the given situation. Even with help, the student may make several major errors in writing equations or in drawing graphs, or may omit one or more major steps of a process. The student attempts to prepare an original design, but it is fragmented and incomplete.
1	The student demonstrates little if any understanding of conic sections and their application to the given situation. Even with assistance, any attempts to write equations or to draw graphs are trivial or irrelevant. Instead of creating a well-planned original design, the student may simply draw shapes at random, ignoring the directive to provide equations.

EVALUATION GUIDES

1. Write a question about $\triangle ABC$ that you can answer using one of the reciprocal trigonometric functions. Show how to use that function to answer the question.

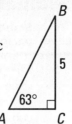

Objectives A

☐ Is able to evaluate reciprocal functions.
☐ Write an appropriate question. (Sample: What is the length of the hypotenuse?)
☐ Shows a correct method of answering the question. (Sample [for the question given]:
$\csc 63° = \frac{AB}{5}$; $AB = 5 \csc 63°$; $AB \approx 5.61$)

2. State two trigonometric identities that involve the cotangent function. Explain how to use an automatic grapher to test the identities. Then prove each identity, taking care to state any restrictions on its domain.

Objective F, G, H

☐ Is able to prove trigonometric identities.
☐ Can use an automatic grapher to test an identity.
☐ Understands singularities of functions.
☐ States two appropriate identities. (Samples: $\cot x \cdot \sec x = \csc x$; $\csc^2 x - \cot^2 x = 1$)
☐ Explains the use of an automatic grapher.
☐ Gives a correct proof of each identity.
☐ Identifies all restrictions on the domains.

3. The circle graphed on the polar coordinate system at the right is symmetric with respect to the polar axis. Give a polar equation for the circle. Now choose a point of the circle *that does not lie on the axis.* Give polar coordinates and rectangular coordinates for this point.

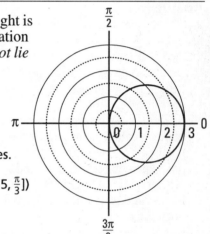

Objectives I, J, K

☐ Is able to interpret graphs of polar equations.
☐ Is able to plot points in a polar coordinate system.
☐ Is able to convert between polar and rectangular coordinates.
☐ Gives a correct equation for the graph. (Sample: $r = 3 \cos \theta$)
☐ Gives polar coordinates for a point of the graph. (Sample [$1.5, \frac{\pi}{3}$])
☐ Gives correct rectangular coordinates for the chosen point.
(Sample [for the given polar coordinates]: $\left(\frac{3}{4}, \frac{3\sqrt{3}}{4}\right)$)

4. State as many facts as you can about the complex number $-5 + 2i$. Be sure to include information about its geometric representation(s) and about different forms.

Objectives C, L

☐ Is able to represent complex numbers in different forms.
☐ Is able to graph complex numbers.
☐ States several significant facts, such as: Its graph in the rectangular coordinate plane is the point (-5, 2).
Its absolute value is $\sqrt{29}$. Its arguments are of the form $\approx 158° + 360°n$, where n is an integer. One pair of polar coordinates is [$\sqrt{29}, \approx 158°$]. A trigonometric form is: $\approx \sqrt{29}(\cos 158° + i \sin 158°)$.

5. Let $z = \frac{1}{2} + \frac{\sqrt{3}}{2} i$. Identify a computation involving z that can be performed using DeMoivre's Theorem. Explain why the theorem makes the computation easier than it might otherwise be. Then perform the computation. Show all your work.

Objectives D

☐ Is able to find powers of complex numbers.
☐ Gives an appropriate computation. (Sample: z^6)
☐ Gives a clear explanation of the advantage of using DeMoivre's Theorem.
☐ Writes a clear set of steps to carry out the computation.
☐ Gives the correct product (1).

EVALUATION GUIDES

Teacher Notes

Objectives I, J, K

Concepts and Skills This activity requires students to:
- plot points in a polar coordinate system.
- convert between rectangular and polar coordinates.
- graph and interpret graphs of polar equations.
- write an article comparing the rectangular and polar coordinate systems.

Guiding Questions
- How do you draw a rectangular coordinate system? polar?
- Can you transform polar graphs by reflection? rotation? translation? size changes?

Answers

a.-d. Answers will vary. Sample are given.

a. i. Each: shows a coordinatized plane; has locations named by an ordered pair; has a central point O; pictures a point P that is exactly the same distance from O, in exactly the same direction.
ii. Grid A: Two perpendicular axes intersect at point O, called the origin. Grid B: Just one polar axis passes through point O, called the pole. Grid A: Point P is located by the unique ordered pair $(3, 4)$. Grid B: Point P is located by the ordered pair $[5, \approx 53°]$, but this pair is not unique.

b. i. $x = 1$: vertical line one unit right of the y-axis; $y = 1$: horizontal line one unit above the x-axis **ii.** $r = 1$: circle of radius 1 centered at the pole; $\theta = 1$; line obtained by rotating the polar axis one radian counterclockwise.

c. i. For any circle, there is an equation of the form $(x - h)^2 + (y - k)^2 = r^2$, (h, k) being the center and r the radius. **ii.** Different equations, such as $r = k$, $r = a \sin \theta$, and $r = a \cos \theta$, yield circles.

d. i. parabolas, ellipses, hyperbolas, sine curves. **ii.** rose curves, cardioids, Archimedean spirals, logarithmic spirals, "loop" curves (limaçons)

e. Answers will vary. Check students' work.

Extension

Have students research a different type of coordinate system — for example, bipolar coordinates, spherical coordinates, or Plücker coordinates — and prepare a presentation describing the structure of the system and comparing it to the rectangular and polar systems.

Evaluation

Level	Standard to be achieved for performance at specified level
5	The student demonstrates an in-depth understanding of a polar coordinate system and its relationship to rectangular coordinates. All responses to the questions are accurate and complete. The student prepares an articulate, informative article, and may offer insights extending considerably beyond the core material taught in the text.
4	The student demonstrates a clear understanding of a polar coordinate system and its relationship in rectangular coordinates. The student answers all the questions thoughtfully, but the responses may contain minor inaccuracies. The article is well-organized and easy to read, but it may lack in some detail.
3	The student demonstrates a fundamental understanding of a polar coordinate system and its relationship to rectangular coordinates, but may need some assistance in answering the questions posed. The responses may contain one or more major errors, or a key concept may be overlooked. The article is essentially informative, but it may be somewhat disorganized.
2	The student demonstrates some understanding of a polar coordinate system and its relationship to rectangular coordinates, but needs considerable assistance in answering the questions posed. Even with help, the responses may contain several major errors, or key concepts may be overlooked. The student attempts to prepare a relevant article, but it is jumbled and not particularly informative.
1	The student demonstrates little if any understanding of a polar coordinate system and its relationship to rectangular coordinates. Even with assistance, any attempts to respond to the questions are trivial or irrelevant. Instead of writing a coherent article, the student may simply create a page of random equations and graphs.

Functions, Statistics, and Trigonometry © Scott Foresman Addison Wesley

EVALUATION GUIDES